I0006676

Ready-Made Visual FoxPro® Applications for File Maintenance

Templates 2000 *for Visual FoxPro®*

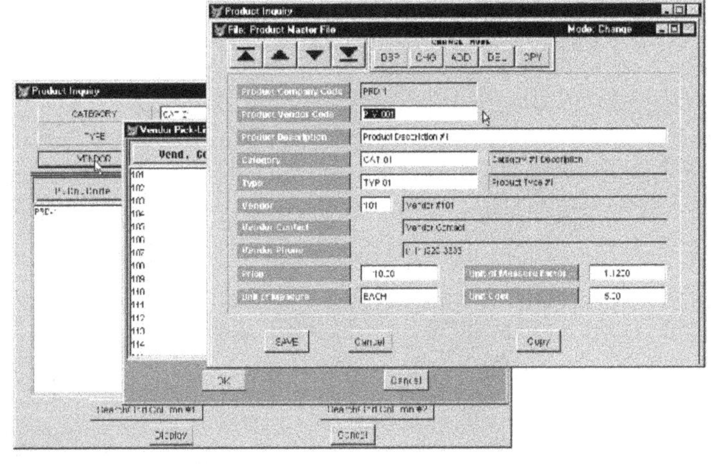

Emilio Aleu

authorHOUSE®

AuthorHouse™
1663 Liberty Drive
Bloomington, IN 47403
www.authorhouse.com
Phone: 1-800-839-8640

First published by AuthorHouse 9/17/2010

ISBN: 978-1-4490-7056-4 (e)
ISBN: 978-1-4490-7055-7 (sc)

Printed in the United States of America

This book is printed on acid-free paper.

List Form

```
*================================================================*
* Form        : _______             (Created from LIST_02.scx )  *
* Procedure   : Init                                             *
* Description : _______  Master File - List                      *
* Application : Sample Application                               *
* Programmer  : _______                                          *
* Date created:                                                  *
*----------------------------------------------------------------*
* See also the method: AD16_CALL_DATA_ENTRY_FORM                 *
*================================================================*
Lparameter na
Public LI_WIDTH_COL1, LI_WIDTH_COL2, LI_WIDTH_COL3
Public LI_WIDTH_COL4, LI_WIDTH_COL5, LI_WIDTH_COL6
Public LI_WIDTH_COL7, LI_WIDTH_COL8, LI_WIDTH_COL9
Public LI_WIDTH_COL10, LI_WIDTH_COL11, LI_WIDTH_COL12
Public LI_WIDTH_COL13, LI_CAPTION_COL13, LI_FRM_CAPTION
Public LI_CAPTION_COL1, LI_CAPTION_COL2, LI_CAPTION_COL3
Public LI_CAPTION_COL4, LI_CAPTION_COL5, LI_CAPTION_COL6
Public LI_CAPTION_COL7, LI_CAPTION_COL8, LI_CAPTION_COL9
Public LI_CAPTION_COL10, LI_CAPTION_COL11, LI_CAPTION_COL12
Public LI_TYPE_COL1, LI_TYPE_COL2, LI_DATABASE, LI_TABLE
Public LI_WITH_SEARCH
Public LI_VIEW1, LI_VIEW2, LI_VIEW3, LI_VIEW4
Public LI_ROW_SOURCE_1, LI_ROW_SOURCE_2
Public LI_ROW_SOURCE_3, LI_ROW_SOURCE_4
Public LI_C1_SW_Caption, LI_C1_SW_Input_Mask
Public LI_C2_SW_Caption, LI_C2_SW_Input_Mask
*---------------------------------------------------------------
* Form Caption:
*---------------------------------------------------------------
LI_FRM_CAPTION      = "File: ______ Master File"

*---------------------------------------------------------------
* Parameters for the List:
*---------------------------------------------------------------
LI_WIDTH_COL1       = 0
LI_WIDTH_COL2       = 0
LI_WIDTH_COL3       = 0
LI_WIDTH_COL4       = 0
LI_WIDTH_COL5       = 0
LI_WIDTH_COL6       = 0
LI_WIDTH_COL7       = 0
LI_WIDTH_COL8       = 0
LI_WIDTH_COL9       = 0
LI_WIDTH_COL10      = 0
LI_CAPTION_COL1     = ""
LI_CAPTION_COL2     = ""
```

```
LI_CAPTION_COL3      = ""
LI_CAPTION_COL4      = ""
LI_CAPTION_COL5      = ""
LI_CAPTION_COL6      = ""
LI_CAPTION_COL7      = ""
LI_CAPTION_COL8      = ""
LI_CAPTION_COL9      = ""
LI_CAPTION_COL10     = ""

                                   && See the database table.
LI_TYPE_COL1         = "CHR"       && "CHR", "NUM", "DATE"
LI_TYPE_COL2         = "CHR"       && "CHR", "NUM", "DATE"

*-------------------------------------------------------------
* Parameters for Database, Views and List Row Source:
*-------------------------------------------------------------

LI_DATABASE          = "C:\TMP2000\DATA\VFP_DATA"

LI_TABLE             = "???_MAST"    && See the AD17_CLEANUP
                                     && Method.

LI_WITH_SEARCH       = .T.

LI_VIEW1             = "V_???_IDX_1"
LI_VIEW2             = "V_???_IDX_2"
LI_VIEW3             = "V_???_SRC_1"
LI_VIEW4             = "V_???_SRC_2"

LI_ROW_SOURCE_1      = "V_???_IDX_1.???_CODE, ???_NAME"
LI_ROW_SOURCE_2      = "V_???_IDX_2.???_CODE, ???_NAME"
LI_ROW_SOURCE_3      = "V_???_SRC_1.???_CODE, ???_NAME"
LI_ROW_SOURCE_4      = "V_???_SRC_2.???_CODE, ???_NAME"

*--------------------------------------------------------------
* For Column #1 Search Window: (If LI_WITH_SEARCH = .T.)
*--------------------------------------------------------------
LI_C1_SW_Caption     = "Search: _____ Code"
LI_C1_SW_Input_Mask = "XXXXX"          && ("9999", "XXXX")
*--------------------------------------------------------------
* For Column #2 Search Window:
*--------------------------------------------------------------
LI_C2_SW_Caption     = "Search: _____ Name"
LI_C2_SW_Input_Mask = "XXXXXXXXXXXXXXXXXXXXXXXXXXXXXXXXXXXX"
*--------------------------------------------------------------
DODEFAULT()
```

```
*===============================================================*
* Form         : C_LIST                                         *
* Description : List Form Parent Class                          *
* Author       : E. Aleu                                        *
* Procedure    : INIT                                           *
* Date created: 04/02/97                                        *
* Date revised: 06/08/97, 12/23/97, 06/12/05                    *
*===============================================================*
 SET TALK OFF
 SET ECHO OFF
 LOCAL TMP_INIT_IDX
 THISFORM.CLOSABLE = .F.

 THISFORM.AD14_BEFORE_INIT

 THISFORM.AD03_FORM_CAPTION

 THISFORM.B01_OPEN_FILE

 THISFORM.B03_SETUP_LIST

 TMP_INIT_IDX = THISFORM.AD13_INIT_INDEX()

 THISFORM.B09_INDEX_USED(TMP_INIT_IDX, .F.)

 THISFORM.AO14_INIT_SET_FOCUS

 THISFORM.AD15_AFTER_INIT

 THISFORM.showtips = .T.

 THISFORM.Refresh



*===============================================================*
* Procedure: LOAD                                               *
*                                                               *
*===============================================================*

 SET TALK OFF
 SET ECHO OFF



*===============================================================*
* Procedure: B01_OPEN_FILE                                      *
*                                                               *
*===============================================================*
```

Source Code

```
SET EXCLUSIVE OFF
SET REPROCESS TO 0
SET MULTILOCKS ON
SET DELETED ON

Thisform.Buffermode = 2      && Optimistic Table Buffering

THISFORM.AF01_OPEN_DATABASE

THISFORM.AF02_OPEN_FILES_VIEWS




*=============================================================*
* Procedure: B02_COMMAND_GROUP_CLICK                          *
*                                                             *
* Options/Methods:                                            *
*                                                             *
*      B80_PB_CANCEL     B85_PB_DISPLAY     B90_PB_PROCESS    *
*      B81_PB_OK         B86_PB_ADD                           *
*      B82_PB_CHANGE     B87_PB_SAVE                          *
*      B83_PB_COPY       B88_PB_PRINT                         *
*      B84_PB_DELETE     B89_PB_EXIT                          *
*                                             See page 157.   *
*=============================================================*
 LPARAMETERS TMP_OPT

 DO CASE
 CASE TMP_OPT = 1                   && ADD
    THISFORM.B86_PB_ADD

 CASE TMP_OPT = 2                   && CHANGE
    THISFORM.B82_PB_CHANGE

 CASE TMP_OPT = 3                   && DISPLAY
    THISFORM.B85_PB_DISPLAY

 CASE TMP_OPT = 4                   && DELETE
    THISFORM.B84_PB_DELETE

 CASE TMP_OPT = 5                   && EXIT
    THISFORM.B89_PB_EXIT

 ENDCASE
```

```
*==============================================================*
* Procedure: B03_SETUP_LIST                                    *
*                                                              *
*==============================================================*
LOCAL TMP_CC, TMP_CW, TMP_RST, TMP_RS, TMP_BC, TMP_NA

TMP_CC = THISFORM.AD05_LIST_COLUMN_COUNT()
THISFORM.AO05_LIST_COLUMN_COUNT(TMP_CC)

TMP_CW = THISFORM.AD06_LIST_COLUMN_WIDTH(TMP_CC)
THISFORM.AO06_LIST_COLUMN_WIDTH(TMP_CW)

THISFORM.AD07_LIST_PB_CAPTION(TMP_CC)

THISFORM.AD11_LIST_FONT

TMP_RST = THISFORM.AD09_LIST_ROW_SOURCE_TYPE()
THISFORM.AO09_LIST_ROW_SOURCE_TYPE(TMP_RST)

TMP_BC = THISFORM.AD12_LIST_BOUND_COLUMN()
THISFORM.AO16_LIST_BOUND_COLUMN(TMP_BC)



*==============================================================*
* Procedure: B04_LIST_COLUMN_PB_CLICK                          *
*                                     See pages 87 and 157.    *
*==============================================================*
 LPARAMETERS TMP_INDEX

 LOCAL TMP_WITH_SEARCH

 TMP_WITH_SEARCH = THISFORM.AD04_WITH_SEARCH_WINDOW()

 THISFORM.B09_INDEX_USED(TMP_INDEX ,TMP_WITH_SEARCH)

 THISFORM.AO01_LIST_REQUERY

 thisform.Refresh



*==============================================================*
* Procedure: B05_LIST_INTERACTIVE_CHG                          *
*                                              See page 87.    *
*==============================================================*
LPARAMETER TMP_ROW_SRC_TYPE
```

```
LOCAL TMP_RST
TMP_RST = TMP_ROW_SRC_TYPE

DO CASE
CASE TMP_RST = 2 OR TMP_RST = 6  && Alias or Field

   Thisform.Refresh

OTHERWISE

    *----------------------------------------
    * For RowSourceType = (0, 1, 3, 4, 5)
    *---------------------------------------
    * Select product
    * Locate for This.Value = Cust_id
    *                        *========
    * Thisform.Refresh

ENDCASE


*==============================================================*
* Procedure: B06_LIST_DBL_CLICK                                *
*                                             See page 87. *
*==============================================================*



*==============================================================*
* Procedure: B07_SETUP_LIST_COLUMN                             *
*                                                              *
*==============================================================*
 LPARAMETERS C1,C2,C3,C4,C5,C6,C7,C8,C9,C10,C11,C12,C13

 LOCAL  C1_W,C2_W,C3_W,C4_W,C5_W,C6_W,C7_W,C8_W,C9_W,C10_W, ;
        C11_W,C12_W
 LOCAL PB1_L, PB1_W, PB2_L, PB2_W, PB3_L, PB3_W, PB4_L, PB4_W
 LOCAL PB5_L, PB5_W, PB6_L, PB6_W, PB7_L, PB7_W, PB8_L, PB8_W
 LOCAL PB9_L, PB9_W, PB10_L, PB10_W, PB11_L, PB11_W, PB12_L
 LOCAL PB12_W PB13_L, PB13_W

 LOCAL TMP_CC, LIST_LEFT, LIST_WIDTH

 TMP_CC     = THISFORM.AD05_LIST_COLUMN_COUNT()
 LIST_LEFT  = THISFORM.A003_RETURN_LIST_LEFT()
 LIST_WIDTH = THISFORM.A004_RETURN_LIST_WIDTH()

 DO CASE
 CASE TMP_CC = 1
```

```
    PB1_L = LIST_LEFT  + 5
    PB1_W = LIST_WIDTH - 31

 CASE TMP_CC = 2

    PB1_W = C1 - 2
    PB1_L = LIST_LEFT + 5
    PB2_W = LIST_WIDTH - PB1_W - 33
    PB2_L  = PB1_L + PB1_W + 4

CASE TMP_CC = 3

     PB1_W = C1 - 1
     PB1_L  = LIST_LEFT + 5
     PB2_W = C2 - 1
     PB2_L  = PB1_L + PB1_W + 4
     PB3_W = LIST_WIDTH - PB1_W - PB2_W - 36
     PB3_L  = PB2_L + PB2_W + 4

CASE TMP_CC = 4
     PB1_W = C1 - 2
     PB1_L  = LIST_LEFT + 5
     PB2_W = C2 - 1
     PB2_L  = PB1_L + PB1_W + 4
     PB3_W = C3 - 1
     PB3_L  = PB2_L + PB2_W + 4
     PB4_W = LIST_WIDTH - PB1_W - PB2_W - PB3_W - 38
     PB4_L  = PB3_L + PB3_W + 4

CASE TMP_CC = 5

     PB1_W = C1 - 2
     PB1_L  = LIST_LEFT + 5
     PB2_W = C2 - 1
     PB2_L  = PB1_L + PB1_W + 4
     PB3_W = C3 - 1
     PB3_L  = PB2_L + PB2_W + 4
     PB4_W = C4 - 1
     PB4_L  = PB3_L + PB3_W + 4
     PB5_W = LIST_WIDTH -PB1_W -PB2_W -PB3_W - PB4_W - 42
     PB5_L  = PB4_L + PB4_W + 4

CASE TMP_CC = 6

     PB1_W = C1 - 2
     PB1_L  = LIST_LEFT + 5

     PB2_W = C2 - 1
     PB2_L  = PB1_L + PB1_W + 4
```

```
        PB3_W = C3 - 1
        PB3_L  = PB2_L + PB2_W + 4

        PB4_W = C4 - 1
        PB4_L  = PB3_L + PB3_W + 4

        PB5_W = C5 - 1
        PB5_L  = PB4_L + PB4_W + 4

        PB6_W = LIST_WIDTH - PB1_W - PB2_W - PB3_W - PB4_W - ;
                PB5_W - 46
        PB6_L  = PB5_L + PB5_W + 4

CASE TMP_CC = 7

        PB1_W = C1 - 2
        PB1_L  = LIST_LEFT + 5

        PB2_W = C2 - 1
        PB2_L  = PB1_L + PB1_W + 4

        PB3_W = C3 - 1
        PB3_L  = PB2_L + PB2_W + 4

        PB4_W = C4 - 1
        PB4_L  = PB3_L + PB3_W + 4

        PB5_W = C5 - 1
        PB5_L  = PB4_L + PB4_W + 4

        PB6_W = C6 - 1
        PB6_L  = PB5_L + PB5_W + 4

        PB7_W = LIST_WIDTH - PB1_W - PB2_W - PB3_W - PB4_W - ;
                PB5_W - PB6_W - 51
        PB7_L  = PB6_L + PB6_W + 4

CASE TMP_CC = 8

        PB1_W = C1 - 2
        PB1_L  = LIST_LEFT + 5

        PB2_W = C2 - 1
        PB2_L  = PB1_L + PB1_W + 4

        PB3_W = C3 - 1
        PB3_L  = PB2_L + PB2_W + 4

        PB4_W = C4 - 1
```

```
        PB4_L  = PB3_L + PB3_W + 4

        PB5_W = C5 - 1
        PB5_L  = PB4_L + PB4_W + 4

        PB6_W = C6 - 1
        PB6_L  = PB5_L + PB5_W + 4

        PB7_W = C7 - 1
        PB7_L  = PB6_L + PB6_W + 4

        PB8_W = LIST_WIDTH - PB1_W - PB2_W - PB3_W - PB4_W - ;
                PB5_W - PB6_W - PB7_W - 55
        PB8_L  = PB7_L + PB7_W + 4

    CASE TMP_CC = 9

        PB1_W = C1 - 2
        PB1_L  = LIST_LEFT + 5

        PB2_W = C2 - 1
        PB2_L  = PB1_L + PB1_W + 4

        PB3_W = C3 - 1
        PB3_L  = PB2_L + PB2_W + 4

        PB4_W = C4 - 1
        PB4_L  = PB3_L + PB3_W + 4

        PB5_W = C5 - 1
        PB5_L  = PB4_L + PB4_W + 4

        PB6_W = C6 - 1
        PB6_L  = PB5_L + PB5_W + 4

        PB7_W = C7 - 1
        PB7_L  = PB6_L + PB6_W + 4
        PB8_W = C8 - 1
        PB8_L  = PB7_L + PB7_W + 4

        PB9_W = LIST_WIDTH - PB1_W - PB2_W - PB3_W - PB4_W - ;
                PB5_W - PB6_W - PB7_W - PB8_W - 60

        PB9_L  = PB8_L + PB8_W + 4

    CASE TMP_CC = 10

        PB1_W = C1 - 2
        PB1_L  = LIST_LEFT + 5
```

```
     PB2_W = C2 - 1
     PB2_L  = PB1_L + PB1_W + 4

     PB3_W = C3 - 1
     PB3_L  = PB2_L + PB2_W + 4

     PB4_W = C4 - 1
     PB4_L  = PB3_L + PB3_W + 4

     PB5_W = C5 - 1
     PB5_L  = PB4_L + PB4_W + 4

     PB6_W = C6 - 1
     PB6_L  = PB5_L + PB5_W + 4

     PB7_W = C7 - 1
     PB7_L  = PB6_L + PB6_W + 4

     PB8_W = C8 - 1
     PB8_L  = PB7_L + PB7_W + 4

     PB9_W = C9 - 1
     PB9_L  = PB8_L + PB8_W + 4

     PB10_W = LIST_WIDTH - PB1_W - PB2_W - PB3_W - PB4_W - ;
              PB5_W - PB6_W - PB7_W - PB8_W - PB9_W - 65

     PB10_L  = PB9_L + PB9_W + 4

CASE TMP_CC = 11

     PB1_W = C1 - 2
     PB1_L  = LIST_LEFT + 5

     PB2_W = C2 - 1
     PB2_L  = PB1_L + PB1_W + 4
     PB3_W = C3 - 1
     PB3_L  = PB2_L + PB2_W + 4

     PB4_W = C4 - 1
     PB4_L  = PB3_L + PB3_W + 4

     PB5_W = C5 - 1
     PB5_L  = PB4_L + PB4_W + 4

     PB6_W = C6 - 1
     PB6_L  = PB5_L + PB5_W + 4

     PB7_W = C7 - 1
     PB7_L  = PB6_L + PB6_W + 4
```

```
        PB8_W = C8 - 1
        PB8_L  = PB7_L + PB7_W + 4

        PB9_W = C9 - 1
        PB9_L  = PB8_L + PB8_W + 4

        PB10_W = C10 - 1
        PB10_L  = PB9_L + PB9_W + 4

        PB11_W = LIST_WIDTH - PB1_W - PB2_W - PB3_W - PB4_W - ;
          PB5_W - PB6_W - PB7_W - PB8_W - PB9_W  - PB10_W -  70
        PB11_L  = PB10_L + PB10_W + 4

    CASE TMP_CC = 12

        PB1_W = C1 - 2
        PB1_L  = LIST_LEFT + 5

        PB2_W = C2 - 1
        PB2_L  = PB1_L + PB1_W + 4

        PB3_W = C3 - 1
        PB3_L  = PB2_L + PB2_W + 4

        PB4_W = C4 - 1
        PB4_L  = PB3_L + PB3_W + 4

        PB5_W = C5 - 1
        PB5_L  = PB4_L + PB4_W + 4

        PB6_W = C6 - 1
        PB6_L  = PB5_L + PB5_W + 4
        PB7_W = C7 - 1
        PB7_L  = PB6_L + PB6_W + 4

        PB8_W = C8 - 1
        PB8_L  = PB7_L + PB7_W + 4

        PB9_W = C9 - 1
        PB9_L  = PB8_L + PB8_W + 4

        PB10_W = C10 - 1
        PB10_L  = PB9_L + PB9_W + 4

        PB11_W = C11 - 1
        PB11_L  = PB10_L + PB10_W + 4

        PB12_W = LIST_WIDTH - PB1_W - PB2_W - PB3_W - PB4_W - ;
            PB5_W - PB6_W - PB7_W - PB8_W - PB9_W  - PB10_W - ;
```

```
        PB11_W - 75
    PB12_L  = PB11_L + PB11_W + 4

CASE TMP_CC = 13

    PB1_W = C1 - 2
    PB1_L  = LIST_LEFT + 5

    PB2_W = C2 - 1
    PB2_L  = PB1_L + PB1_W + 4

    PB3_W = C3 - 1
    PB3_L  = PB2_L + PB2_W + 4

    PB4_W = C4 - 1
    PB4_L  = PB3_L + PB3_W + 4

    PB5_W = C5 - 1
    PB5_L  = PB4_L + PB4_W + 4

    PB6_W = C6 - 1
    PB6_L  = PB5_L + PB5_W + 4

    PB7_W = C7 - 1
    PB7_L  = PB6_L + PB6_W + 4

    PB8_W = C8 - 1
    PB8_L  = PB7_L + PB7_W + 4

    PB9_W = C9 - 1
    PB9_L  = PB8_L + PB8_W + 4

    PB10_W = C10 - 1
    PB10_L  = PB9_L + PB9_W + 4

    PB11_W = C11 - 1
    PB11_L  = PB10_L + PB10_W + 4

    PB12_W = C12 - 1
    PB12_L  = PB11_L + PB11_W + 4

    PB13_W = LIST_WIDTH - PB1_W - PB2_W - PB3_W - PB4_W - ;
        PB5_W - PB6_W - PB7_W - PB8_W - PB9_W  - PB10_W - ;
        PB11_W - PB12_W - 75

    PB13_L  = PB12_L + PB12_W + 4

ENDCASE

THISFORM.A008_LIST_COLUMN_PB_WIDTH( TMP_CC,PB1_L,PB1_W, ;
```

```
   PB2_L, PB2_W,PB3_L,PB3_W, PB4_L,PB4_W,PB5_L,PB5_W,PB6_L, ;
   PB6_W,PB7_L, PB7_W,PB8_L,PB8_W,PB9_L, PB9_W, PB10_L, ;
   PB10_W,PB11_L,PB11_W, PB12_L, PB12_W, PB13_L, PB13_W )

ON ERROR



*============================================================*
* Procedure: B08_LIST_PB_ADJUST_CLICK                        *
*                                             See page 87. *
*============================================================*
 LOCAL C1,C2,C3,C4,C5,C6,C7,C8,C9,C10,C11,C12,C13
 LOCAL C1_W, C2_W, C3_W, C4_W, C5_W, C6_W, C7_W,C8_W,C9_W, ;
       C10_W,C11_W,C12_W
 LOCAL TMP_CC, TMP_RTN_CW , TMP_CW , C13_W

 TMP_CC = THISFORM.AD05_LIST_COLUMN_COUNT()

 DO FORM C:\TMP2000\PRGS_ETC\T_ADJUST.SCX WITH ;
         TMP_CC TO TMP_RTN_CW

 IF LEN(ALLTRIM(TMP_RTN_CW)) > 0

 DO CASE
 CASE TMP_CC = 1
     C1_W  = SUBSTR(TMP_RTN_CW,1,3)
     C1 = VAL(C1_W)
     TMP_CW = C1_W

 CASE TMP_CC = 2
     C1_W = SUBSTR(TMP_RTN_CW,1,3)
     C2_W = SUBSTR(TMP_RTN_CW,4,3)
     C1 = VAL(C1_W)
     C2 = VAL(C2_W)
     TMP_CW = C1_W + ',' + C2_W

 CASE TMP_CC = 3
     C1_W  = SUBSTR(TMP_RTN_CW,1,3)
     C2_W  = SUBSTR(TMP_RTN_CW,4,3)
     C3_W  = SUBSTR(TMP_RTN_CW,7,3)
     C1 = VAL(C1_W)
     C2 = VAL(C2_W)
     C3 = VAL(C3_W)
     TMP_CW = C1_W + ',' + C2_W + ',' + C3_W

 CASE TMP_CC = 4
     C1_W  = SUBSTR(TMP_RTN_CW,1,3)
     C2_W  = SUBSTR(TMP_RTN_CW,4,3)
     C3_W  = SUBSTR(TMP_RTN_CW,7,3)
```

```
    C4_W   = SUBSTR(TMP_RTN_CW,10,3)
    C1 = VAL(C1_W)
    C2 = VAL(C2_W)
    C3 = VAL(C3_W)
    C4 = VAL(C4_W)
    TMP_CW = C1_W + ',' + C2_W + ',' + C3_W  + ',' + C4_W

CASE TMP_CC = 5
    C1_W   = SUBSTR(TMP_RTN_CW,1,3)
    C2_W   = SUBSTR(TMP_RTN_CW,4,3)
    C3_W   = SUBSTR(TMP_RTN_CW,7,3)
    C4_W   = SUBSTR(TMP_RTN_CW,10,3)
    C5_W   = SUBSTR(TMP_RTN_CW,13,3)
    C1 = VAL(C1_W)
    C2 = VAL(C2_W)
    C3 = VAL(C3_W)
    C4 = VAL(C4_W)
    C5 = VAL(C5_W)
    TMP_CW = C1_W + ',' + C2_W + ',' + C3_W  + ',' + C4_W + ;
             ',' + C5_W

CASE TMP_CC = 6
    C1_W   = SUBSTR(TMP_RTN_CW,1,3)
    C2_W   = SUBSTR(TMP_RTN_CW,4,3)
    C3_W   = SUBSTR(TMP_RTN_CW,7,3)
    C4_W   = SUBSTR(TMP_RTN_CW,10,3)
    C5_W   = SUBSTR(TMP_RTN_CW,13,3)
    C6_W   = SUBSTR(TMP_RTN_CW,16,3)
    C1 = VAL(C1_W)
    C2 = VAL(C2_W)
    C3 = VAL(C3_W)
    C4 = VAL(C4_W)
    C5 = VAL(C5_W)
    C6 = VAL(C6_W)
    TMP_CW = C1_W + ',' + C2_W + ',' + C3_W  + ',' + C4_W + ;
             ',' + C5_W + ',' + C6_W

CASE TMP_CC = 7
    C1_W   = SUBSTR(TMP_RTN_CW,1,3)
    C2_W   = SUBSTR(TMP_RTN_CW,4,3)
    C3_W   = SUBSTR(TMP_RTN_CW,7,3)
    C4_W   = SUBSTR(TMP_RTN_CW,10,3)
    C5_W   = SUBSTR(TMP_RTN_CW,13,3)
    C6_W   = SUBSTR(TMP_RTN_CW,16,3)
    C7_W   = SUBSTR(TMP_RTN_CW,19,3)
    C1 = VAL(C1_W)
    C2 = VAL(C2_W)
    C3 = VAL(C3_W)
    C4 = VAL(C4_W)
    C5 = VAL(C5_W)
```

```
    C6 = VAL(C6_W)
    C7 = VAL(C7_W)
    TMP_CW = C1_W + ',' + C2_W + ',' + C3_W  + ',' + C4_W + ;
            ',' + C5_W + ',' + C6_W + ',' + C7_W

CASE TMP_CC = 8
    C1_W   = SUBSTR(TMP_RTN_CW,1,3)
    C2_W   = SUBSTR(TMP_RTN_CW,4,3)
    C3_W   = SUBSTR(TMP_RTN_CW,7,3)
    C4_W   = SUBSTR(TMP_RTN_CW,10,3)
    C5_W   = SUBSTR(TMP_RTN_CW,13,3)
    C6_W   = SUBSTR(TMP_RTN_CW,16,3)
    C7_W   = SUBSTR(TMP_RTN_CW,19,3)
    C8_W   = SUBSTR(TMP_RTN_CW,22,3)
    C1 = VAL(C1_W)
    C2 = VAL(C2_W)
    C3 = VAL(C3_W)
    C4 = VAL(C4_W)
    C5 = VAL(C5_W)
    C6 = VAL(C6_W)
    C7 = VAL(C7_W)
    C8 = VAL(C8_W)
    TMP_CW = C1_W + ',' + C2_W + ',' + C3_W  + ',' + C4_W + ;
             ',' + C5_W + ',' + C6_W + ',' + C7_W  + ',' +   ;
             C8_W

CASE TMP_CC = 9
    C1_W   = SUBSTR(TMP_RTN_CW,1,3)
    C2_W   = SUBSTR(TMP_RTN_CW,4,3)
    C3_W   = SUBSTR(TMP_RTN_CW,7,3)
    C4_W   = SUBSTR(TMP_RTN_CW,10,3)
    C5_W   = SUBSTR(TMP_RTN_CW,13,3)
    C6_W   = SUBSTR(TMP_RTN_CW,16,3)
    C7_W   = SUBSTR(TMP_RTN_CW,19,3)
    C8_W   = SUBSTR(TMP_RTN_CW,22,3)
    C9_W   = SUBSTR(TMP_RTN_CW,25,3)
    C1 = VAL(C1_W)
    C2 = VAL(C2_W)
    C3 = VAL(C3_W)
    C4 = VAL(C4_W)
    C5 = VAL(C5_W)
    C6 = VAL(C6_W)
    C7 = VAL(C7_W)
    C8 = VAL(C8_W)
    C9 = VAL(C9_W)
    TMP_CW = C1_W + ',' + C2_W + ',' + C3_W  + ',' + C4_W + ;
             ',' + C5_W + ',' + C6_W + ',' + C7_W  + ',' +  ;
             C8_W + ',' + C9_W

  CASE TMP_CC = 10
```

```
    C1_W  = SUBSTR(TMP_RTN_CW,1,3)
    C2_W  = SUBSTR(TMP_RTN_CW,4,3)
    C3_W  = SUBSTR(TMP_RTN_CW,7,3)
    C4_W  = SUBSTR(TMP_RTN_CW,10,3)
    C5_W  = SUBSTR(TMP_RTN_CW,13,3)
    C6_W  = SUBSTR(TMP_RTN_CW,16,3)
    C7_W  = SUBSTR(TMP_RTN_CW,19,3)
    C8_W  = SUBSTR(TMP_RTN_CW,22,3)
    C9_W  = SUBSTR(TMP_RTN_CW,25,3)
    C10_W = SUBSTR(TMP_RTN_CW,28,3)
    C1 = VAL(C1_W)
    C2 = VAL(C2_W)
    C3 = VAL(C3_W)
    C4 = VAL(C4_W)
    C5 = VAL(C5_W)
    C6 = VAL(C6_W)
    C7 = VAL(C7_W)
    C8 = VAL(C8_W)
    C9 = VAL(C9_W)
    C10 = VAL(C10_W)
    TMP_CW = C1_W + ',' + C2_W + ',' + C3_W  + ',' + C4_W + ;
             ',' + C5_W + ',' + C6_W + ',' + C7_W  + ',' +  ;
             C8_W + ',' + C9_W + ',' + C10_W

 CASE TMP_CC = 11
    C1_W  = SUBSTR(TMP_RTN_CW,1,3)
    C2_W  = SUBSTR(TMP_RTN_CW,4,3)
    C3_W  = SUBSTR(TMP_RTN_CW,7,3)
    C4_W  = SUBSTR(TMP_RTN_CW,10,3)
    C5_W  = SUBSTR(TMP_RTN_CW,13,3)
    C6_W  = SUBSTR(TMP_RTN_CW,16,3)
    C7_W  = SUBSTR(TMP_RTN_CW,19,3)
    C8_W  = SUBSTR(TMP_RTN_CW,22,3)
    C9_W  = SUBSTR(TMP_RTN_CW,25,3)
    C10_W = SUBSTR(TMP_RTN_CW,28,3)
    C11_W = SUBSTR(TMP_RTN_CW,31,3)
    C1 = VAL(C1_W)
    C2 = VAL(C2_W)
    C3 = VAL(C3_W)
    C4 = VAL(C4_W)
    C5 = VAL(C5_W)
    C6 = VAL(C6_W)
    C7 = VAL(C7_W)
    C8 = VAL(C8_W)
    C9 = VAL(C9_W)
    C10 = VAL(C10_W)
    C11 = VAL(C11_W)
    TMP_CW = C1_W + ',' + C2_W + ',' + C3_W  + ',' + C4_W + ;
             ',' + C5_W + ',' + C6_W + ',' + C7_W  + ',' +  ;
             C8_W + ',' + C9_W + ',' + C10_W + ',' + C11_W
```

```
 CASE TMP_CC = 12
    C1_W   = SUBSTR(TMP_RTN_CW,1,3)
    C2_W   = SUBSTR(TMP_RTN_CW,4,3)
    C3_W   = SUBSTR(TMP_RTN_CW,7,3)
    C4_W   = SUBSTR(TMP_RTN_CW,10,3)
    C5_W   = SUBSTR(TMP_RTN_CW,13,3)
    C6_W   = SUBSTR(TMP_RTN_CW,16,3)
    C7_W   = SUBSTR(TMP_RTN_CW,19,3)
    C8_W   = SUBSTR(TMP_RTN_CW,22,3)
    C9_W   = SUBSTR(TMP_RTN_CW,25,3)
    C10_W  = SUBSTR(TMP_RTN_CW,28,3)
    C11_W  = SUBSTR(TMP_RTN_CW,31,3)
    C12_W  = SUBSTR(TMP_RTN_CW,34,3)
    C1 = VAL(C1_W)
    C2 = VAL(C2_W)
    C3 = VAL(C3_W)
    C4 = VAL(C4_W)
    C5 = VAL(C5_W)
    C6 = VAL(C6_W)
    C7 = VAL(C7_W)
    C8 = VAL(C8_W)
    C9 = VAL(C9_W)
    C10 = VAL(C10_W)
    C11 = VAL(C11_W)
    C12 = VAL(C12_W)
    TMP_CW = C1_W + ',' + C2_W + ',' + C3_W  + ',' + C4_W + ;
             ',' + C5_W + ',' + C6_W + ',' + C7_W  + ',' +  ;
             C8_W + ',' + C9_W + ',' + C10_W + ',' + C11_W  ;
             + ',' + C12_W

CASE TMP_CC = 13
    C1_W   = SUBSTR(TMP_RTN_CW,1,3)
    C2_W   = SUBSTR(TMP_RTN_CW,4,3)
    C3_W   = SUBSTR(TMP_RTN_CW,7,3)
    C4_W   = SUBSTR(TMP_RTN_CW,10,3)
    C5_W   = SUBSTR(TMP_RTN_CW,13,3)
    C6_W   = SUBSTR(TMP_RTN_CW,16,3)
    C7_W   = SUBSTR(TMP_RTN_CW,19,3)
    C8_W   = SUBSTR(TMP_RTN_CW,22,3)
    C9_W   = SUBSTR(TMP_RTN_CW,25,3)
    C10_W  = SUBSTR(TMP_RTN_CW,28,3)
    C11_W  = SUBSTR(TMP_RTN_CW,31,3)
    C12_W  = SUBSTR(TMP_RTN_CW,34,3)
    C13_W  = SUBSTR(TMP_RTN_CW,37,3)
    C1 = VAL(C1_W)
    C2 = VAL(C2_W)
    C3 = VAL(C3_W)
    C4 = VAL(C4_W)
    C5 = VAL(C5_W)
    C6 = VAL(C6_W)
```

```
        C7 = VAL(C7_W)
        C8 = VAL(C8_W)
        C9 = VAL(C9_W)
        C10 = VAL(C10_W)
        C11 = VAL(C11_W)
        C12 = VAL(C12_W)
        C13 = VAL(C13_W)
        TMP_CW = C1_W + ',' + C2_W + ',' + C3_W  + ',' + C4_W + ;
                 ',' + C5_W + ',' + C6_W + ',' + C7_W  + ',' +  ;
                 C8_W + ',' + C9_W + ',' + C10_W + ',' + C11_W  ;
                 + ',' + C12_W

   ENDCASE
   THISFORM.A006_LIST_COLUMN_WIDTH(TMP_CW)
   THISFORM.B07_SETUP_LIST_COLUMN(C1,C2,C3,C4,C5,C6,C7,C8,C9,
                                  C10,C11,C12,C13)

ENDIF




*==============================================================*
* Procedure: B09_INDEX_USED                                    *
*                                                              *
*==============================================================*
LPARAMETERS TMP_INDEX_USED, TMP_WITH_SEARCH
LOCAL TMP_CC

 IF TMP_WITH_SEARCH = .F.

    DO CASE
    CASE TMP_INDEX_USED = 1
        THISFORM.AF03_VIEW_IDX1
    CASE TMP_INDEX_USED = 2
        THISFORM.AF04_VIEW_IDX2
    ENDCASE

 ELSE

    DO CASE
    CASE TMP_INDEX_USED = 1
       THISFORM.AF05_VIEW_SEARCH_IDX1
    CASE TMP_INDEX_USED = 2
       THISFORM.AF06_VIEW_SEARCH_IDX2
    ENDCASE

 ENDIF
```

```
 TMP_CC = THISFORM.AD05_LIST_COLUMN_COUNT()

 DO CASE
   CASE TMP_INDEX_USED = 1
      THISFORM.AO12_INIT_PB_COLOR_IDX1(TMP_CC)
      THISFORM.LABEL_IDX.CAPTION = "1"
   CASE TMP_INDEX_USED = 2
      THISFORM.AO13_INIT_PB_COLOR_IDX2(TMP_CC)
      THISFORM.LABEL_IDX.CAPTION = "2"
 ENDCASE


*==============================================================*
* Procedure: B82_PB_CHANGE                                     *
*                                                              *
*==============================================================*
 LOCAL TMP_L_VAL, TMP_IDX_NO

 TMP_L_VAL = THISFORM.AO02_LIST_VALUE()
IF LEN(TRIM(TMP_L_VAL)) > 0

    THISFORM.AD16_CALL_DATA_ENTRY_FORM("CHG", TMP_L_VAL)

    TMP_IDX_NO = VAL(THISFORM.LABEL_IDX.CAPTION)
    THISFORM.B09_INDEX_USED(TMP_IDX_NO,.F.)
    THISFORM.AO01_LIST_REQUERY
    thisform.Refresh

 ELSE
      WAIT WINDOW NOWAIT " Select a valid record. "
 ENDIF


*==============================================================*
* Procedure: B83_PB_COPY                                       *
*                                                              *
*==============================================================*
 LOCAL TMP_L_VAL, TMP_IDX_NO

 TMP_L_VAL = THISFORM.AO02_LIST_VALUE()

 IF LEN(TRIM(TMP_L_VAL)) > 0

    THISFORM.AD16_CALL_DATA_ENTRY_FORM("CPY", TMP_L_VAL)

    TMP_IDX_NO = VAL(THISFORM.LABEL_IDX.CAPTION)
    THISFORM.B09_INDEX_USED(TMP_IDX_NO, .F.)
```

```
    THISFORM.A001_LIST_REQUERY
    Thisform.Refresh

 ELSE
    WAIT WINDOW NOWAIT " Select a valid record. "
 ENDIF



*==============================================================*
* Procedure: B84_PB_DELETE                                     *
*                                                              *
*==============================================================*
 LOCAL TMP_L_VAL, TMP_IDX_NO

 TMP_L_VAL = THISFORM.A002_LIST_VALUE()
IF LEN(TRIM(TMP_L_VAL)) > 0

     THISFORM.AD16_CALL_DATA_ENTRY_FORM("DEL", TMP_L_VAL)

     TMP_IDX_NO = VAL(THISFORM.LABEL_IDX.CAPTION)
     THISFORM.B09_INDEX_USED(TMP_IDX_NO, .F.)
     THISFORM.A001_LIST_REQUERY
     Thisform.Refresh

  ELSE
      WAIT WINDOW NOWAIT " Select a valid record. "
  ENDIF


*==============================================================*
* Procedure: B85_PB_DISPLAY                                    *
*                                                              *
*==============================================================*
 LOCAL TMP_L_VAL, TMP_IDX_NO

 TMP_L_VAL = THISFORM.A002_LIST_VALUE()

 IF LEN(TRIM(TMP_L_VAL)) > 0

    THISFORM.AD16_CALL_DATA_ENTRY_FORM("DSP", TMP_L_VAL)

    TMP_IDX_NO = VAL(THISFORM.LABEL_IDX.CAPTION)
    THISFORM.B09_INDEX_USED(TMP_IDX_NO, .F.)
    THISFORM.A001_LIST_REQUERY
    THISFORM.Refresh

 ELSE
```

```
   WAIT WINDOW NOWAIT " Select a valid record. "
 ENDIF


*=============================================================*
* Procedure: B86_PB_ADD                                        *
*                                                              *
*=============================================================*
LOCAL TMP_IDX_NO

THISFORM.AD16_CALL_DATA_ENTRY_FORM("ADD", " ")

TMP_IDX_NO = VAL(THISFORM.LABEL_IDX.CAPTION)
THISFORM.B09_INDEX_USED(TMP_IDX_NO,.F.)
THISFORM.A001_LIST_REQUERY
THISFORM.Refresh



*=============================================================*
* Procedure: B87_PB_SAVE                                       *
*                                                              *
*=============================================================*


*=============================================================*
* Procedure: B88_PB_PRINT                                      *
*                                                              *
*=============================================================*



*=============================================================*
* Procedure: B89_PB_EXIT                                       *
*                                                              *
*=============================================================*

 Thisform.AD17_CLEANUP

 CLOSE DATABASES

 THISFORM.RELEASE


*=============================================================*
* Procedure : AD01_FORMS_PROPERTIES                            *
*                                                              *
* Description: The following form properties were changed     *
*              using the Property Window:                      *
*                                                              *
```

```
*                ShowWindow  = 2 As Top Level Form             *
*                WindowType  = 1 Modal                         *
*                DataSession = 2 Private Data Session          *
*                                                              *
*                Height= 425, Width= 630, Top = 0, Left = 0    *
*                                                              *
*==============================================================*


*==============================================================*
* Procedure: AD03_FORM_CAPTION                                 *
*                                                              *
*==============================================================*

Thisform.Caption = LI_FRM_CAPTION



*==============================================================*
* Procedure: AD04_WITH_SEARCH_WINDOW                           *
*                                                              *
*==============================================================*
Lparameters na

Local with_search


    with_search = LI_WITH_SEARCH     && .T. or .F.


*------------------------------
* Do not change the code below.
*------------------------------

 If with_search = .T.
   Return .T.
 Else
   Return .F.
 Endif



*==============================================================*
* Procedure: AD05_LIST_COLUMN_COUNT                            *
*                                                              *
*==============================================================*
 Local column_count
```

```
    column_count = 2
                  *==


*-------------------------------
* Do not change the code below.
*-------------------------------

 Return column_count




*==============================================================*
* Procedure: AD06_LIST_COLUMN_WIDTH                            *
*                                                              *
*==============================================================*
Lparameters cc

Local c1,c2,c3,c4,c5,c6,c7,c8,c9,c10,c11,c12,c13
Local cw, c1_w, c2_w ,c3_w, c4_w, c5_w, c6_w, c7_w
Local c8_W ,c9_w, c10_w, c11_w, c12_w , c13_w

      *------------------
      * Column Width
      *------------------
      c1  = LI_WIDTH_COL1
      c2  = LI_WIDTH_COL2
      c3  = LI_WIDTH_COL3
      c4  = LI_WIDTH_COL4
      c5  = LI_WIDTH_COL5
      c6  = LI_WIDTH_COL6
      c7  = LI_WIDTH_COL7
      c8  = LI_WIDTH_COL8
      c9  = LI_WIDTH_COL9
      c10 = LI_WIDTH_COL10
    * c11 = 0
    * c12 = 0
    * c13 = 0
           *==


 *-------------------------------
 * Do not change the code below.
 *-------------------------------

 DO CASE
 CASE CC = 1
```

```
    C1_W = ALLTRIM(STR(C1))
    CW    =  C1_W
CASE CC = 2
    C1_W = ALLTRIM(STR(C1))
    C2_W = ALLTRIM(STR(C2))
    CW =  C1_W + ',' + C2_W
CASE CC = 3
    C1_W = ALLTRIM(STR(C1))
    C2_W = ALLTRIM(STR(C2))
    C3_W = ALLTRIM(STR(C3))
    CW    = C1_W + ',' + C2_W + ',' + C3_W

CASE CC = 4
    C1_W = ALLTRIM(STR(C1))
    C2_W = ALLTRIM(STR(C2))
    C3_W = ALLTRIM(STR(C3))
    C4_W = ALLTRIM(STR(C4))
    CW = C1_W + ',' + C2_W + ',' + C3_W  + ',' + C4_W

CASE CC = 5
    C1_W = ALLTRIM(STR(C1))
    C2_W = ALLTRIM(STR(C2))
    C3_W = ALLTRIM(STR(C3))
    C4_W = ALLTRIM(STR(C4))
    C5_W = ALLTRIM(STR(C5))
    CW = C1_W + ',' + C2_W + ',' + C3_W  + ',' + C4_W  + ;
         ',' + C5_W

CASE CC = 6
    C1_W = ALLTRIM(STR(C1))
    C2_W = ALLTRIM(STR(C2))
    C3_W = ALLTRIM(STR(C3))
    C4_W = ALLTRIM(STR(C4))
    C5_W = ALLTRIM(STR(C5))
    C6_W = ALLTRIM(STR(C6))

    CW = C1_W + ',' + C2_W + ',' + C3_W  + ',' + C4_W + ;
         ',' + C5_W + ',' + C6_W

CASE CC = 7
    C1_W = ALLTRIM(STR(C1))
    C2_W = ALLTRIM(STR(C2))
    C3_W = ALLTRIM(STR(C3))
    C4_W = ALLTRIM(STR(C4))
    C5_W = ALLTRIM(STR(C5))
    C6_W = ALLTRIM(STR(C6))
    C7_W = ALLTRIM(STR(C7))

    CW = C1_W + ',' + C2_W + ',' + C3_W  + ',' + C4_W +  ;
         ',' + C5_W + ',' + C6_W + ',' + C7_W
```

```
CASE CC = 8
   C1_W = ALLTRIM(STR(C1))
   C2_W = ALLTRIM(STR(C2))
   C3_W = ALLTRIM(STR(C3))
   C4_W = ALLTRIM(STR(C4))
   C5_W = ALLTRIM(STR(C5))
   C6_W = ALLTRIM(STR(C6))
   C7_W = ALLTRIM(STR(C7))
   C8_W = ALLTRIM(STR(C8))
   CW = C1_W + ',' + C2_W + ',' + C3_W  + ',' + C4_W + ;
        ',' + C5_W + C6_W + ',' + C7_W  + ',' + C8_W

CASE CC = 9
   C1_W = ALLTRIM(STR(C1))
   C2_W = ALLTRIM(STR(C2))
   C3_W = ALLTRIM(STR(C3))
   C4_W = ALLTRIM(STR(C4))
   C5_W = ALLTRIM(STR(C5))
   C6_W = ALLTRIM(STR(C6))
   C7_W = ALLTRIM(STR(C7))
   C8_W = ALLTRIM(STR(C8))
   C9_W = ALLTRIM(STR(C9))

   CW = C1_W + ',' + C2_W + ',' + C3_W  + ',' + C4_W + ;
         ',' + C5_W + ',' + C6_W + ',' + C7_W  + ',' + ;
         C8_W + ',' + C9_W

CASE CC = 10

   C1_W = ALLTRIM(STR(C1))
   C2_W = ALLTRIM(STR(C2))
   C3_W = ALLTRIM(STR(C3))
   C4_W = ALLTRIM(STR(C4))
   C5_W = ALLTRIM(STR(C5))
   C6_W = ALLTRIM(STR(C6))
   C7_W = ALLTRIM(STR(C7))
   C8_W = ALLTRIM(STR(C8))
   C9_W = ALLTRIM(STR(C9))
   C10_W = ALLTRIM(STR(C10))

   CW = C1_W + ',' + C2_W + ',' + C3_W  + ',' + C4_W + ;
        ',' + C5_W + C6_W + ',' + C7_W  + ',' + C8_W + ;
        ',' + C9_W + C10_W

CASE CC = 11

   C1_W = ALLTRIM(STR(C1))
   C2_W = ALLTRIM(STR(C2))
   C3_W = ALLTRIM(STR(C3))
```

```
    C4_W = ALLTRIM(STR(C4))
    C5_W = ALLTRIM(STR(C5))
    C6_W = ALLTRIM(STR(C6))
    C7_W = ALLTRIM(STR(C7))
    C8_W = ALLTRIM(STR(C8))
    C9_W = ALLTRIM(STR(C9))
    C10_W = ALLTRIM(STR(C10))
    C11_W = ALLTRIM(STR(C11))

    CW = C1_W + ',' + C2_W + ',' + C3_W  + ',' + C4_W + ;
         ',' + C5_W + C6_W + ',' + C7_W  + ',' + C8_W + ;
         ',' + C9_W + C10_W + ',' + C11_W

 CASE CC = 12
    C1_W = ALLTRIM(STR(C1))
    C2_W = ALLTRIM(STR(C2))
    C3_W = ALLTRIM(STR(C3))
    C4_W = ALLTRIM(STR(C4))
    C5_W = ALLTRIM(STR(C5))
    C6_W = ALLTRIM(STR(C6))
    C7_W = ALLTRIM(STR(C7))
    C8_W = ALLTRIM(STR(C8))
    C9_W = ALLTRIM(STR(C9))
    C10_W = ALLTRIM(STR(C10))
    C11_W = ALLTRIM(STR(C11))
    C12_W = ALLTRIM(STR(C12))

    CW = C1_W + ',' + C2_W + ',' + C3_W  + ',' + C4_W + ;
         ',' + C5_W + C6_W + ',' + C7_W  + ',' + C8_W + ;
         ',' + C9_W + C10_W + ',' + C11_W  + ',' + C12_W

CASE CC = 13
    C1_W = ALLTRIM(STR(C1))
    C2_W = ALLTRIM(STR(C2))
    C3_W = ALLTRIM(STR(C3))
    C4_W = ALLTRIM(STR(C4))
    C5_W = ALLTRIM(STR(C5))
    C6_W = ALLTRIM(STR(C6))
    C7_W = ALLTRIM(STR(C7))
    C8_W = ALLTRIM(STR(C8))
    C9_W = ALLTRIM(STR(C9))
    C10_W = ALLTRIM(STR(C10))
    C11_W = ALLTRIM(STR(C11))
    C12_W = ALLTRIM(STR(C12))
    C13_W = ALLTRIM(STR(C13))

    CW = C1_W + ',' + C2_W + ',' + C3_W  + ',' + C4_W + ;
         ',' + C5_W + ',' + C6_W + ',' + C7_W  + ',' + ;
          C8_W + ',' + C9_W + ',' + C10_W + ',' + C11_W ;
          + ',' + C12_W + ',' + C13_W
```

```
ENDCASE

THISFORM.B07_SETUP_LIST_COLUMN(C1,C2,C3,C4,C5,C6,C7,C8, ;
                               C9,C10,C11,C12,C13)

RETURN CW  && Column Width


*==============================================================*
* Procedure  : AD07_LIST_PB_CAPTION                            *
*                                                              *
*==============================================================*
Lparameters cc

Local c1, c2, c3, c4, c5, c6, c7, c8, c9, c10, c11, c12, c13

    *-------------------------
    * Column Name/ PB Caption
    *-------------------------
    c1  =  LI_CAPTION_COL1
    c2  =  LI_CAPTION_COL2
    c3  =  LI_CAPTION_COL3
    c4  =  LI_CAPTION_COL4
    c5  =  LI_CAPTION_COL5
    c6  =  LI_CAPTION_COL6
    c7  =  LI_CAPTION_COL7
    c8  =  LI_CAPTION_COL8
    c9  =  LI_CAPTION_COL9
    c10 =  LI_CAPTION_COL10
    c11 =  " "
    c12 =  " "
    c13 =  " "
          *=======

*-------------------------------
* Do not change the code below.
*-------------------------------

Thisform.ao07_list_pb_caption(cc,c1,c2,c3,c4,c5,c6,c7,;
                              c8,c9,c10,c11,c12,c13)


*==============================================================*
* Procedure  : AD09_LIST_ROW_SOURCE_TYPE                       *
*                                                              *
*  SourceType   Description    RowSource                       *
*  ----------   ------------   --------------------------      *
*      6          Field        "USERS.user_id, user_name"      *
*==============================================================*
```

Source Code

```
Lparameters na
Local row_source_type

   row_source_type = 6      && Field
                   *==

RETURN row_source_type




*=============================================================*
* Procedure: AD11_LIST_FONT                                   *
*                                                             *
*=============================================================*
Local font_name, font_size


   font_name = "Arial"   &&
   font_size = 8         && 9
            *=======

*-------------------------------
* Do not change the code below.
*-------------------------------

Thisform.ao11_list_font(font_name,font_size)



*=============================================================*
* Procedure   : AD12_LIST_BOUND_COLUMN                        *
* Description: Determines which column is bound to the        *
*              Value Property.                                *
*=============================================================*
Local bound_column


    bound_column = 1
                 *==

RETURN bound_column


*=============================================================*
* Procedure   : AD13_INIT_INDEX                               *
* Description: Selects initial index (1) or (2). Also,        *
*              selects initial color of command buttons.      *
*=============================================================*
Lparameters na
```

```
Local index_used

    index_used  = 1      && Select index: 1 or 2
                  *===

RETURN index_used



*============================================================*
* Procedure: AD14_BEFORE_INIT                                *
*                                                            *
*============================================================*

Public PVP_COL_1  && Parameterized View Parameter
Public PVP_COL_2  && Parameterized View Parameter
      *=========

 DO CASE
 CASE li_type_col1 = "CHR"
                           PVP_COL_1 = " "
 CASE li_type_col1 = "NUM"
                           PVP_COL_1 = 0
 CASE li_type_col1 = "DATE"
                           PVP_COL_1 = CTOD("00/00/00")
 ENDCASE

 DO CASE
 CASE li_type_col2 = "CHR"
                           PVP_COL_2 = " "
 CASE li_type_col2 = "NUM"
                           PVP_COL_2 = 0
 CASE li_type_col2 = "DATE"
                           PVP_COL_2 = CTOD("00/00/00")
 ENDCASE



*============================================================*
* Procedure: AD15_AFTER_INIT                                 *
*                                                            *
*============================================================*
```

Source Code

```
*===============================================================*
* Procedure: AD16_CALL_DATA_ENTRY_FORM                          *
*                                                               *
*===============================================================*
Lparameters maint_mode, sel_rec

   *    DO FORM ________.SCX with maint_mode, sel_rec
            *========
```

```
*===============================================================*
* Procedure  : AD17_CLEANUP                                     *
* Description: Used to erase, "Pack", deleted records.          *
*===============================================================*

CLOSE DATABASES

DO FORM t_pack.scx WITH li_database, li_table
                        *==========  ========
***                     First parameter  = Database
***                     Second parameter = Table Name
***                                              (Not View)
```

```
*===============================================================*
* Procedure: AF01_OPEN_DATABASE                                 *
*                                                               *
*===============================================================*
* Local dbase1
* dbase1      = " "


*------------------------------
* Do not change the code below.
*------------------------------

OPEN DATABASE &li_database


NODEFAULT    &&  Optional - (Just in case.)
```

```
*===============================================================*
* Procedure: AF02_OPEN_FILES_VIEWS                              *
*                                                               *
*===============================================================*
* Local file1, file2, file3, file4

* file1      = ""
* file2      = ""
* file3      = ""
* file4      = ""
*--------------------------------------------------------------
 SELECT 0
 USE &LI_VIEW1 ALIAS &LI_VIEW1
 CURSORSETPROP('BUFFERING', 5)  && Optimistic Table Buffering
 *-------------------------------------------------------------
 *-------------------------------------------------------------
 SELECT 0
 USE &LI_VIEW2 ALIAS &LI_VIEW2
 CURSORSETPROP('BUFFERING', 5)  && Optimistic Table Buffering
 *-------------------------------------------------------------
 *-------------------------------------------------------------
 SELECT 0
 USE &LI_VIEW3 ALIAS &LI_VIEW3  NODATA
 CURSORSETPROP('BUFFERING', 5)  && Optimistic Table Buffering
 *-------------------------------------------------------------
 *-------------------------------------------------------------
 SELECT 0
 USE &LI_VIEW4 ALIAS &LI_VIEW4  NODATA
 CURSORSETPROP('BUFFERING', 5)  && Optimistic Table Buffering
 *-------------------------------------------------------------

 NODEFAULT



*===============================================================*
* Procedure  : AF03_VIEW_IDX1                                   *
* Description: Opens the view with sort order 1,                *
*              and sets the row source.                         *
*===============================================================*
Local row_source, no_err

 * view_1     = " "
 * row_source = " "


 *-------------------------------
 * Do not change the code below.
 *-------------------------------
```

```
 Select &LI_VIEW1
 Use
 Select 0
 Use &LI_VIEW1 Alias &LI_VIEW1
 Cursorsetprop('Buffering', 5) && Optimistic Table Buffering

 no_err = .T.
 no_err = Thisform.ao10_list_row_source(LI_ROW_SOURCE_1)
If no_err = .f.
   Thisform.ao01_list_requery
   Thisform.Refresh
   no_err = Thisform.ao10_list_row_source(LI_ROW_SOURCE_1)
 Endif

 On Error

 Thisform.ao15_list_reset_value




*==============================================================*
* Procedure  : AF04_VIEW_IDX2                                  *
* Description: Opens the view with sort order 2,               *
*              and sets the row source.                        *
*==============================================================*
Local row_source, view_2, no_err

 *  view_2     = " "
 *  row_source = " "

 *-------------------------------
 * Do not change the code below.
 *-------------------------------

 Select &LI_VIEW2
 Use
 Select 0
 Use &LI_VIEW2 Alias &LI_VIEW2
 Cursorsetprop('Buffering', 5) && Optimistic Table Buffering

 no_err = .T.
 no_err = Thisform.ao10_list_row_source(LI_ROW_SOURCE_2)

 If no_err = .f.
   Thisform.ao01_list_requery
   Thisform.Refresh
   no_err = Thisform.ao10_list_row_source(LI_ROW_SOURCE_2)
 Endif
```

```
On Error

Thisform.ao15_list_reset_value




*=================================================================*
* Procedure  : AF05_VIEW_SEARCH_IDX1                              *
* Description: Opens the view with sort order 1, and              *
*              sets the row source. (Using Search Window.)        *
*=================================================================*
Local f_caption, input_mask, parm1, no_err

 *  parm_view   = " "
 *  row_source = " "

 *-----------------------------------------------------------
 * For Search Window:                                        *
 *-----------------------------------------------------------
 f_caption   = LI_C1_SW_Caption     && Search Window Caption
 input_mask = LI_C1_SW_Input_Mask && ("9999", "XXXX", etc.)
                *=======

 DO FORM t_search.scx WITH input_mask, f_caption  TO parm1

 DO CASE
 CASE li_type_col1 = "CHR"
                          PVP_COL_1 = Alltrim(PARM1)
 CASE li_type_col1 = "NUM"
                          PVP_COL_1 = VAL(Alltrim(PARM1))
 CASE li_type_col1 = "DATE"
                          PVP_COL_1 = CTOD(Alltrim(PARM1))
 ENDCASE


 *------------------------------
 * Do not change the code below.
 *------------------------------
 Select &LI_VIEW3
 Use
 Select 0
 Use &LI_VIEW3 Alias &LI_VIEW3
 Cursorsetprop('Buffering', 5) && Optimistic Table Buffering

 no_err = .T.
 no_err = Thisform.ao10_list_row_source(LI_ROW_SOURCE_3)

 If no_err = .f.
   Thisform.ao01_list_requery
```

```
  Thisform.Refresh
  no_err = Thisform.ao10_list_row_source(LI_ROW_SOURCE_3)
Endif

On Error
Thisform.ao15_list_reset_value



*===============================================================*
* Procedure   : AF06_VIEW_SEARCH_IDX2                         *
* Description: Opens the view with sort order 2, and          *
*              sets the row source. (Using Search Window.)    *
*===============================================================*
Local f_caption, input_mask, parm1, no_err

*   parm_view  = " "
*   row_source = " "


*-----------------------------------------------------------
* For Search Window:                                        *
*-----------------------------------------------------------
f_caption  = LI_C2_SW_Caption     && Search Window Caption
input_mask = LI_C2_SW_Input_Mask && ("9999", "XXXX", etc.)
             *=======

DO FORM t_search.scx WITH input_mask, f_caption TO parm1

DO CASE
CASE li_type_col2 = "CHR"
                          PVP_COL_2 = Alltrim(PARM1)
CASE li_type_col2 = "NUM"
                          PVP_COL_2 = VAL(Alltrim(PARM1))
CASE li_type_col2 = "DATE"
                          PVP_COL_2 = CTOD(Alltrim(PARM1))
ENDCASE

*----------------------------
* Do not change code below.
*----------------------------
Select &LI_VIEW4
Use
Select 0
Use &LI_VIEW4 Alias &LI_VIEW4
Cursorsetprop('Buffering', 5) && Optimistic Table Buffering

no_err = .T.
no_err = Thisform.ao10_list_row_source(LI_ROW_SOURCE_4)
```

```
 If no_err = .f.
   Thisform.ao01_list_requery
   Thisform.Refresh
   no_err = Thisform.ao10_list_row_source(LI_ROW_SOURCE_4)
 Endif

 On Error
 Thisform.ao15_list_reset_value



*==============================================================*
* Procedure: AO01_LIST_REQUERY                                 *
*                                                              *
*==============================================================*

Thisform.CONTAIN_LIST_021.List1.Requery
        *================




*==============================================================*
* Procedure: AO02_LIST_VALUE                                   *
*                                                              *
*==============================================================*
Lparameters na
Local  lst_val


       lst_val = Thisform.CONTAIN_LIST_021.List1.Value
                                 *=================

RETURN lst_val



*==============================================================*
* Procedure: AO03_RETURN_LIST_LEFT                             *
*                                                              *
*==============================================================*
Lparameters na
Local  ll

       ll = Thisform.CONTAIN_LIST_021.List1.Left
                            *================

RETURN ll
```

Source Code

```
*==============================================================*
* Procedure: A004_RETURN_LIST_WIDTH                            *
*                                                              *
*==============================================================*
Lparameters na
Local  lw

       lw = Thisform.CONTAIN_LIST_021.List1.Width
                    *================

RETURN lw


*==============================================================*
* Procedure: A005_LIST_COLUMN_COUNT                            *
*                                                              *
*==============================================================*
Lparameters cc

     Thisform.CONTAIN_LIST_021.List1.ColumnCount = cc
            *================



*==============================================================*
* Procedure: A006_LIST_COLUMN_WIDTH                            *
*                                                              *
*==============================================================*
Lparameters cw

     Thisform.CONTAIN_LIST_021.List1.ColumnWidths = cw
            *================


*==============================================================*
* Procedure: A007_LIST_PB_CAPTION                              *
*                                                              *
*==============================================================*
Lparameters cc,c1,c2,c3,c4,c5,c6,c7,c8,c9,c10,c11,c12,c13

 If cc >= 1
       Thisform.CONTAIN_LIST_021.Command1.Caption  = c1
 Endif        && =================
 If cc >= 2
       Thisform.CONTAIN_LIST_021.Command2.Caption  = c2
 Endif        && =================
 If cc >= 3
       THISFORM.CONTAIN_LIST_021.Command3.Caption  = c3
 Endif        && =================
 If cc >= 4
```

```
        Thisform.CONTAIN_LIST_021.Command4.Caption  = c4
 Endif       && =================
 If cc >= 5
        Thisform.CONTAIN_LIST_021.Command5.Caption  = c5
 Endif       && =================
 If cc >= 6
        THISFORM.CONTAIN_LIST_021.Command6.Caption  = c6
 Endif       && =================
 If cc >= 7
        Thisform.CONTAIN_LIST_021.Command7.Caption  = c7
 Endif       && =================
If cc >= 8
        Thisform.CONTAIN_LIST_021.Command8.Caption  = c8
 Endif       && =================
 If cc >= 9
        THISFORM.CONTAIN_LIST_021.Command9.Caption  = c9
 Endif       && =================
 If cc >= 10
        Thisform.CONTAIN_LIST_021.Command10.Caption = c10
 Endif       && =================
 If cc >= 11
        Thisform.CONTAIN_LIST_021.Command11.Caption = c11
 Endif       && =================
 If cc >= 12
        THISFORM.CONTAIN_LIST_021.Command12.Caption = c12
 Endif       && =================
 If cc >= 13
        THISFORM.CONTAIN_LIST_021.Command13.Caption = c13
 Endif       && =================




*============================================================*
* Procedure: AO08_LIST_COLUMN_PB_WIDTH                       *
*                                                            *
*============================================================*
Lparameters cc,pb1_l, pb1_w, pb2_l, pb2_w, pb3_l, pb3_w,   ;
   pb4_l, pb4_w, pb5_l, pb5_w, pb6_l, pb6_w, pb7_l, pb7_w, ;
   pb8_l, pb8_w, pb9_l, pb9_w, pb10_l, pb10_w, pb11_l,     ;
   pb11_w, pb12_l, pb12_w, pb13_l, pb13_w

 IF cc >= 1
     On Error Return
     With Thisform.CONTAIN_LIST_021.Command1
                  *================
       .Left  = pb1_l
       .Width = pb1_w
     Endwith
 ENDIF
```

```
 IF cc >= 2
     On Error Return
     With Thisform.CONTAIN_LIST_021.Command2
                  *=================
       .Left  = pb2_l
       .Width = pb2_w
     Endwith
 ENDIF
IF cc >= 3
     On Error Return
     With Thisform.CONTAIN_LIST_021.Command3
                  *=================
       .Left  = pb3_l
       .Width = pb3_w
     Endwith
 ENDIF

 IF cc >= 4
     On error Return
     With Thisform.CONTAIN_LIST_021.Command4
                  *=================
       .Left  = pb4_l
       .Width = pb4_w
     Endwith
 ENDIF

 IF cc >= 5
     On Error Return
     With Thisform.CONTAIN_LIST_021.Command5
                  *=================
       .Left  = pb5_l
       .Width = pb5_w
     Endwith
 ENDIF

 IF cc >= 6
     On Error Return
     With Thisform.CONTAIN_LIST_021.Command6
                  *=================
       .Left  = pb6_l
       .Width = pb6_w
     Endwith
 ENDIF

 IF cc >= 7
     On error Return
     With Thisform.CONTAIN_LIST_021.Command7
                  *=================
       .Left  = pb7_l
```

```
        .Width = pb7_w
    Endwith
ENDIF

IF cc >= 8
    On Error Return
    With Thisform.CONTAIN_LIST_021.Command8
                 *=================
        .Left  = pb8_l
        .Width = pb8_w
    Endwith
ENDIF

IF cc >= 9
    On Error Return
    With Thisform.CONTAIN_LIST_021.Command9
                 *=================
        .Left  = pb9_l
        .Width = pb9_w
    Endwith
ENDIF

IF cc >= 10
    On Error Return
    With Thisform.CONTAIN_LIST_021.Command10
                 *=================
        .Left  = pb10_l
        .Width = pb10_w
    Endwith
ENDIF

IF cc >= 11
    On Error Return
    With Thisform.CONTAIN_LIST_021.Command11
                 *=================
        .Left  = pb11_l
        .Width = pb11_w
    Endwith
ENDIF

IF cc >= 12
    On error Return
    With Thisform.CONTAIN_LIST_021.Command12
                 *=================
        .Left  = pb12_l
        .Width = pb12_w
    Endwith
ENDIF
```

```
 IF cc >= 13
     On Error Return
     With Thisform.CONTAIN_LIST_021.Command13
                  *=================
        .Left  = pb13_l
        .Width = pb13_w
     Endwith
 ENDIF


*==============================================================*
* Procedure: AO09_LIST_ROW_SOURCE_TYPE                         *
*                                                              *
*==============================================================*
Lparameters row_source_type

Thisform.CONTAIN_LIST_021.List1.RowSourceType = row_source_type
        *=================


*==============================================================*
* Procedure: AO10_LIST_ROW_SOURCE                              *
*                                                              *
*==============================================================*
Lparameters row_source

On Error Return .F.

     Thisform.CONTAIN_LIST_021.List1.RowSource  = row_source
             *=================

RETURN .T.


*==============================================================*
* Procedure: AO11_LIST_FONT                                    *
*                                                              *
*==============================================================*
Lparameters font_name, font_size

  Thisform.CONTAIN_LIST_021.List1.FontName  = font_name
  Thisform.CONTAIN_LIST_021.List1.FontSize  = font_size
          *=================


*==============================================================*
* Procedure: AO12_INIT_PB_COLOR_IDX1                           *
*                                                              *
*==============================================================*
```

```
Lparameters cc

  Thisform.CONTAIN_LIST_021.Command1.Forecolor = RGB(64,0,128)
          *=================                    && Blue

If cc > 1
  Thisform.CONTAIN_LIST_021.Command2.Forecolor = RGB(0,0,0)
          *=================                    && Black
Endif



*==============================================================*
* Procedure: A013_INIT_PB_COLOR_IDX2                           *
*                                                              *
*==============================================================*
Lparameters cc

 Thisform.CONTAIN_LIST_021.Command1.Forecolor = RGB(0,0,0)
         *=================                     && Black

If cc > 1
  Thisform.CONTAIN_LIST_021.Command2.Forecolor = RGB(64,0,128)
            *=================                  && Blue
Endif



*==============================================================*
* Procedure: A014_INIT_SET_FOCUS                               *
*                                                              *
*==============================================================*

 Thisform.CONTAIN_LIST_021.List1.SetFocus()
         *=================



*==============================================================*
* Procedure: A015_LIST_RESET_VALUE                             *
*                                                              *
*==============================================================*

 Thisform.CONTAIN_LIST_021.List1.Value = ""
         *=================
```

Source Code

```
*==============================================================*
* Procedure: AO16_LIST_BOUND_COLUMN                            *
*                                                              *
*==============================================================*
Lparameters bc

Thisform.CONTAIN_LIST_021.list1.BoundColumn  = bc
        *=================
```

Pick-List Form

```
*==============================================================*
* Form        : _______          (Created from A_P_LST1.scx ) *
* Description : _______ Pick-List                              *
* Application : Sample Application                             *
* Procedure   : Init                                           *
* Author      : E. Aleu                                        *
* Date created: 06/08/97                                       *
*--------------------------------------------------------------*
* See also the method:  AD16_CALL_DATA_ENTRY_FORM              *
*==============================================================*
Lparameters NA
Public PL_WIDTH_COL1, PL_WIDTH_COL2, PL_WIDTH_COL3
Public PL_WIDTH_COL4, PL_WIDTH_COL5, PL_WIDTH_COL6
Public PL_WIDTH_COL7, PL_WIDTH_COL8, PL_WIDTH_COL9
Public PL_WIDTH_COL10, PL_CAPTION_COL1, PL_CAPTION_COL2
Public PL_CAPTION_COL3, PL_CAPTION_COL4, PL_CAPTION_COL5
Public PL_CAPTION_COL6, PL_CAPTION_COL7, PL_CAPTION_COL8
Public PL_CAPTION_COL9, PL_CAPTION_COL10, PL_FRM_CAPTION
Public PL_TYPE_COL1, PL_TYPE_COL2
Public PL_DATABASE, PL_TABLE
Public PL_WITH_SEARCH
Public PL_VIEW1, PL_VIEW2, PL_VIEW3, PL_VIEW4
Public PL_ROW_SOURCE_1, PL_ROW_SOURCE_2
Public PL_ROW_SOURCE_3, PL_ROW_SOURCE_4
Public PL_C1_SW_Caption, PL_C1_SW_Input_Mask
Public PL_C2_SW_Caption, PL_C2_SW_Input_Mask
*--------------------------------------------------------------
* Form Caption:
*--------------------------------------------------------------

PL_FRM_CAPTION       = "File: ______ Master File"

*-------------------------------------------------------------
* Parameters for the List:
*-------------------------------------------------------------
PL_WIDTH_COL1        = 0
PL_WIDTH_COL2        = 0
PL_WIDTH_COL3        = 0
PL_WIDTH_COL4        = 0
PL_WIDTH_COL5        = 0
PL_WIDTH_COL6        = 0
PL_WIDTH_COL7        = 0
PL_WIDTH_COL8        = 0
PL_WIDTH_COL9        = 0
PL_WIDTH_COL10       = 0
PL_CAPTION_COL1      = "______ Code"
PL_CAPTION_COL2      = "______ Name"
```

```
PL_CAPTION_COL3      = ""
PL_CAPTION_COL4      = ""
PL_CAPTION_COL5      = ""
PL_CAPTION_COL6      = ""
PL_CAPTION_COL7      = ""
PL_CAPTION_COL8      = ""
PL_CAPTION_COL9      = ""
PL_CAPTION_COL10     = ""
                                   && See the database table.
PL_TYPE_COL1         = "CHR"       && "CHR", "NUM", "DATE"
PL_TYPE_COL2         = "CHR"       && "CHR", "NUM", "DATE"

*-------------------------------------------------------------
* Parameters for Database, Views and List Row Source:
*-------------------------------------------------------------
PL_DATABASE        = "C:\TMP2000\DATA\VFP_DATA"

PL_TABLE           = ""            && Not required.
                                   && See AD17_CLEANUP

PL_WITH_SEARCH     = .T.

PL_VIEW1           = "V_???_PLST_IDX_1"
PL_VIEW2           = "V_???_PLST_IDX_2"
PL_VIEW3           = "V_???_PLST_SRC_1"
PL_VIEW4           = "V_???_PLST_SRC_2"


PL_ROW_SOURCE_1      = "V_???_PLST_IDX_1.???_CODE, ???_DESC"
PL_ROW_SOURCE_2      = "V_???_PLST_IDX_2.???_CODE, ???_DESC"
PL_ROW_SOURCE_3      = "V_???_PLST_SRC_1.???_CODE, ???_DESC"
PL_ROW_SOURCE_4      = "V_???_PLST_SRC_2.???_CODE, ???_DESC"

*-------------------------------------------------------------
* For Column #1 Search Window: (If PL_WITH_SEARCH = .T.)
*-------------------------------------------------------------
PL_C1_SW_Caption     = "Search: _____ Code"
PL_C1_SW_Input_Mask = "XXXXX"         && ("9999", "XXXX")

*-------------------------------------------------------------
* For Column #2 Search Window:
*-------------------------------------------------------------
PL_C2_SW_Caption     = "Search: _____ Name"
PL_C2_SW_Input_Mask = "XXXXXXXXXXXXXXXXXXXXXXXXXXXXXXXXXXXX"
*-------------------------------------------------------------

DODEFAULT()
```

```
*==============================================================*
* Form         : C_P_LST1                                      *
* Description : Pick-List Form Parent Class                    *
* Procedure    : INIT                                          *
* Author       : E. Aleu                                       *
* Date created: 04/02/97                                       *
* Date Revised: 06/08/97, 12/23/97, 06/12/05, 8/13/05          *
*==============================================================*
SET TALK OFF
SET ECHO OFF
LOCAL TMP_INIT_IDX

PUBLIC TMP_PL1_RTN
TMP_PL1_RTN = ""


THISFORM.CLOSABLE = .F.

THISFORM.AD14_BEFORE_INIT

THISFORM.AD03_FORM_CAPTION

THISFORM.B01_OPEN_FILE

THISFORM.B03_SETUP_LIST

TMP_INIT_IDX = THISFORM.AD13_INIT_INDEX()

THISFORM.B09_INDEX_USED(TMP_INIT_IDX, .F.)

THISFORM.A014_INIT_SET_FOCUS

THISFORM.AD15_AFTER_INIT

THISFORM.showtips = .T.

THISFORM.Refresh


*==============================================================*
* Procedure: LOAD                                              *
*                                                              *
*==============================================================*

 SET TALK OFF
 SET ECHO OFF
```

```
*=================================================================*
* Procedure: UNLOAD                                               *
*                                                                 *
*=================================================================*
 Close Databases

 Return  TMP_PL1_RTN


*=================================================================*
* Procedure: B01_OPEN_FILE                                        *
*                                                                 *
*=================================================================*
SET EXCLUSIVE OFF
SET REPROCESS TO 0
SET MULTILOCKS ON
SET DELETED ON

Thisform.Buffermode = 2      && Optimistic Table Buffering

THISFORM.AF01_OPEN_DATABASE

THISFORM.AF02_OPEN_FILES_VIEWS


*=================================================================*
* Procedure: B02_COMMAND_GROUP_CLICK                              *
*                                                                 *
* Options/Methods:                                                *
*                                                                 *
*     B80_PB_CANCEL      B85_PB_DISPLAY     B90_PB_PROCESS        *
*     B81_PB_OK          B86_PB_ADD                               *
*     B82_PB_CHANGE      B87_PB_SAVE                              *
*     B83_PB_COPY        B88_PB_PRINT                             *
*     B84_PB_DELETE      B89_PB_EXIT                              *
*                                                  See page 157.  *
*=================================================================*
 LPARAMETERS TMP_OPT

 DO CASE
 CASE TMP_OPT = 1                 && OK - Select
   THISFORM.B81_PB_OK

 CASE TMP_OPT = 2                 && CANCEL
   THISFORM.B80_PB_CANCEL

 CASE TMP_OPT = 3                 && ADD
    THISFORM.B86_PB_ADD
CASE TMP_OPT = 4                 && CHANGE
    THISFORM.B82_PB_CHANGE
```

```
 CASE TMP_OPT = 5                && DISPLAY
    THISFORM.B85_PB_DISPLAY

 CASE TMP_OPT = 6                && DELETE
    THISFORM.B84_PB_DELETE
 ENDCASE


*============================================================*
* Procedure: B03_SETUP_LIST                                  *
*                                                            *
*============================================================*
LOCAL TMP_CC, TMP_CW, TMP_RST, TMP_RS, TMP_BC, TMP_NA

TMP_CC = THISFORM.AD05_LIST_COLUMN_COUNT()
THISFORM.AO05_LIST_COLUMN_COUNT(TMP_CC)

TMP_CW = THISFORM.AD06_LIST_COLUMN_WIDTH(TMP_CC)
THISFORM.AO06_LIST_COLUMN_WIDTH(TMP_CW)

THISFORM.AD07_LIST_PB_CAPTION(TMP_CC)

THISFORM.AD11_LIST_FONT

TMP_RST = THISFORM.AD09_LIST_ROW_SOURCE_TYPE()
THISFORM.AO09_LIST_ROW_SOURCE_TYPE(TMP_RST)

TMP_BC = THISFORM.AD12_LIST_BOUND_COLUMN()
THISFORM.AO16_LIST_BOUND_COLUMN(TMP_BC)


*============================================================*
* Procedure: B04_LIST_COLUMN_PB_CLICK                        *
*                                  See pages 87 and 157.     *
*============================================================*
 LPARAMETERS TMP_INDEX

 LOCAL TMP_WITH_SEARCH

 TMP_WITH_SEARCH = THISFORM.AD04_WITH_SEARCH_WINDOW()

 THISFORM.B09_INDEX_USED(TMP_INDEX ,TMP_WITH_SEARCH)

 THISFORM.AO01_LIST_REQUERY

 thisform.Refresh
```

```
*==============================================================*
* Procedure: B05_LIST_INTERACTIVE_CHG                          *
*                                               See page 87.  *
*==============================================================*
LPARAMETER TMP_ROW_SRC_TYPE

LOCAL TMP_RST
TMP_RST = TMP_ROW_SRC_TYPE

DO CASE
CASE TMP_RST = 2 OR TMP_RST = 6  && Alias or Field

   Thisform.Refresh

OTHERWISE

    *----------------------------------------
    * For RowSourceType = (0, 1, 3, 4, 5)
    *---------------------------------------
    * Select product
    * Locate for This.Value = Cust_id
    *                        *========
    * Thisform.Refresh

ENDCASE


*==============================================================*
* Procedure: B06_LIST_DBL_CLICK                                *
*                                               See page 87.  *
*==============================================================*
 LOCAL TMP_L_VAL

 TMP_L_VAL = THISFORM.A002_LIST_VALUE()

 IF LEN(TRIM(TMP_L_VAL)) > 0

      TMP_PL_RTN = TMP_L_VAL
      Thisform.AD17_CLEANUP
      THISFORM.RELEASE

  ELSE
       Messagebox(" Select a valid record. ")
  ENDIF


*==============================================================*
* Procedure: B07_SETUP_LIST_COLUMN                             *
*                                                              *
*==============================================================*
```

```
LPARAMETERS C1,C2,C3,C4,C5,C6,C7,C8,C9,C10,C11,C12,C13

LOCAL  C1_W,C2_W,C3_W,C4_W,C5_W,C6_W,C7_W,C8_W,C9_W,C10_W, ;
       C11_W,C12_W
LOCAL PB1_L, PB1_W, PB2_L, PB2_W, PB3_L, PB3_W, PB4_L, PB4_W
LOCAL PB5_L, PB5_W, PB6_L, PB6_W, PB7_L, PB7_W, PB8_L, PB8_W
LOCAL PB9_L, PB9_W, PB10_L, PB10_W, PB11_L, PB11_W, PB12_L
LOCAL PB12_W PB13_L, PB13_W

LOCAL TMP_CC, LIST_LEFT, LIST_WIDTH
TMP_CC     = THISFORM.AD05_LIST_COLUMN_COUNT()
LIST_LEFT  = THISFORM.AO03_RETURN_LIST_LEFT()
LIST_WIDTH = THISFORM.AO04_RETURN_LIST_WIDTH()

DO CASE
CASE TMP_CC = 1

   PB1_L = LIST_LEFT  + 5
   PB1_W = LIST_WIDTH - 31

CASE TMP_CC = 2

   PB1_W = C1 - 2
   PB1_L = LIST_LEFT + 5
   PB2_W = LIST_WIDTH - PB1_W - 33
   PB2_L  = PB1_L + PB1_W + 4

CASE TMP_CC = 3

     PB1_W = C1 - 1
     PB1_L  = LIST_LEFT + 5
     PB2_W = C2 - 1
     PB2_L  = PB1_L + PB1_W + 4
     PB3_W = LIST_WIDTH - PB1_W - PB2_W - 36
     PB3_L  = PB2_L + PB2_W + 4

CASE TMP_CC = 4
     PB1_W = C1 - 2
     PB1_L  = LIST_LEFT + 5
     PB2_W = C2 - 1
     PB2_L  = PB1_L + PB1_W + 4
     PB3_W = C3 - 1
     PB3_L  = PB2_L + PB2_W + 4
     PB4_W = LIST_WIDTH - PB1_W - PB2_W - PB3_W - 38
     PB4_L  = PB3_L + PB3_W + 4
CASE TMP_CC = 5

     PB1_W = C1 - 2
     PB1_L  = LIST_LEFT + 5
     PB2_W = C2 - 1
```

```
    PB2_L  = PB1_L + PB1_W + 4
    PB3_W = C3 - 1
    PB3_L  = PB2_L + PB2_W + 4
    PB4_W = C4 - 1
    PB4_L  = PB3_L + PB3_W + 4
    PB5_W = LIST_WIDTH -PB1_W -PB2_W -PB3_W - PB4_W - 42
    PB5_L  = PB4_L + PB4_W + 4

CASE TMP_CC = 6

    PB1_W = C1 - 2
    PB1_L  = LIST_LEFT + 5

    PB2_W = C2 - 1
    PB2_L  = PB1_L + PB1_W + 4

    PB3_W = C3 - 1
    PB3_L  = PB2_L + PB2_W + 4

    PB4_W = C4 - 1
    PB4_L  = PB3_L + PB3_W + 4

    PB5_W = C5 - 1
    PB5_L  = PB4_L + PB4_W + 4

    PB6_W = LIST_WIDTH - PB1_W - PB2_W - PB3_W - PB4_W - ;
            PB5_W - 46
    PB6_L  = PB5_L + PB5_W + 4

CASE TMP_CC = 7

    PB1_W = C1 - 2
    PB1_L  = LIST_LEFT + 5

    PB2_W = C2 - 1
    PB2_L  = PB1_L + PB1_W + 4

    PB3_W = C3 - 1
    PB3_L  = PB2_L + PB2_W + 4

    PB4_W = C4 - 1
    PB4_L  = PB3_L + PB3_W + 4
    PB5_W = C5 - 1
    PB5_L  = PB4_L + PB4_W + 4

    PB6_W = C6 - 1
    PB6_L  = PB5_L + PB5_W + 4

    PB7_W = LIST_WIDTH - PB1_W - PB2_W - PB3_W - PB4_W - ;
            PB5_W - PB6_W - 51
```

```
      PB7_L  = PB6_L + PB6_W + 4

CASE TMP_CC = 8

      PB1_W = C1 - 2
      PB1_L  = LIST_LEFT + 5

      PB2_W = C2 - 1
      PB2_L  = PB1_L + PB1_W + 4

      PB3_W = C3 - 1
      PB3_L  = PB2_L + PB2_W + 4

      PB4_W = C4 - 1
      PB4_L  = PB3_L + PB3_W + 4

      PB5_W = C5 - 1
      PB5_L  = PB4_L + PB4_W + 4

      PB6_W = C6 - 1
      PB6_L  = PB5_L + PB5_W + 4

      PB7_W = C7 - 1
      PB7_L  = PB6_L + PB6_W + 4

      PB8_W = LIST_WIDTH - PB1_W - PB2_W - PB3_W - PB4_W - ;
              PB5_W - PB6_W - PB7_W - 55
      PB8_L  = PB7_L + PB7_W + 4

CASE TMP_CC = 9

      PB1_W = C1 - 2
      PB1_L  = LIST_LEFT + 5

      PB2_W = C2 - 1
      PB2_L  = PB1_L + PB1_W + 4

      PB3_W = C3 - 1
      PB3_L  = PB2_L + PB2_W + 4

      PB4_W = C4 - 1
      PB4_L  = PB3_L + PB3_W + 4

      PB5_W = C5 - 1
      PB5_L  = PB4_L + PB4_W + 4

      PB6_W = C6 - 1
      PB6_L  = PB5_L + PB5_W + 4

      PB7_W = C7 - 1
```

```
    PB7_L  = PB6_L + PB6_W + 4

    PB8_W = C8 - 1
    PB8_L  = PB7_L + PB7_W + 4

    PB9_W = LIST_WIDTH - PB1_W - PB2_W - PB3_W - PB4_W - ;
            PB5_W - PB6_W - PB7_W - PB8_W - 60

    PB9_L  = PB8_L + PB8_W + 4

CASE TMP_CC = 10

    PB1_W = C1 - 2
    PB1_L  = LIST_LEFT + 5

    PB2_W = C2 - 1
    PB2_L  = PB1_L + PB1_W + 4

    PB3_W = C3 - 1
    PB3_L  = PB2_L + PB2_W + 4

    PB4_W = C4 - 1
    PB4_L  = PB3_L + PB3_W + 4

    PB5_W = C5 - 1
    PB5_L  = PB4_L + PB4_W + 4

    PB6_W = C6 - 1
    PB6_L  = PB5_L + PB5_W + 4

    PB7_W = C7 - 1
    PB7_L  = PB6_L + PB6_W + 4

    PB8_W = C8 - 1
    PB8_L  = PB7_L + PB7_W + 4

    PB9_W = C9 - 1
    PB9_L  = PB8_L + PB8_W + 4
    PB10_W = LIST_WIDTH - PB1_W - PB2_W - PB3_W - PB4_W - ;
             PB5_W - PB6_W - PB7_W - PB8_W - PB9_W - 65

    PB10_L  = PB9_L + PB9_W + 4

CASE TMP_CC = 11

    PB1_W = C1 - 2
    PB1_L  = LIST_LEFT + 5

    PB2_W = C2 - 1
    PB2_L  = PB1_L + PB1_W + 4
```

```
    PB3_W = C3 - 1
    PB3_L  = PB2_L + PB2_W + 4

    PB4_W = C4 - 1
    PB4_L  = PB3_L + PB3_W + 4

    PB5_W = C5 - 1
    PB5_L  = PB4_L + PB4_W + 4

    PB6_W = C6 - 1
    PB6_L  = PB5_L + PB5_W + 4

    PB7_W = C7 - 1
    PB7_L  = PB6_L + PB6_W + 4

    PB8_W = C8 - 1
    PB8_L  = PB7_L + PB7_W + 4

    PB9_W = C9 - 1
    PB9_L  = PB8_L + PB8_W + 4

    PB10_W = C10 - 1
    PB10_L  = PB9_L + PB9_W + 4

    PB11_W = LIST_WIDTH - PB1_W - PB2_W - PB3_W - PB4_W - ;
      PB5_W - PB6_W - PB7_W - PB8_W - PB9_W  - PB10_W -  70
    PB11_L  = PB10_L + PB10_W + 4

CASE TMP_CC = 12

    PB1_W = C1 - 2
    PB1_L  = LIST_LEFT + 5

    PB2_W = C2 - 1
    PB2_L  = PB1_L + PB1_W + 4

    PB3_W = C3 - 1
    PB3_L  = PB2_L + PB2_W + 4

    PB4_W = C4 - 1
    PB4_L  = PB3_L + PB3_W + 4

    PB5_W = C5 - 1
    PB5_L  = PB4_L + PB4_W + 4

    PB6_W = C6 - 1
    PB6_L  = PB5_L + PB5_W + 4

    PB7_W = C7 - 1
```

```
     PB7_L  = PB6_L + PB6_W + 4

     PB8_W = C8 - 1
     PB8_L  = PB7_L + PB7_W + 4

     PB9_W = C9 - 1
     PB9_L  = PB8_L + PB8_W + 4

     PB10_W = C10 - 1
     PB10_L  = PB9_L + PB9_W + 4

     PB11_W = C11 - 1
     PB11_L  = PB10_L + PB10_W + 4

     PB12_W = LIST_WIDTH - PB1_W - PB2_W - PB3_W - PB4_W - ;
         PB5_W - PB6_W - PB7_W - PB8_W - PB9_W  - PB10_W - ;
         PB11_W - 75
     PB12_L  = PB11_L + PB11_W + 4

CASE TMP_CC = 13

     PB1_W = C1 - 2
     PB1_L  = LIST_LEFT + 5

     PB2_W = C2 - 1
     PB2_L  = PB1_L + PB1_W + 4

     PB3_W = C3 - 1
     PB3_L  = PB2_L + PB2_W + 4

     PB4_W = C4 - 1
     PB4_L  = PB3_L + PB3_W + 4

     PB5_W = C5 - 1
     PB5_L  = PB4_L + PB4_W + 4

     PB6_W = C6 - 1
     PB6_L  = PB5_L + PB5_W + 4

     PB7_W = C7 - 1
     PB7_L  = PB6_L + PB6_W + 4

     PB8_W = C8 - 1
     PB8_L  = PB7_L + PB7_W + 4

     PB9_W = C9 - 1
     PB9_L  = PB8_L + PB8_W + 4

     PB10_W = C10 - 1
     PB10_L  = PB9_L + PB9_W + 4
```

```
      PB11_W = C11 - 1
      PB11_L  = PB10_L + PB10_W + 4

      PB12_W = C12 - 1
      PB12_L  = PB11_L + PB11_W + 4

      PB13_W = LIST_WIDTH - PB1_W - PB2_W - PB3_W - PB4_W - ;
          PB5_W - PB6_W - PB7_W - PB8_W - PB9_W  - PB10_W - ;
          PB11_W - PB12_W - 75

      PB13_L  = PB12_L + PB12_W + 4

ENDCASE

THISFORM.AO08_LIST_COLUMN_PB_WIDTH( TMP_CC,PB1_L,PB1_W, ;
   PB2_L, PB2_W,PB3_L,PB3_W, PB4_L,PB4_W,PB5_L,PB5_W,PB6_L, ;
   PB6_W,PB7_L, PB7_W,PB8_L,PB8_W,PB9_L, PB9_W, PB10_L, ;
   PB10_W,PB11_L,PB11_W, PB12_L, PB12_W, PB13_L, PB13_W )

ON ERROR


*==============================================================*
* Procedure: B08_LIST_PB_ADJUST_CLICK                          *
*                                              See page 87. *
*==============================================================*
 LOCAL C1,C2,C3,C4,C5,C6,C7,C8,C9,C10,C11,C12,C13
 LOCAL C1_W, C2_W, C3_W, C4_W, C5_W, C6_W, C7_W,C8_W,C9_W, ;
       C10_W,C11_W,C12_W
 LOCAL TMP_CC, TMP_RTN_CW , TMP_CW , C13_W

 TMP_CC = THISFORM.AD05_LIST_COLUMN_COUNT()
DO FORM C:\TMP2000\PRGS_ETC\T_ADJUST.SCX WITH ;
         TMP_CC TO TMP_RTN_CW

 IF LEN(ALLTRIM(TMP_RTN_CW)) > 0

 DO CASE
 CASE TMP_CC = 1
     C1_W   = SUBSTR(TMP_RTN_CW,1,3)
     C1 = VAL(C1_W)
     TMP_CW = C1_W

 CASE TMP_CC = 2
     C1_W = SUBSTR(TMP_RTN_CW,1,3)
     C2_W = SUBSTR(TMP_RTN_CW,4,3)
     C1 = VAL(C1_W)
     C2 = VAL(C2_W)
     TMP_CW = C1_W + ',' + C2_W
```

```
CASE TMP_CC = 3
    C1_W   = SUBSTR(TMP_RTN_CW,1,3)
    C2_W   = SUBSTR(TMP_RTN_CW,4,3)
    C3_W   = SUBSTR(TMP_RTN_CW,7,3)
    C1 = VAL(C1_W)
    C2 = VAL(C2_W)
    C3 = VAL(C3_W)
    TMP_CW = C1_W + ',' + C2_W + ',' + C3_W

CASE TMP_CC = 4
    C1_W   = SUBSTR(TMP_RTN_CW,1,3)
    C2_W   = SUBSTR(TMP_RTN_CW,4,3)
    C3_W   = SUBSTR(TMP_RTN_CW,7,3)
    C4_W   = SUBSTR(TMP_RTN_CW,10,3)
    C1 = VAL(C1_W)
    C2 = VAL(C2_W)
    C3 = VAL(C3_W)
    C4 = VAL(C4_W)
    TMP_CW = C1_W + ',' + C2_W + ',' + C3_W  + ',' + C4_W
CASE TMP_CC = 5
    C1_W   = SUBSTR(TMP_RTN_CW,1,3)
    C2_W   = SUBSTR(TMP_RTN_CW,4,3)
    C3_W   = SUBSTR(TMP_RTN_CW,7,3)
    C4_W   = SUBSTR(TMP_RTN_CW,10,3)
    C5_W   = SUBSTR(TMP_RTN_CW,13,3)
    C1 = VAL(C1_W)
    C2 = VAL(C2_W)
    C3 = VAL(C3_W)
    C4 = VAL(C4_W)
    C5 = VAL(C5_W)
    TMP_CW = C1_W + ',' + C2_W + ',' + C3_W  + ',' + C4_W + ;
             ',' + C5_W

CASE TMP_CC = 6
    C1_W   = SUBSTR(TMP_RTN_CW,1,3)
    C2_W   = SUBSTR(TMP_RTN_CW,4,3)
    C3_W   = SUBSTR(TMP_RTN_CW,7,3)
    C4_W   = SUBSTR(TMP_RTN_CW,10,3)
    C5_W   = SUBSTR(TMP_RTN_CW,13,3)
    C6_W   = SUBSTR(TMP_RTN_CW,16,3)
    C1 = VAL(C1_W)
    C2 = VAL(C2_W)
    C3 = VAL(C3_W)
    C4 = VAL(C4_W)
    C5 = VAL(C5_W)
    C6 = VAL(C6_W)
    TMP_CW = C1_W + ',' + C2_W + ',' + C3_W  + ',' + C4_W + ;
             ',' + C5_W + ',' + C6_W
```

```
CASE TMP_CC = 7
    C1_W  = SUBSTR(TMP_RTN_CW,1,3)
    C2_W  = SUBSTR(TMP_RTN_CW,4,3)
    C3_W  = SUBSTR(TMP_RTN_CW,7,3)
    C4_W  = SUBSTR(TMP_RTN_CW,10,3)
    C5_W  = SUBSTR(TMP_RTN_CW,13,3)
    C6_W  = SUBSTR(TMP_RTN_CW,16,3)
    C7_W  = SUBSTR(TMP_RTN_CW,19,3)
    C1 = VAL(C1_W)
    C2 = VAL(C2_W)
    C3 = VAL(C3_W)
    C4 = VAL(C4_W)
    C5 = VAL(C5_W)
    C6 = VAL(C6_W)
    C7 = VAL(C7_W)
    TMP_CW = C1_W + ',' + C2_W + ',' + C3_W  + ',' + C4_W + ;
            ',' + C5_W + ',' + C6_W + ',' + C7_W

CASE TMP_CC = 8
    C1_W  = SUBSTR(TMP_RTN_CW,1,3)
    C2_W  = SUBSTR(TMP_RTN_CW,4,3)
    C3_W  = SUBSTR(TMP_RTN_CW,7,3)
    C4_W  = SUBSTR(TMP_RTN_CW,10,3)
    C5_W  = SUBSTR(TMP_RTN_CW,13,3)
    C6_W  = SUBSTR(TMP_RTN_CW,16,3)
    C7_W  = SUBSTR(TMP_RTN_CW,19,3)
    C8_W  = SUBSTR(TMP_RTN_CW,22,3)
    C1 = VAL(C1_W)
    C2 = VAL(C2_W)
    C3 = VAL(C3_W)
    C4 = VAL(C4_W)
    C5 = VAL(C5_W)
    C6 = VAL(C6_W)
    C7 = VAL(C7_W)
    C8 = VAL(C8_W)
    TMP_CW = C1_W + ',' + C2_W + ',' + C3_W  + ',' + C4_W + ;
             ',' + C5_W + ',' + C6_W + ',' + C7_W  + ',' +    ;
             C8_W

CASE TMP_CC = 9
    C1_W  = SUBSTR(TMP_RTN_CW,1,3)
    C2_W  = SUBSTR(TMP_RTN_CW,4,3)
    C3_W  = SUBSTR(TMP_RTN_CW,7,3)
    C4_W  = SUBSTR(TMP_RTN_CW,10,3)
    C5_W  = SUBSTR(TMP_RTN_CW,13,3)
    C6_W  = SUBSTR(TMP_RTN_CW,16,3)
    C7_W  = SUBSTR(TMP_RTN_CW,19,3)
    C8_W  = SUBSTR(TMP_RTN_CW,22,3)
    C9_W  = SUBSTR(TMP_RTN_CW,25,3)
    C1 = VAL(C1_W)
```

```
    C2 = VAL(C2_W)
    C3 = VAL(C3_W)
    C4 = VAL(C4_W)
    C5 = VAL(C5_W)
    C6 = VAL(C6_W)
    C7 = VAL(C7_W)
    C8 = VAL(C8_W)
    C9 = VAL(C9_W)
    TMP_CW = C1_W + ',' + C2_W + ',' + C3_W  + ',' + C4_W + ;
             ',' + C5_W + ',' + C6_W + ',' + C7_W  + ',' +  ;
             C8_W + ',' + C9_W

  CASE TMP_CC = 10
    C1_W  = SUBSTR(TMP_RTN_CW,1,3)
    C2_W  = SUBSTR(TMP_RTN_CW,4,3)
    C3_W  = SUBSTR(TMP_RTN_CW,7,3)
    C4_W  = SUBSTR(TMP_RTN_CW,10,3)
    C5_W  = SUBSTR(TMP_RTN_CW,13,3)
    C6_W  = SUBSTR(TMP_RTN_CW,16,3)
    C7_W  = SUBSTR(TMP_RTN_CW,19,3)
    C8_W  = SUBSTR(TMP_RTN_CW,22,3)
    C9_W  = SUBSTR(TMP_RTN_CW,25,3)
    C10_W = SUBSTR(TMP_RTN_CW,28,3)
    C1 = VAL(C1_W)
    C2 = VAL(C2_W)
    C3 = VAL(C3_W)
    C4 = VAL(C4_W)
    C5 = VAL(C5_W)
    C6 = VAL(C6_W)
    C7 = VAL(C7_W)
    C8 = VAL(C8_W)
    C9 = VAL(C9_W)
    C10 = VAL(C10_W)
    TMP_CW = C1_W + ',' + C2_W + ',' + C3_W  + ',' + C4_W + ;
             ',' + C5_W + ',' + C6_W + ',' + C7_W  + ',' +  ;
             C8_W + ',' + C9_W + ',' + C10_W

 CASE TMP_CC = 11
    C1_W  = SUBSTR(TMP_RTN_CW,1,3)
    C2_W  = SUBSTR(TMP_RTN_CW,4,3)
    C3_W  = SUBSTR(TMP_RTN_CW,7,3)
    C4_W  = SUBSTR(TMP_RTN_CW,10,3)
    C5_W  = SUBSTR(TMP_RTN_CW,13,3)
    C6_W  = SUBSTR(TMP_RTN_CW,16,3)
    C7_W  = SUBSTR(TMP_RTN_CW,19,3)
    C8_W  = SUBSTR(TMP_RTN_CW,22,3)
    C9_W  = SUBSTR(TMP_RTN_CW,25,3)
    C10_W = SUBSTR(TMP_RTN_CW,28,3)
    C11_W = SUBSTR(TMP_RTN_CW,31,3)
    C1 = VAL(C1_W)
```

```
    C2 = VAL(C2_W)
    C3 = VAL(C3_W)
    C4 = VAL(C4_W)
    C5 = VAL(C5_W)
    C6 = VAL(C6_W)
    C7 = VAL(C7_W)
    C8 = VAL(C8_W)
    C9 = VAL(C9_W)
    C10 = VAL(C10_W)
    C11 = VAL(C11_W)
    TMP_CW = C1_W + ',' + C2_W + ',' + C3_W  + ',' + C4_W + ;
             ',' + C5_W + ',' + C6_W + ',' + C7_W  + ',' +  ;
             C8_W + ',' + C9_W + ',' + C10_W + ',' + C11_W

 CASE TMP_CC = 12
    C1_W  = SUBSTR(TMP_RTN_CW,1,3)
    C2_W  = SUBSTR(TMP_RTN_CW,4,3)
    C3_W  = SUBSTR(TMP_RTN_CW,7,3)
    C4_W  = SUBSTR(TMP_RTN_CW,10,3)
    C5_W  = SUBSTR(TMP_RTN_CW,13,3)
    C6_W  = SUBSTR(TMP_RTN_CW,16,3)
    C7_W  = SUBSTR(TMP_RTN_CW,19,3)
    C8_W  = SUBSTR(TMP_RTN_CW,22,3)
    C9_W  = SUBSTR(TMP_RTN_CW,25,3)
    C10_W = SUBSTR(TMP_RTN_CW,28,3)
    C11_W = SUBSTR(TMP_RTN_CW,31,3)
    C12_W = SUBSTR(TMP_RTN_CW,34,3)
    C1 = VAL(C1_W)
    C2 = VAL(C2_W)
    C3 = VAL(C3_W)
    C4 = VAL(C4_W)
    C5 = VAL(C5_W)
    C6 = VAL(C6_W)
    C7 = VAL(C7_W)
    C8 = VAL(C8_W)
    C9 = VAL(C9_W)
    C10 = VAL(C10_W)
    C11 = VAL(C11_W)
    C12 = VAL(C12_W)
    TMP_CW = C1_W + ',' + C2_W + ',' + C3_W  + ',' + C4_W + ;
             ',' + C5_W + ',' + C6_W + ',' + C7_W  + ',' +  ;
             C8_W + ',' + C9_W + ',' + C10_W + ',' + C11_W  ;
             + ',' + C12_W
CASE TMP_CC = 13
    C1_W  = SUBSTR(TMP_RTN_CW,1,3)
    C2_W  = SUBSTR(TMP_RTN_CW,4,3)
    C3_W  = SUBSTR(TMP_RTN_CW,7,3)
    C4_W  = SUBSTR(TMP_RTN_CW,10,3)
    C5_W  = SUBSTR(TMP_RTN_CW,13,3)
    C6_W  = SUBSTR(TMP_RTN_CW,16,3)
```

```
    C7_W  = SUBSTR(TMP_RTN_CW,19,3)
    C8_W  = SUBSTR(TMP_RTN_CW,22,3)
    C9_W  = SUBSTR(TMP_RTN_CW,25,3)
    C10_W = SUBSTR(TMP_RTN_CW,28,3)
    C11_W = SUBSTR(TMP_RTN_CW,31,3)
    C12_W = SUBSTR(TMP_RTN_CW,34,3)
    C13_W = SUBSTR(TMP_RTN_CW,37,3)
    C1 = VAL(C1_W)
    C2 = VAL(C2_W)
    C3 = VAL(C3_W)
    C4 = VAL(C4_W)
    C5 = VAL(C5_W)
    C6 = VAL(C6_W)
    C7 = VAL(C7_W)
    C8 = VAL(C8_W)
    C9 = VAL(C9_W)
    C10 = VAL(C10_W)
    C11 = VAL(C11_W)
    C12 = VAL(C12_W)
    C13 = VAL(C13_W)
    TMP_CW = C1_W + ',' + C2_W + ',' + C3_W  + ',' + C4_W + ;
             ',' + C5_W + ',' + C6_W + ',' + C7_W  + ',' +  ;
             C8_W + ',' + C9_W + ',' + C10_W + ',' + C11_W  ;
             + ',' + C12_W
  ENDCASE
  THISFORM.A006_LIST_COLUMN_WIDTH(TMP_CW)
  THISFORM.B07_SETUP_LIST_COLUMN(C1,C2,C3,C4,C5,C6,C7,C8,C9,
                                 C10,C11,C12,C13)

ENDIF



*==============================================================*
* Procedure: B09_INDEX_USED                                    *
*                                                              *
*==============================================================*
LPARAMETERS TMP_INDEX_USED, TMP_WITH_SEARCH
LOCAL TMP_CC

 IF TMP_WITH_SEARCH = .F.

    DO CASE
    CASE TMP_INDEX_USED = 1
        THISFORM.AF03_VIEW_IDX1
    CASE TMP_INDEX_USED = 2
        THISFORM.AF04_VIEW_IDX2
    ENDCASE

 ELSE
```

```
   DO CASE
   CASE TMP_INDEX_USED = 1
      THISFORM.AF05_VIEW_SEARCH_IDX1
   CASE TMP_INDEX_USED = 2
      THISFORM.AF06_VIEW_SEARCH_IDX2
   ENDCASE

ENDIF


TMP_CC = THISFORM.AD05_LIST_COLUMN_COUNT()

DO CASE
  CASE TMP_INDEX_USED = 1
     THISFORM.AO12_INIT_PB_COLOR_IDX1(TMP_CC)
     THISFORM.LABEL_IDX.CAPTION = "1"
  CASE TMP_INDEX_USED = 2
     THISFORM.AO13_INIT_PB_COLOR_IDX2(TMP_CC)
     THISFORM.LABEL_IDX.CAPTION = "2"
ENDCASE


*==============================================================*
* Procedure: B80_PB_CANCEL                                     *
*                                                              *
*==============================================================*

 TMP_PL1_RTN = "CANCEL"

 CLOSE DATABASES

 THISFORM.RELEASE



*==============================================================*
* Procedure: B81_PB_OK                                         *
*                                                              *
*==============================================================*
LOCAL TMP_L_VAL

TMP_L_VAL = THISFORM.AO02_LIST_VALUE()

IF LEN(TRIM(TMP_L_VAL)) > 0

   TMP_PL1_RTN = TMP_L_VAL
   thisform.AD17_CLEANUP
   CLOSE DATABASES
   THISFORM.RELEASE
```

```
ELSE
    WAIT WINDOW " Select a valid record. "
    RETURN
ENDIF

THISFORM.RELEASE



*==============================================================*
* Procedure: B82_PB_CHANGE                                     *
*                                                              *
*==============================================================*
LOCAL TMP_L_VAL, TMP_IDX_NO

TMP_L_VAL = THISFORM.A002_LIST_VALUE()

IF LEN(TRIM(TMP_L_VAL)) > 0

   THISFORM.AD16_CALL_DATA_ENTRY_FORM("CHG", TMP_L_VAL)

   TMP_IDX_NO = VAL(THISFORM.LABEL_IDX.CAPTION)
   THISFORM.B09_INDEX_USED(TMP_IDX_NO,.F.)
   THISFORM.A001_LIST_REQUERY
   thisform.Refresh

ELSE
     WAIT WINDOW NOWAIT " Select a valid record. "

ENDIF



*==============================================================*
* Procedure: B83_PB_COPY                                       *
*                                                              *
*==============================================================*
LOCAL TMP_L_VAL, TMP_IDX_NO

TMP_L_VAL = THISFORM.A002_LIST_VALUE()

IF LEN(TRIM(TMP_L_VAL)) > 0

   THISFORM.AD16_CALL_DATA_ENTRY_FORM("CPY", TMP_L_VAL)

   TMP_IDX_NO = VAL(THISFORM.LABEL_IDX.CAPTION)
   THISFORM.B09_INDEX_USED(TMP_IDX_NO, .F.)
   THISFORM.A001_LIST_REQUERY
```

```
   Thisform.Refresh

ELSE
   WAIT WINDOW NOWAIT " Select a valid record. "

ENDIF



*==============================================================*
* Procedure: B84_PB_DELETE                                     *
*                                                              *
*==============================================================*
LOCAL TMP_L_VAL, TMP_IDX_NO

TMP_L_VAL = THISFORM.A002_LIST_VALUE()


IF LEN(TRIM(TMP_L_VAL)) > 0

    THISFORM.AD16_CALL_DATA_ENTRY_FORM("DEL", TMP_L_VAL)

    TMP_IDX_NO = VAL(THISFORM.LABEL_IDX.CAPTION)
    THISFORM.B09_INDEX_USED(TMP_IDX_NO, .F.)
    THISFORM.A001_LIST_REQUERY
    Thisform.Refresh

 ELSE
     WAIT WINDOW NOWAIT " Select a valid record. "
 ENDIF
```

```
*==============================================================*
* Procedure: B85_PB_DISPLAY                                    *
*                                                              *
*==============================================================*
 LOCAL TMP_L_VAL, TMP_IDX_NO

 TMP_L_VAL = THISFORM.AO02_LIST_VALUE()

 IF LEN(TRIM(TMP_L_VAL)) > 0

    THISFORM.AD16_CALL_DATA_ENTRY_FORM("DSP", TMP_L_VAL)

    TMP_IDX_NO = VAL(THISFORM.LABEL_IDX.CAPTION)
    THISFORM.B09_INDEX_USED(TMP_IDX_NO, .F.)
    THISFORM.AO01_LIST_REQUERY
    THISFORM.Refresh

 ELSE
    WAIT WINDOW NOWAIT " Select a valid record. "

 ENDIF


*==============================================================*
* Procedure: B86_PB_ADD                                        *
*                                                              *
*==============================================================*
LOCAL TMP_IDX_NO

THISFORM.AD16_CALL_DATA_ENTRY_FORM("ADD", " ")

TMP_IDX_NO = VAL(THISFORM.LABEL_IDX.CAPTION)
THISFORM.B09_INDEX_USED(TMP_IDX_NO,.F.)
THISFORM.AO01_LIST_REQUERY
THISFORM.Refresh


*==============================================================*
* Procedure: B87_PB_SAVE                                       *
*                                                              *
*==============================================================*


*==============================================================*
* Procedure: B88_PB_PRINT                                      *
*                                                              *
*==============================================================*
```

```
*===============================================================*
* Procedure: B89_PB_EXIT                                        *
*                                                               *
*===============================================================*
 Thisform.AD17_CLEANUP
 CLOSE DATABASES
 THISFORM.RELEASE


*===============================================================*
* Procedure : AD01_FORMS_PROPERTIES                             *
*                                                               *
* Description: The following form properties are changed       *
*              using the Property Window:                       *
*                                                               *
*   ShowWindow  = 1 In Top Level Form                           *
*   WindowType  = 1 Modal                                       *
*   DataSession = 2 Private Data Session                        *
*                                                               *
*   AutoCenter  = .T.                                           *
*                        Height= 324, Width= 488                *
*                                                               *
*===============================================================*



*===============================================================*
* Procedure: AD03_FORM_CAPTION                                  *
*                                                               *
*===============================================================*

Thisform.Caption = PL_FRM_CAPTION



*===============================================================*
* Procedure: AD04_WITH_SEARCH_WINDOW                            *
*                                                               *
*===============================================================*
lparameters na
local with_search

    with_search = PL_WITH_SEARCH      && .T. or .F.

 IF with_search = .T.
   Return .T.
 ELSE
   Return .F.
 ENDIF
```

```
*==================================================================*
* Procedure: AD05_LIST_COLUMN_COUNT                                *
*                                                                  *
*==================================================================*
 local column_count


    column_count = 2
                   *==



*--------------------------------
* Do not change the code below.
*--------------------------------

 Return column_count




*==================================================================*
* Procedure: AD06_LIST_COLUMN_WIDTH                                *
*                                                                  *
*==================================================================*
Lparameters cc

 Local c1,c2,c3,c4,c5,c6,c7,c8,c9,c10,c11,c12,c13
 Local cw, c1_w, c2_w ,c3_w, c4_w, c5_w, c6_w, c7_w
 Local c8_W ,c9_w, c10_w, c11_w, c12_w , c13_w

      *-------------------
      * Column Width
      *-------------------
      c1  = PL_WIDTH_COL1
      c2  = PL_WIDTH_COL2
      c3  = PL_WIDTH_COL3
      c4  = PL_WIDTH_COL4
      c5  = PL_WIDTH_COL5
      c6  = PL_WIDTH_COL6
      c7  = PL_WIDTH_COL7
      c8  = PL_WIDTH_COL8
      c9  = PL_WIDTH_COL9
      c10 = PL_WIDTH_COL10
      c11 = 0
      c12 = 0
      c13 = 0
           *==
*--------------------------------
* Do not change the code below.
*--------------------------------
```

```
DO CASE
CASE CC = 1
   C1_W = ALLTRIM(STR(C1))
   CW   =  C1_W
CASE CC = 2
   C1_W = ALLTRIM(STR(C1))
   C2_W = ALLTRIM(STR(C2))
   CW =  C1_W + ',' + C2_W
CASE CC = 3
   C1_W = ALLTRIM(STR(C1))
   C2_W = ALLTRIM(STR(C2))
   C3_W = ALLTRIM(STR(C3))
   CW   = C1_W + ',' + C2_W + ',' + C3_W

CASE CC = 4
   C1_W = ALLTRIM(STR(C1))
   C2_W = ALLTRIM(STR(C2))
   C3_W = ALLTRIM(STR(C3))
   C4_W = ALLTRIM(STR(C4))
   CW = C1_W + ',' + C2_W + ',' + C3_W + ',' + C4_W

CASE CC = 5
   C1_W = ALLTRIM(STR(C1))
   C2_W = ALLTRIM(STR(C2))
   C3_W = ALLTRIM(STR(C3))
   C4_W = ALLTRIM(STR(C4))
   C5_W = ALLTRIM(STR(C5))
   CW = C1_W + ',' + C2_W + ',' + C3_W + ',' + C4_W  + ;
        ',' + C5_W

CASE CC = 6
   C1_W = ALLTRIM(STR(C1))
   C2_W = ALLTRIM(STR(C2))
   C3_W = ALLTRIM(STR(C3))
   C4_W = ALLTRIM(STR(C4))
   C5_W = ALLTRIM(STR(C5))
   C6_W = ALLTRIM(STR(C6))

 CW = C1_W + ',' + C2_W + ',' + C3_W + ',' + C4_W + ',' ;
      + C5_W  + ',' + C6_W

CASE CC = 7
   C1_W = ALLTRIM(STR(C1))
   C2_W = ALLTRIM(STR(C2))
   C3_W = ALLTRIM(STR(C3))
   C4_W = ALLTRIM(STR(C4))
   C5_W = ALLTRIM(STR(C5))
   C6_W = ALLTRIM(STR(C6))
   C7_W = ALLTRIM(STR(C7))
```

```
 CW = C1_W + ',' + C2_W + ',' + C3_W  + ',' + C4_W + ;
      ',' + C5_W + ',' + C6_W + ',' + C7_W

CASE CC = 8
   C1_W = ALLTRIM(STR(C1))
   C2_W = ALLTRIM(STR(C2))
   C3_W = ALLTRIM(STR(C3))
   C4_W = ALLTRIM(STR(C4))
   C5_W = ALLTRIM(STR(C5))
   C6_W = ALLTRIM(STR(C6))
   C7_W = ALLTRIM(STR(C7))
   C8_W = ALLTRIM(STR(C8))

 CW = C1_W + ',' + C2_W + ',' + C3_W  + ',' + C4_W + ;
      ',' + C5_W + ',' + C6_W + ',' + C7_W  + ',' + C8_W

CASE CC = 9
   C1_W = ALLTRIM(STR(C1))
   C2_W = ALLTRIM(STR(C2))
   C3_W = ALLTRIM(STR(C3))
   C4_W = ALLTRIM(STR(C4))
   C5_W = ALLTRIM(STR(C5))
   C6_W = ALLTRIM(STR(C6))
   C7_W = ALLTRIM(STR(C7))
   C8_W = ALLTRIM(STR(C8))
   C9_W = ALLTRIM(STR(C9))

 CW = C1_W + ',' + C2_W + ',' + C3_W  + ',' + C4_W + ;
      ',' + C5_W + ',' + C6_W + ',' + C7_W + ',' + C8_W ;
       + ',' + C9_W

CASE CC = 10

   C1_W = ALLTRIM(STR(C1))
   C2_W = ALLTRIM(STR(C2))
   C3_W = ALLTRIM(STR(C3))
   C4_W = ALLTRIM(STR(C4))
   C5_W = ALLTRIM(STR(C5))
   C6_W = ALLTRIM(STR(C6))
   C7_W = ALLTRIM(STR(C7))
   C8_W = ALLTRIM(STR(C8))
   C9_W = ALLTRIM(STR(C9))
   C10_W = ALLTRIM(STR(C10))

 CW = C1_W + ',' + C2_W + ',' + C3_W  + ',' + C4_W + ;
      ',' + C5_W + ',' + C6_W + ',' + C7_W  + ',' + C8_W ;
      + ',' + C9_W + ',' + C10_W
```

```
CASE CC = 11

   C1_W = ALLTRIM(STR(C1))
   C2_W = ALLTRIM(STR(C2))
   C3_W = ALLTRIM(STR(C3))
   C4_W = ALLTRIM(STR(C4))
   C5_W = ALLTRIM(STR(C5))
   C6_W = ALLTRIM(STR(C6))
   C7_W = ALLTRIM(STR(C7))
   C8_W = ALLTRIM(STR(C8))
   C9_W = ALLTRIM(STR(C9))
   C10_W = ALLTRIM(STR(C10))
   C11_W = ALLTRIM(STR(C11))

 CW = C1_W + ',' + C2_W + ',' + C3_W  + ',' + C4_W + ;
      ',' + C5_W + ',' + C6_W + ',' + C7_W  + ',' + ;
      C8_W + ',' + C9_W + ',' + C10_W + ',' + C11_W

CASE CC = 12
   C1_W = ALLTRIM(STR(C1))
   C2_W = ALLTRIM(STR(C2))
   C3_W = ALLTRIM(STR(C3))
   C4_W = ALLTRIM(STR(C4))
   C5_W = ALLTRIM(STR(C5))
   C6_W = ALLTRIM(STR(C6))
   C7_W = ALLTRIM(STR(C7))
   C8_W = ALLTRIM(STR(C8))
   C9_W = ALLTRIM(STR(C9))
   C10_W = ALLTRIM(STR(C10))
   C11_W = ALLTRIM(STR(C11))
   C12_W = ALLTRIM(STR(C12))

 CW = C1_W + ',' + C2_W + ',' + C3_W  + ',' + C4_W + ;
      ',' + C5_W + ',' + C6_W + ',' + C7_W  + ',' + ;
      C8_W + ',' + C9_W + ',' + C10_W + ',' + C11_W + ;
      ',' + C12_W

CASE CC = 13
   C1_W = ALLTRIM(STR(C1))
   C2_W = ALLTRIM(STR(C2))
   C3_W = ALLTRIM(STR(C3))
   C4_W = ALLTRIM(STR(C4))
   C5_W = ALLTRIM(STR(C5))
   C6_W = ALLTRIM(STR(C6))
   C7_W = ALLTRIM(STR(C7))
   C8_W = ALLTRIM(STR(C8))
   C9_W = ALLTRIM(STR(C9))
   C10_W = ALLTRIM(STR(C10))
   C11_W = ALLTRIM(STR(C11))
   C12_W = ALLTRIM(STR(C12))
```

```
    C13_W = ALLTRIM(STR(C13))

  CW = C1_W + ',' + C2_W + ',' + C3_W + ',' + C4_W + ;
       ',' + C5_W + ',' + C6_W + ',' + C7_W + ',' + ;
       C8_W + ',' + C9_W + ',' + C10_W + ',' + C11_W + ;
       ',' + C12_W + ',' + C13_W
ENDCASE

THISFORM.B07_SETUP_LIST_COLUMN(C1,C2,C3,C4,C5,C6,C7, ;
                               C8,C9,C10,C11,C12,C13)
RETURN CW  && Column Width


*===============================================================*
* Procedure: AD07_LIST_PB_CAPTION                               *
*                                                               *
*===============================================================*
Lparameters cc
Local c1, c2, c3, c4, c5, c6, c7, c8, c9, c10, c11, c12, c13

    *------------------------
    * Column Name/ PB Caption
    *------------------------
    c1  =  PL_CAPTION_COL1
    c2  =  PL_CAPTION_COL2
    c3  =  PL_CAPTION_COL3
    c4  =  PL_CAPTION_COL4
    c5  =  PL_CAPTION_COL5
    c6  =  PL_CAPTION_COL6
    c7  =  PL_CAPTION_COL7
    c8  =  PL_CAPTION_COL8
    c9  =  PL_CAPTION_COL9
    c10 =  PL_CAPTION_COL10
    c11 =  " "
    c12 =  " "
    c13 =  " "
          *=======

Thisform.ao07_list_pb_caption(cc,c1,c2,c3,c4,c5,c6,c7,c8, ;
                              c9,c10,c11,c12,c13)



*===============================================================*
* Procedure: AD09_LIST_ROW_SOURCE_TYPE                          *
*                                                               *
* Example:                                                      *
*                                                               *
*    SourceType   Description    RowSource                      *
*    ----------   ------------   -----------------------        *
```

```
*       6          Field       "USERS.user_id, user_nam"   *
*                                                           *
*===========================================================*
Lparameters na

Local row_source_type


    row_source_type = 6      && Field
                     *==


 *------------------------------
 * Do not change the code below.
 *------------------------------

 Return row_source_type




*===========================================================*
* Procedure: AD11_LIST_FONT                                 *
*                                                           *
*===========================================================*
 local font_name, font_size


    font_name = "Arial"   &&
    font_size = 8         && 9
              *=======



 *------------------------------
 * Do not change the code below.
 *------------------------------

 Thisform.ao11_list_font(font_name,font_size)



*===========================================================*
* Procedure   : AD12_LIST_BOUND_COLUMN                      *
* Description: Determines which column is bound to the      *
*             Value Property.                               *
*===========================================================*
 Local bound_column
```

```
    bound_column = 1
                  *==

Return bound_column



*============================================================*
* Procedure: AD13_INIT_INDEX                                 *
*                                                            *
*============================================================*
Lparameters na
Local index_used


    index_used  = 1     && Select index, 1 or 2.
                *===

Return index_used


*============================================================*
* Procedure: AD14_BEFORE_INIT                                *
*                                                            *
*============================================================*
Public PL_COL_1  && Parameterized View Parameter
Public PL_COL_2  && Parameterized View Parameter
      *=======
DO CASE
CASE pl_type_col1 = "CHR"
                           PL_COL_1 = " "
CASE pl_type_col1 = "NUM"
                           PL_COL_1 = 0
ENDCASE

DO CASE
CASE pl_type_col2 = "CHR"
                           PL_COL_2 = " "
CASE pl_type_col2 = "NUM"
                           PL_COL_2 = 0
ENDCASE



*============================================================*
* Procedure: AD15_AFTER_INIT                                 *
*                                                            *
*============================================================*
```

```
*==============================================================*
* Procedure: AD16_CALL_DATA_ENTRY_FORM                         *
*                                                              *
*==============================================================*
Lparameters maint_mode, sel_rec

   * DO FORM ________.scx WITH maint_mode, sel_rec
         *=========
```

```
*==============================================================*
* Procedure: AD17_CLEANUP                                      *
*                                                              *
*==============================================================*



*==============================================================*
* Procedure: AF01_OPEN_DATABASE                                *
*                                                              *
*==============================================================*

* Local dbase1
* dbase1  = " "


 *------------------------------
 * Do not change the code below.
 *------------------------------

 Open Database &PL_DATABASE

 NoDefault



*==============================================================*
* Procedure: AF02_OPEN_FILES_VIEWS                             *
*                                                              *
*==============================================================*
* Local FILE1, FILE2, FILE3, FILE4

* FILE1     = &P_VIEW1
* FILE2     = &P_VIEW2
* FILE3     = &P_VIEW3
* FILE4     = &P_VIEW4

 *-----------------------------------------------------------
 SELECT 0
 USE &PL_VIEW1 ALIAS &PL_VIEW1
 CURSORSETPROP('BUFFERING', 5)  && Optimistic Table Buffering
 *-----------------------------------------------------------
 *-----------------------------------------------------------
 SELECT 0
 USE &PL_VIEW2 ALIAS &PL_VIEW2
 CURSORSETPROP('BUFFERING', 5)  && Optimistic Table Buffering
 *-----------------------------------------------------------
 *-----------------------------------------------------------
 SELECT 0
```

```
USE &PL_VIEW3 ALIAS &PL_VIEW3  NODATA
CURSORSETPROP('BUFFERING', 5)  && Optimistic Table Buffering
*-------------------------------------------------------------
*-------------------------------------------------------------
SELECT 0
USE &PL_VIEW4 ALIAS &PL_VIEW4  NODATA
CURSORSETPROP('BUFFERING', 5)  && Optimistic Table Buffering
*-------------------------------------------------------------

NODEFAULT    &&  Optional  - (just in case)



*==============================================================*
* Procedure: AF03_VIEW_IDX1                                    *
*                                                              *
*==============================================================*
local row_source, no_err

 * view_1     = " "
 * row_source = " "



 *-------------------------------
 * Do not change the code below.
 *-------------------------------

 Select &PL_VIEW1
 Use
 Select 0
 Use &PL_VIEW1 Alias &PL_VIEW1
 Cursorsetprop('Buffering', 5) && Optimistic Table Buffering

 no_err = .T.
 no_err = Thisform.ao10_list_row_source(PL_ROW_SOURCE_1)

 If no_err = .f.
   thisform.ao01_list_requery
   thisform.Refresh
   no_err = Thisform.ao10_list_row_source(PL_ROW_SOURCE_1)
 Endif

 On Error

 Thisform.ao15_list_reset_value
```

```
*==============================================================*
* Procedure: AF04_VIEW_IDX2                                    *
*                                                              *
*==============================================================*
Local row_source, view_2, no_err

 *  view_2     = " "
 *  row_source = " "

 *------------------------------
 * Do not change the code below.
 *------------------------------

 Select &PL_VIEW2
 Use
 Select 0
 Use &PL_VIEW2 Alias &PL_VIEW2
 Cursorsetprop('Buffering', 5) && Optimistic Table Buffering

 no_err = .T.
 no_err = Thisform.ao10_list_row_source(PL_ROW_SOURCE_2)
If no_err = .f.
   Thisform.ao01_list_requery
   Thisform.Refresh
   no_err = Thisform.ao10_list_row_source(PL_ROW_SOURCE_2)
 Endif

 On Error

 Thisform.ao15_list_reset_value




*==============================================================*
* Procedure  : AF05_VIEW_SEARCH_IDX1                           *
*                                                              *
*==============================================================*
Local f_caption, input_mask, parm1, no_err

 *  parm_view  = " "
 *  row_source = " "


 *-----------------------------------------------------
 * For Search Window:                                  *
 *-----------------------------------------------------
 f_caption  = PL_C1_SW_Caption
 input_mask = PL_C1_SW_Input_Mask  && ("9999", "XXXX")
            *====================
```

```
 DO FORM t_search.scx WITH input_mask, f_caption TO parm1


 DO CASE
 CASE PL_TYPE_COL1 = "CHR"
                            PL_COL_1 = Alltrim(PARM1)
 CASE PL_TYPE_COL1 = "NUM"
                            PL_COL_1 = VAL(Alltrim(PARM1))
 ENDCASE


 *-------------------------------
 * Do not change the code below.
 *-------------------------------
 Select &PL_VIEW3
 Use
 Select 0
 Use &PL_VIEW3 Alias &PL_VIEW3
 Cursorsetprop('Buffering', 5) && Optimistic Table Buffering
no_err = .T.
 no_err = Thisform.ao10_list_row_source(PL_ROW_SOURCE_3)

 If no_err = .f.
   Thisform.ao01_list_requery
   Thisform.Refresh
   no_err = Thisform.ao10_list_row_source(PL_ROW_SOURCE_3)
 Endif

 On Error

 Thisform.ao15_list_reset_value




*==============================================================*
* Procedure: AF06_VIEW_SEARCH_IDX2                             *
*                                                              *
*==============================================================*
 Local f_caption, input_mask, parm1, no_err

 *   parm_view  = " "
 *   row_source = " "


 *---------------------------------------------------------
 * For Search Window:                                      *
 *---------------------------------------------------------
 f_caption  = PL_C2_SW_Caption
 input_mask = PL_C2_SW_Input_Mask  && ("9999", "XXXX")
```

```
        *====================

 DO FORM t_search.scx WITH input_mask, f_caption TO parm1


 DO CASE
 CASE PL_type_col2 = "CHR"
                          PL_COL_2 = Alltrim(parm1)
 CASE PL_type_col2 = "NUM"
                          PL_COL_2 = VAL(Alltrim(parm1))
 ENDCASE


*----------------------------
* Do not change code below.
*----------------------------
Select &PL_VIEW4
Use
Select 0
Use &PL_VIEW4 Alias &PL_VIEW4
Cursorsetprop('Buffering', 5) && Optimistic Table Buffering

no_err = .T.
no_err = Thisform.ao10_list_row_source(PL_ROW_SOURCE_4)

If no_err = .f.
  Thisform.ao01_list_requery
  Thisform.Refresh
  no_err = Thisform.ao10_list_row_source(PL_ROW_SOURCE_4)
Endif

On Error

Thisform.ao15_list_reset_value


*============================================================*
* Procedure: AO01_LIST_REQUERY                               *
*                                                            *
*============================================================*

 Thisform.CONTAIN_P_LST21.P_List1.Requery
        *=================
```

```
*=============================================================*
* Procedure: A002_LIST_VALUE                                  *
*                                                             *
*=============================================================*
 Lparameters na
 Local lst_val


     lst_val = Thisform.CONTAIN_P_LST21.P_list1.Value
                        *================


 Return lst_val



*=============================================================*
* Procedure: A003_RETURN_LIST_LEFT                            *
*                                                             *
*=============================================================*
 Lparameters na
 Local ll

    ll = Thisform.CONTAIN_P_LST21.P_list1.Left
                  *================

 Return ll




*=============================================================*
* Procedure: A004_RETURN_LIST_WIDTH                           *
*                                                             *
*=============================================================*
 Lparameters na
 Local lw


      lw = Thisform.CONTAIN_P_LST21.P_List1.Width
                    *================


 Return lw



*=============================================================*
* Procedure: A005_LIST_COLUMN_COUNT                           *
*                                                             *
*=============================================================*
```

```
Lparameters cc

     Thisform.CONTAIN_P_LST21.P_list1.ColumnCount = cc
             *======================


*============================================================*
* Procedure: A006_LIST_COLUMN_WIDTH                           *
*                                                             *
*============================================================*
 Lparameters cw

     Thisform.CONTAIN_P_LST21.P_list1.ColumnWidths = cw
             *=================


*============================================================*
* Procedure: A007_LIST_PB_CAPTION                             *
*                                                             *
*============================================================*
 Lparameters cc, c1, c2, c3, c4, c5, c6, c7, c8, c9, c10, ;
             c11, c12, c13

 If cc >= 1
       Thisform.CONTAIN_P_LST21.Command1.Caption  = c1
 Endif       && ================
 If cc >= 2
       Thisform.CONTAIN_P_LST21.Command2.Caption  = c2
 Endif       && ================
 If cc >= 3
       Thisform.CONTAIN_P_LST21.Command3.Caption  = c3
 Endif       && ================
 If cc >= 4
       Thisform.CONTAIN_P_LST21.Command4.Caption  = c4
 Endif       && ================
 If cc >= 5
       Thisform.CONTAIN_P_LST21.Command5.Caption  = c5
 Endif       && ================
 If cc >= 6
       Thisform.CONTAIN_P_LST21.Command6.Caption  = c6
 Endif       && ================
 If cc >= 7
       Thisform.CONTAIN_P_LST21.Command7.Caption  = c7
 Endif       && ================
 If cc >= 8
       Thisform.CONTAIN_P_LST21.Command8.Caption  = c8
 Endif       && ================
 If cc >= 9
       Thisform.CONTAIN_P_LST21.Command9.Caption  = c9
 Endif       && ================
```

```
If cc >= 10
      Thisform.CONTAIN_P_LST21.Command10.Caption = c10
Endif        && ================
If cc >= 11
      Thisform.CONTAIN_P_LST21.Command11.Caption = c11
Endif        && ================
If cc >= 12
      Thisform.CONTAIN_P_LST21.Command12.Caption = c12
Endif        && ================
If cc >= 13
      Thisform.CONTAIN_P_LST21.Command13.Caption = c13
Endif        && ================
```

```
*===============================================================*
* Procedure: AO08_LIST_COLUMN_PB_WIDTH                          *
*                                                               *
*===============================================================*
 Lparameters cc,pb1_l, pb1_w, pb2_l, pb2_w, pb3_l, pb3_w, ;
 pb4_l, pb4_w, pb5_l, pb5_w, pb6_l, pb6_w, pb7_l, pb7_w, ;
 pb8_l, pb8_w, pb9_l, pb9_w, pb10_l, pb10_w, pb11_l, pb11_w, ;
 pb12_l, pb12_w, pb13_l, pb13_w

 If cc >= 1
     On Error Return
     With Thisform.CONTAIN_P_LST21.Command1
                    *================
       .Left  = pb1_l
       .Width = pb1_w
     Endwith
 Endif

 If cc >= 2
     On Error Return
     With Thisform.CONTAIN_P_LST21.Command2
                    *================
       .Left  = pb2_l
       .Width = pb2_w
     Endwith
 Endif

 If cc >= 3
     On Error Return
     With Thisform.CONTAIN_P_LST21.Command3
                    *================
       .Left  = pb3_l
       .Width = pb3_w
     Endwith
 Endif

 If cc >= 4
     On Error Return
     With Thisform.CONTAIN_P_LST21.Command4
                    *================
       .Left  = pb4_l
       .Width = pb4_w
     Endwith
 Endif

 If cc >= 5
     On Error Return
     With Thisform.CONTAIN_P_LST21.Command5
                    *================
```

```
        .Left  = pb5_l
        .Width = pb5_w
    Endwith
Endif

If cc >= 6
    On Error Return
    With Thisform.CONTAIN_P_LST21.Command6
                 *=================
        .Left  = pb6_l
        .Width = pb6_w
    Endwith
Endif

If cc >= 7
    On Error Return
    With Thisform.CONTAIN_P_LST21.Command7
                 *=================
        .Left  = pb7_l
        .Width = pb7_w
    Endwith
Endif

If cc >= 8
    On Error Return
    With Thisform.CONTAIN_P_LST21.Command8
                 *=================
        .Left  = pb8_l
        .Width = pb8_w
    Endwith
Endif

If cc >= 9
    On Error Return
    With Thisform.CONTAIN_P_LST21.Command9
                 *================
        .Left  = pb9_l
        .Width = pb9_w
    Endwith
Endif

If cc >= 10
    On Error Return
    With Thisform.CONTAIN_P_LST21.Command10
                 *================
        .Left  = pb10_l
        .Width = pb10_w
    Endwith
Endif
If cc >= 11
```

```
     On Error Return
     With Thisform.CONTAIN_P_LST21.Command11
                   *================
       .Left  = pb11_l
       .Width = pb11_w
     Endwith
 Endif

 If cc >= 12
     On Error Return
     With Thisform.CONTAIN_P_LST21.Command12
                   *===============
       .Left  = pb12_l
       .Width = pb12_w
     Endwith
 Endif

 If cc >= 13
     On Error Return
     With Thisform.CONTAIN_P_LST21.Command13
                   *===============
       .Left  = pb13_l
       .Width = pb13_w
     Endwith
 Endif


*==============================================================*
* Procedure: A009_LIST_ROW_SOURCE_TYPE                         *
*                                                              *
*==============================================================*
 Lparameters row_source_type

 Thisform.CONTAIN_P_LST21.P_List1.RowSourceType = row_source_
type
         *=================


*==============================================================*
* Procedure: A010_LIST_ROW_SOURCE                              *
*                                                              *
*==============================================================*
 Lparameters row_source

 On Error Return .F.

     Thisform.CONTAIN_P_LST21.P_list1.RowSource  = row_source
             *=================
 Return .T.
```

```
*===============================================================*
* Procedure: AO11_LIST_FONT                                      *
*                                                                *
*===============================================================*
 Lparameters font_name, font_size

    Thisform.CONTAIN_P_LST21.P_list1.FontName  = font_name
    Thisform.CONTAIN_P_LST21.P_List1.FontSize  = font_size
            *=================



*===============================================================*
* Procedure: AO12_INIT_PB_COLOR_IDX1                             *
*                                                                *
*===============================================================*
 Lparameters cc

  Thisform.CONTAIN_P_LST21.Command1.Forecolor = RGB(64,0,128)
            *=================                  && BLUE

  If cc > 1
    Thisform.CONTAIN_P_LST21.Command2.Forecolor = RGB(0,0,0)
            *=================                    && BLACK
  Endif



*===============================================================*
* Procedure: AO13_INIT_PB_COLOR_IDX2                             *
*                                                                *
*===============================================================*
 Lparameters cc

    Thisform.CONTAIN_P_LST21.Command1.Forecolor = RGB(0,0,0)
            *=================                     && BLACK

  If cc > 1
    Thisform.CONTAIN_P_LST21.Command2.Forecolor = RGB(64,0,128)
            *=================                     && BLUE
  Endif
```

```
*=============================================================*
* Procedure: A014_INIT_SET_FOCUS                              *
*                                                             *
*=============================================================*
ON ERROR DO ERROR_PROC_01

  Thisform.CONTAIN_P_LST21.P_list1.SetFocus()
         *================
```

```
*=============================================================*
* Procedure: A015_LIST_RESET_VALUE                            *
*                                                             *
*=============================================================*

 Thisform.CONTAIN_P_LST21.P_List1.Value = ""
        *=================
```

```
*=============================================================*
* Procedure: A016_LIST_BOUND_COLUMN                           *
*                                                             *
*=============================================================*
 Lparameters bc

 Thisform.CONTAIN_P_LST21.P_list1.BoundColumn  = bc
        *==================
```

Source Code Example for the Contain_list_02 Control

```
*==============================================================*
* Class     : Contain_list_02                                  *
* Object    : List1                                            *
* Procedure: DblClick                                          *
*==============================================================*

THISFORM.B06_LIST_DBL_CLICK

*==============================================================*
* Class     : Contain_list_02                                  *
* Object    : List1                                            *
* Procedure: InteractiveChange                                 *
*==============================================================*
LOCAL RS_TYPE

RS_TYPE = THIS.RowSourceType

THISFORM.B05_LIST_INTERACTIVE_CHG(RS_TYPE)

*==============================================================*
* Class     : Contain_list_02                                  *
* Object    : Command1                                         *
* Procedure: Click                                             *
*==============================================================*

THISFORM.B04_LIST_COLUMN_PB_CLICK(1)

THISFORM.SETALL('FORECOLOR',RGB(0,0,0),'CommandButton')

THIS.ForeColor = RGB(64,0,128)

*==============================================================*
* Class     : Contain_list_02                                  *
* Object    : Command1 ("Command2")                            *
* Procedure: Click                                             *
*==============================================================*

THISFORM.B04_LIST_column_PB_CLICK(2)

THISFORM.SETALL('FORECOLOR',RGB(0,0,0),'CommandButton')

THIS.ForeColor = RGB(64,0,128)

*==============================================================*
* Class     : Contain_list_02                                  *
* Object    : PB_ADJUST                                        *
* Procedure: Click                                             *
*==============================================================*

THISFORM.B08_LIST_PB_ADJUST_CLICK
```

Query List Form

```
*==============================================================*
* Form        : _______          (Created from A_Q_LST1.scx ) *
* Description : _______________                                *
* Application : Sample Application                             *
* Procedure   : Init                                           *
* Programmer  : E. Aleu                                        *
* Date created: _______                                        *
* Date revised:                                                *
*--------------------------------------------------------------*
* To add Pick-Lists and retrieve information from other       *
* database tables, see the following methods:                  *
*                                                              *
*       1.) AF02_OPEN_FILES_VIEWS                              *
*       2.) AD14_BEFORE_INIT                                   *
*       3.) AD22_QRY_TEXTBOX_VALIDATE                          *
*       4.) AD21_QRY_PICKLIST_CALL                             *
*--------------------------------------------------------------*
* See also the method:                                         *
*           1.) AD16_CALL_DATA_ENTRY_FORM                      *
*==============================================================*
Lparameters na

Public QR_FRM_CAPTION
Public QR_WIDTH_COL1, QR_WIDTH_COL2, QR_WIDTH_COL3
Public QR_WIDTH_COL4, QR_WIDTH_COL5, QR_WIDTH_COL6
Public QR_WIDTH_COL7, QR_WIDTH_COL8, QR_WIDTH_COL9
Public QR_WIDTH_COL10, QR_WIDTH_COL11, QR_WIDTH_COL12
Public QR_WIDTH_COL13, QR_CAPTION_COL1, QR_CAPTION_COL2
Public QR_CAPTION_COL3, QR_CAPTION_COL4, QR_CAPTION_COL5
Public QR_CAPTION_COL6, QR_CAPTION_COL7, QR_CAPTION_COL8
Public QR_CAPTION_COL9, QR_CAPTION_COL10, QR_CAPTION_COL11
Public QR_CAPTION_COL12, QR_CAPTION_COL13
Public QR_TYPE_COL1, QR_TYPE_COL2
Public QR_LIST_COL_COUNT
Public QR_DATABASE, QR_TABLE
Public QR_WITH_SEARCH
Public QR_VIEW1, QR_VIEW2, QR_VIEW3, QR_VIEW4
Public QR_ROW_SOURCE_1, QR_ROW_SOURCE_2, QR_ROW_SOURCE_3
Public QR_ROW_SOURCE_4
Public QR_C1_SW_Caption
Public QR_C1_SW_Input_Mask
Public QR_C2_SW_Caption
Public QR_C2_SW_Input_Mask
Public QR_QTY_QRY_PARMS
Public QR_PARM_1, QR_PARM_2, QR_PARM_3, QR_PARM_4
Public QR_PARM_5
Public QR_TYPE_PARM1, QR_TYPE_PARM2, QR_TYPE_PARM3
```

```
Public QR_TYPE_PARM4, QR_TYPE_PARM5

*--------------------------------------------------------------
* Form Caption:
*--------------------------------------------------------------
QR_FRM_CAPTION         = "______ Inquiry"

*--------------------------------------------------------------
* Parameters for the List:
*--------------------------------------------------------------
QR_LIST_COL_COUNT      = 2

QR_WIDTH_COL1          = 100
QR_WIDTH_COL2          = 300
QR_WIDTH_COL3          = 0
QR_WIDTH_COL4          = 0
QR_WIDTH_COL5          = 0
QR_WIDTH_COL6          = 0
QR_WIDTH_COL7          = 0
QR_WIDTH_COL8          = 0
QR_WIDTH_COL9          = 0
QR_WIDTH_COL10         = 0
QR_WIDTH_COL11         = 0
QR_WIDTH_COL12         = 0
QR_WIDTH_COL13         = 0

QR_CAPTION_COL1        = "Code"
QR_CAPTION_COL2        = "______ Name"
QR_CAPTION_COL3        = ""
QR_CAPTION_COL4        = ""
QR_CAPTION_COL5        = ""
QR_CAPTION_COL6        = ""
QR_CAPTION_COL7        = ""
QR_CAPTION_COL8        = ""
QR_CAPTION_COL9        = ""
QR_CAPTION_COL10       = ""
QR_CAPTION_COL11       = ""
QR_CAPTION_COL12       = ""
QR_CAPTION_COL13       = ""

QR_TYPE_COL1           = "CHR"      && "CHR", "NUM", "DATE"
QR_TYPE_COL2           = "CHR"      && "CHR", "NUM", "DATE"

*--------------------------------------------------------------
* Parameters for the Query:
* (Parameterized View Parameters)
*--------------------------------------------------------------
QR_QTY_QRY_PARMS       = 1

QR_PARM_1              = "QRY_???_REGION" && See view: V_?_QSRC_1
```

```
QR_PARM_2            = ""                  &&  "      "
QR_PARM_3            = ""                  &&  "      "
QR_PARM_4            = ""                  &&  "      "
QR_PARM_5            = ""                  &&  "      "

QR_TYPE_PARM1        = "CHR"               && "CHR", "NUM", "DATE"
QR_TYPE_PARM2        = ""                  &&   "       "
QR_TYPE_PARM3        = ""                  &&   "       "
QR_TYPE_PARM4        = ""                  &&   "       "
QR_TYPE_PARM5        = ""                  &&   "       "

*---------------------------------------------------------------
* Parameters for Database, Views and List Row Source:
*---------------------------------------------------------------
QR_DATABASE          = "C:\TMP2000\DATA\VFP_DATA"

QR_TABLE             = ""             && Not required.
                                      ** See method: AD17_CLEANUP
QR_WITH_SEARCH       = .T.

QR_VIEW1             = "V_???_QIDX_1"
QR_VIEW2             = "V_???_QIDX_2"
QR_VIEW3             = "V_???_QSRC_1"
QR_VIEW4             = "V_???_QSRC_2"

QR_ROW_SOURCE_1      = "V_???_QIDX_1.???_CODE, ???_NAME"
QR_ROW_SOURCE_2      = "V_???_QIDX_2.???_CODE, ???_NAME"
QR_ROW_SOURCE_3      = "V_???_QSRC_1.???_CODE, ???_NAME"
QR_ROW_SOURCE_4      = "V_???_QSRC_2.???_CODE, ???_NAME"

*---------------------------------------------------------------
* For Column #1 Search Window:
*---------------------------------------------------------------
QR_C1_SW_Caption     = "Search : _____ Code"
QR_C1_SW_Input_Mask = "XXXXXX"  && ("9999", "XXXX")

*---------------------------------------------------------------
* For Column #2 Search Window:
*---------------------------------------------------------------
QR_C2_SW_Caption     = "Search : _____ Name"
QR_C2_SW_Input_Mask = "XXXXXXXXXXXXXXXXXXXXXXXXXXXXXXXXXXXXXX"

*---------------------------------------------------------------
* Captions and InputMasks for the Query:
*---------------------------------------------------------------
Thisform.CONTAIN_QRY_11.Command1.Caption      = "___"
* Thisform.CONTAIN_QRY_31.Command2.Caption    = ""
* Thisform.CONTAIN_QRY_31.Command3.Caption    = ""
* Thisform.CONTAIN_QRY_31.Command4.Caption    = ""
* Thisform.CONTAIN_QRY_31.Command5.Caption    = ""
```

```
          *==============                     *===========

Thisform.CONTAIN_QRY_11.qry_txt_1.InputMask   = "XXXXX"
* Thisform.CONTAIN_QRY_31.qry_txt_2.InputMask = ""
* Thisform.CONTAIN_QRY_31.qry_txt_3.InputMask = ""
* Thisform.CONTAIN_QRY_31.qry_txt_4.InputMask = ""
* Thisform.CONTAIN_QRY_31.qry_txt_5.InputMask = ""
          *==============                     *===========

DODEFAULT()


*============================================================*
* Form       : C_QRY_LIST                                    *
* Description: Query List Form                               *
* Procedure  : INIT                                          *
* Author     : E. Aleu                                       *
* Date created : 04/02/97                                    *
* Date Revised : 06/08/97, 12/23/97, 08/17/05                *
*============================================================*
LOCAL TMP_INIT_IDX

THISFORM.CLOSABLE = .F.

THISFORM.AD14_BEFORE_INIT

THISFORM.AD03_FORM_CAPTION

THISFORM.B01_OPEN_FILE

THISFORM.B03_SETUP_LIST

THISFORM.B20_SETUP_QUERY

THISFORM.AO14_INIT_SET_FOCUS

THISFORM.AD15_AFTER_INIT

THISFORM.showtips = .T.

THISFORM.Refresh



*============================================================*
* Procedure: LOAD                                            *
*                                                            *
*============================================================*
 SET TALK OFF
 SET ECHO OFF
```

```
*==============================================================*
* Procedure: B01_OPEN_FILE                                     *
*                                                              *
*==============================================================*
SET EXCLUSIVE OFF
SET REPROCESS TO 0
SET MULTILOCKS ON
SET DELETED ON

Thisform.Buffermode = 2     && Optimistic Table Buffering

THISFORM.AF01_OPEN_DATABASE

THISFORM.AF02_OPEN_FILES_VIEWS



*==============================================================*
* Procedure: B02_COMMAND_GROUP_CLICK                           *
*                                                              *
* Options/Methods:                                             *
*                                                              *
*  B80_PB_CANCEL     B85_PB_DISPLAY      B90_PB_PROCESS        *
*  B81_PB_OK         B86_PB_ADD                                *
*  B82_PB_CHANGE     B87_PB_SAVE                               *
*  B83_PB_COPY       B88_PB_PRINT                              *
*  B84_PB_DELETE     B89_PB_EXIT                See page 157.  *
*==============================================================*
 LPARAMETERS TMP_OPT

 DO CASE
 CASE TMP_OPT = 1                 && ADD
    THISFORM.B86_PB_ADD
 CASE TMP_OPT = 2                 && CHANGE
    THISFORM.B82_PB_CHANGE
 CASE TMP_OPT = 3                 && DISPLAY
    THISFORM.B85_PB_DISPLAY
 CASE TMP_OPT = 4                 && DELETE
    THISFORM.B84_PB_DELETE
 CASE TMP_OPT = 5                 && EXIT
    THISFORM.B89_PB_EXIT
 ENDCASE


*==============================================================*
* Procedure: B03_SETUP_LIST                                    *
*                                                              *
*==============================================================*
```

```
LOCAL TMP_CC, TMP_CW, TMP_RST, TMP_RS, TMP_BC, TMP_NA

TMP_CC = THISFORM.AD05_LIST_COLUMN_COUNT()
THISFORM.AO05_LIST_COLUMN_COUNT(TMP_CC)

TMP_CW = THISFORM.AD06_LIST_COLUMN_WIDTH(TMP_CC)
THISFORM.AO06_LIST_COLUMN_WIDTH(TMP_CW)

THISFORM.AD07_LIST_PB_CAPTION(TMP_CC)

THISFORM.AD11_LIST_FONT

TMP_RST = THISFORM.AD09_LIST_ROW_SOURCE_TYPE()
THISFORM.AO09_LIST_ROW_SOURCE_TYPE(TMP_RST)

TMP_BC = THISFORM.AD12_LIST_BOUND_COLUMN()
THISFORM.AO16_LIST_BOUND_COLUMN(TMP_BC)




*==============================================================*
* Procedure: B04_LIST_COLUMN_PB_CLICK                          *
*                                      See pages 87 and 157.  *
*==============================================================*
 LPARAMETERS TMP_INDEX

 LOCAL TMP_WITH_SEARCH

 TMP_WITH_SEARCH = THISFORM.AD04_WITH_SEARCH_WINDOW()

 THISFORM.B09_INDEX_USED(TMP_INDEX, TMP_WITH_SEARCH)

 THISFORM.AO01_LIST_REQUERY

 Thisform.Refresh



*==============================================================*
* Procedure: B05_LIST_INTERACTIVE_CHG                          *
*                                               See page 87.  *
*==============================================================*
LPARAMETER TMP_ROW_SRC_TYPE

LOCAL TMP_RST
TMP_RST = TMP_ROW_SRC_TYPE

DO CASE
```

```
CASE TMP_RST = 2 OR TMP_RST = 6  && ALIAS OR FIELD

   Thisform.Refresh

OTHERWISE

    *-----------------------------------------
    * For RowSourceType = (0, 1, 3, 4, 5).
    *-----------------------------------------
    * Select product
    * Locate for This.Value = Cust_id
    *                        *========
    * Thisform.Refresh

ENDCASE



*==============================================================*
* Procedure: B06_LIST_DBL_CLICK                                *
*                                             See page 87.     *
*==============================================================*



*==============================================================*
* Procedure: B07_SETUP_LIST_COLUMN                             *
*                                                              *
*==============================================================*
 LPARAMETERS C1,C2,C3,C4,C5,C6,C7,C8,C9,C10,C11,C12,C13

 LOCAL  C1_W,C2_W,C3_W,C4_W,C5_W,C6_W,C7_W,C8_W,C9_W,C10_W, ;
        C11_W,C12_W
 LOCAL PB1_L, PB1_W, PB2_L, PB2_W, PB3_L, PB3_W, PB4_L, PB4_W
 LOCAL PB5_L, PB5_W, PB6_L, PB6_W, PB7_L, PB7_W, PB8_L, PB8_W
 LOCAL PB9_L, PB9_W, PB10_L, PB10_W, PB11_L, PB11_W, PB12_L
 LOCAL PB12_W PB13_L, PB13_W

 LOCAL TMP_CC, LIST_LEFT, LIST_WIDTH
TMP_CC      = THISFORM.AD05_LIST_COLUMN_COUNT()
 LIST_LEFT  = THISFORM.AO03_RETURN_LIST_LEFT()
 LIST_WIDTH = THISFORM.AO04_RETURN_LIST_WIDTH()

 DO CASE
 CASE TMP_CC = 1

    PB1_L = LIST_LEFT  + 5
    PB1_W = LIST_WIDTH - 31

 CASE TMP_CC = 2
```

```
    PB1_W = C1 - 2
    PB1_L = LIST_LEFT + 5
    PB2_W = LIST_WIDTH - PB1_W - 33
    PB2_L  = PB1_L + PB1_W + 4

CASE TMP_CC = 3

     PB1_W = C1 - 1
     PB1_L  = LIST_LEFT + 5
     PB2_W = C2 - 1
     PB2_L  = PB1_L + PB1_W + 4
     PB3_W = LIST_WIDTH - PB1_W - PB2_W - 36
     PB3_L  = PB2_L + PB2_W + 4

CASE TMP_CC = 4
     PB1_W = C1 - 2
     PB1_L  = LIST_LEFT + 5
     PB2_W = C2 - 1
     PB2_L  = PB1_L + PB1_W + 4
     PB3_W = C3 - 1
     PB3_L  = PB2_L + PB2_W + 4
     PB4_W = LIST_WIDTH - PB1_W - PB2_W - PB3_W - 38
     PB4_L  = PB3_L + PB3_W + 4

CASE TMP_CC = 5

     PB1_W = C1 - 2
     PB1_L  = LIST_LEFT + 5
     PB2_W = C2 - 1
     PB2_L  = PB1_L + PB1_W + 4
     PB3_W = C3 - 1
     PB3_L  = PB2_L + PB2_W + 4
     PB4_W = C4 - 1
     PB4_L  = PB3_L + PB3_W + 4
     PB5_W = LIST_WIDTH -PB1_W -PB2_W -PB3_W - PB4_W - 42
     PB5_L  = PB4_L + PB4_W + 4

CASE TMP_CC = 6

     PB1_W = C1 - 2
     PB1_L  = LIST_LEFT + 5

     PB2_W = C2 - 1
     PB2_L  = PB1_L + PB1_W + 4

     PB3_W = C3 - 1
     PB3_L  = PB2_L + PB2_W + 4

     PB4_W = C4 - 1
```

```
     PB4_L  = PB3_L + PB3_W + 4

     PB5_W = C5 - 1
     PB5_L  = PB4_L + PB4_W + 4

     PB6_W = LIST_WIDTH - PB1_W - PB2_W - PB3_W - PB4_W - ;
             PB5_W - 46
     PB6_L  = PB5_L + PB5_W + 4

CASE TMP_CC = 7

     PB1_W = C1 - 2
     PB1_L  = LIST_LEFT + 5

     PB2_W = C2 - 1
     PB2_L  = PB1_L + PB1_W + 4

     PB3_W = C3 - 1
     PB3_L  = PB2_L + PB2_W + 4

     PB4_W = C4 - 1
     PB4_L  = PB3_L + PB3_W + 4

     PB5_W = C5 - 1
     PB5_L  = PB4_L + PB4_W + 4

     PB6_W = C6 - 1
     PB6_L  = PB5_L + PB5_W + 4

     PB7_W = LIST_WIDTH - PB1_W - PB2_W - PB3_W - PB4_W - ;
             PB5_W - PB6_W - 51
     PB7_L  = PB6_L + PB6_W + 4

CASE TMP_CC = 8

     PB1_W = C1 - 2
     PB1_L  = LIST_LEFT + 5

     PB2_W = C2 - 1
     PB2_L  = PB1_L + PB1_W + 4

     PB3_W = C3 - 1
     PB3_L  = PB2_L + PB2_W + 4

     PB4_W = C4 - 1
     PB4_L  = PB3_L + PB3_W + 4

     PB5_W = C5 - 1
     PB5_L  = PB4_L + PB4_W + 4
```

```
    PB6_W = C6 - 1
    PB6_L  = PB5_L + PB5_W + 4

    PB7_W = C7 - 1
    PB7_L  = PB6_L + PB6_W + 4

    PB8_W = LIST_WIDTH - PB1_W - PB2_W - PB3_W - PB4_W - ;
            PB5_W - PB6_W - PB7_W - 55
    PB8_L  = PB7_L + PB7_W + 4

CASE TMP_CC = 9

    PB1_W = C1 - 2
    PB1_L  = LIST_LEFT + 5

    PB2_W = C2 - 1
    PB2_L  = PB1_L + PB1_W + 4

    PB3_W = C3 - 1
    PB3_L  = PB2_L + PB2_W + 4

    PB4_W = C4 - 1
    PB4_L  = PB3_L + PB3_W + 4

    PB5_W = C5 - 1
    PB5_L  = PB4_L + PB4_W + 4

    PB6_W = C6 - 1
    PB6_L  = PB5_L + PB5_W + 4

    PB7_W = C7 - 1
    PB7_L  = PB6_L + PB6_W + 4
    PB8_W = C8 - 1
    PB8_L  = PB7_L + PB7_W + 4

    PB9_W = LIST_WIDTH - PB1_W - PB2_W - PB3_W - PB4_W - ;
            PB5_W - PB6_W - PB7_W - PB8_W - 60

    PB9_L  = PB8_L + PB8_W + 4

CASE TMP_CC = 10

    PB1_W = C1 - 2
    PB1_L  = LIST_LEFT + 5

    PB2_W = C2 - 1
    PB2_L  = PB1_L + PB1_W + 4

    PB3_W = C3 - 1
    PB3_L  = PB2_L + PB2_W + 4
```

```
     PB4_W = C4 - 1
     PB4_L  = PB3_L + PB3_W + 4

     PB5_W = C5 - 1
     PB5_L  = PB4_L + PB4_W + 4

     PB6_W = C6 - 1
     PB6_L  = PB5_L + PB5_W + 4

     PB7_W = C7 - 1
     PB7_L  = PB6_L + PB6_W + 4

     PB8_W = C8 - 1
     PB8_L  = PB7_L + PB7_W + 4

     PB9_W = C9 - 1
     PB9_L  = PB8_L + PB8_W + 4

     PB10_W = LIST_WIDTH - PB1_W - PB2_W - PB3_W - PB4_W - ;
              PB5_W - PB6_W - PB7_W - PB8_W - PB9_W - 65

     PB10_L  = PB9_L + PB9_W + 4

CASE TMP_CC = 11

     PB1_W = C1 - 2
     PB1_L  = LIST_LEFT + 5

     PB2_W = C2 - 1
     PB2_L  = PB1_L + PB1_W + 4
     PB3_W = C3 - 1
     PB3_L  = PB2_L + PB2_W + 4

     PB4_W = C4 - 1
     PB4_L  = PB3_L + PB3_W + 4

     PB5_W = C5 - 1
     PB5_L  = PB4_L + PB4_W + 4

     PB6_W = C6 - 1
     PB6_L  = PB5_L + PB5_W + 4

     PB7_W = C7 - 1
     PB7_L  = PB6_L + PB6_W + 4

     PB8_W = C8 - 1
     PB8_L  = PB7_L + PB7_W + 4

     PB9_W = C9 - 1
```

```
     PB9_L   = PB8_L + PB8_W + 4

     PB10_W = C10 - 1
     PB10_L   = PB9_L + PB9_W + 4

     PB11_W = LIST_WIDTH - PB1_W - PB2_W - PB3_W - PB4_W - ;
       PB5_W - PB6_W - PB7_W - PB8_W - PB9_W  - PB10_W -  70
     PB11_L   = PB10_L + PB10_W + 4

CASE TMP_CC = 12

     PB1_W = C1 - 2
     PB1_L   = LIST_LEFT + 5

     PB2_W = C2 - 1
     PB2_L   = PB1_L + PB1_W + 4

     PB3_W = C3 - 1
     PB3_L   = PB2_L + PB2_W + 4

     PB4_W = C4 - 1
     PB4_L   = PB3_L + PB3_W + 4

     PB5_W = C5 - 1
     PB5_L   = PB4_L + PB4_W + 4

     PB6_W = C6 - 1
     PB6_L   = PB5_L + PB5_W + 4
     PB7_W = C7 - 1
     PB7_L   = PB6_L + PB6_W + 4

     PB8_W = C8 - 1
     PB8_L   = PB7_L + PB7_W + 4

     PB9_W = C9 - 1
     PB9_L   = PB8_L + PB8_W + 4

     PB10_W = C10 - 1
     PB10_L   = PB9_L + PB9_W + 4

     PB11_W = C11 - 1
     PB11_L   = PB10_L + PB10_W + 4

     PB12_W = LIST_WIDTH - PB1_W - PB2_W - PB3_W - PB4_W - ;
         PB5_W - PB6_W - PB7_W - PB8_W - PB9_W  - PB10_W - ;
         PB11_W - 75
     PB12_L   = PB11_L + PB11_W + 4

CASE TMP_CC = 13
```

```
    PB1_W = C1 - 2
    PB1_L  = LIST_LEFT + 5

    PB2_W = C2 - 1
    PB2_L  = PB1_L + PB1_W + 4

    PB3_W = C3 - 1
    PB3_L  = PB2_L + PB2_W + 4

    PB4_W = C4 - 1
    PB4_L  = PB3_L + PB3_W + 4

    PB5_W = C5 - 1
    PB5_L  = PB4_L + PB4_W + 4

    PB6_W = C6 - 1
    PB6_L  = PB5_L + PB5_W + 4

    PB7_W = C7 - 1
    PB7_L  = PB6_L + PB6_W + 4

    PB8_W = C8 - 1
    PB8_L  = PB7_L + PB7_W + 4

    PB9_W = C9 - 1
    PB9_L  = PB8_L + PB8_W + 4

    PB10_W = C10 - 1
    PB10_L  = PB9_L + PB9_W + 4

    PB11_W = C11 - 1
    PB11_L  = PB10_L + PB10_W + 4

    PB12_W = C12 - 1
    PB12_L  = PB11_L + PB11_W + 4

    PB13_W = LIST_WIDTH - PB1_W - PB2_W - PB3_W - PB4_W - ;
        PB5_W - PB6_W - PB7_W - PB8_W - PB9_W  - PB10_W - ;
        PB11_W - PB12_W - 75

    PB13_L  = PB12_L + PB12_W + 4

ENDCASE

THISFORM.A008_LIST_COLUMN_PB_WIDTH( TMP_CC,PB1_L,PB1_W, ;
   PB2_L, PB2_W,PB3_L,PB3_W, PB4_L,PB4_W,PB5_L,PB5_W,PB6_L, ;
   PB6_W,PB7_L, PB7_W,PB8_L,PB8_W,PB9_L, PB9_W, PB10_L, ;
   PB10_W,PB11_L,PB11_W, PB12_L, PB12_W, PB13_L, PB13_W )

ON ERROR
```

```
*===================================================================*
* Procedure: B08_LIST_PB_ADJUST_CLICK                               *
*                                                     See page 87. *
*===================================================================*
 LOCAL C1,C2,C3,C4,C5,C6,C7,C8,C9,C10,C11,C12,C13
 LOCAL C1_W, C2_W, C3_W, C4_W, C5_W, C6_W, C7_W,C8_W,C9_W, ;
       C10_W,C11_W,C12_W
 LOCAL TMP_CC, TMP_RTN_CW , TMP_CW , C13_W

 TMP_CC = THISFORM.AD05_LIST_COLUMN_COUNT()

 DO FORM C:\TMP2000\PRGS_ETC\T_ADJUST.SCX WITH ;
         TMP_CC TO TMP_RTN_CW

 IF LEN(ALLTRIM(TMP_RTN_CW)) > 0

 DO CASE
 CASE TMP_CC = 1
     C1_W   = SUBSTR(TMP_RTN_CW,1,3)
     C1 = VAL(C1_W)
     TMP_CW = C1_W

 CASE TMP_CC = 2
     C1_W = SUBSTR(TMP_RTN_CW,1,3)
     C2_W = SUBSTR(TMP_RTN_CW,4,3)
     C1 = VAL(C1_W)
     C2 = VAL(C2_W)
     TMP_CW = C1_W + ',' + C2_W

 CASE TMP_CC = 3
     C1_W   = SUBSTR(TMP_RTN_CW,1,3)
     C2_W   = SUBSTR(TMP_RTN_CW,4,3)
     C3_W   = SUBSTR(TMP_RTN_CW,7,3)
     C1 = VAL(C1_W)
     C2 = VAL(C2_W)
     C3 = VAL(C3_W)
     TMP_CW = C1_W + ',' + C2_W + ',' + C3_W

 CASE TMP_CC = 4
     C1_W   = SUBSTR(TMP_RTN_CW,1,3)
     C2_W   = SUBSTR(TMP_RTN_CW,4,3)
     C3_W   = SUBSTR(TMP_RTN_CW,7,3)
     C4_W   = SUBSTR(TMP_RTN_CW,10,3)
     C1 = VAL(C1_W)
     C2 = VAL(C2_W)
     C3 = VAL(C3_W)
     C4 = VAL(C4_W)
     TMP_CW = C1_W + ',' + C2_W + ',' + C3_W  + ',' + C4_W

 CASE TMP_CC = 5
```

```
    C1_W  = SUBSTR(TMP_RTN_CW,1,3)
    C2_W  = SUBSTR(TMP_RTN_CW,4,3)
    C3_W  = SUBSTR(TMP_RTN_CW,7,3)
    C4_W  = SUBSTR(TMP_RTN_CW,10,3)
    C5_W  = SUBSTR(TMP_RTN_CW,13,3)
    C1 = VAL(C1_W)
    C2 = VAL(C2_W)
    C3 = VAL(C3_W)
    C4 = VAL(C4_W)
    C5 = VAL(C5_W)
    TMP_CW = C1_W + ',' + C2_W + ',' + C3_W  + ',' + C4_W + ;
             ',' + C5_W

CASE TMP_CC = 6
    C1_W  = SUBSTR(TMP_RTN_CW,1,3)
    C2_W  = SUBSTR(TMP_RTN_CW,4,3)
    C3_W  = SUBSTR(TMP_RTN_CW,7,3)
    C4_W  = SUBSTR(TMP_RTN_CW,10,3)
    C5_W  = SUBSTR(TMP_RTN_CW,13,3)
    C6_W  = SUBSTR(TMP_RTN_CW,16,3)
    C1 = VAL(C1_W)
    C2 = VAL(C2_W)
    C3 = VAL(C3_W)
    C4 = VAL(C4_W)
    C5 = VAL(C5_W)
    C6 = VAL(C6_W)
    TMP_CW = C1_W + ',' + C2_W + ',' + C3_W  + ',' + C4_W + ;
             ',' + C5_W + ',' + C6_W

CASE TMP_CC = 7
    C1_W  = SUBSTR(TMP_RTN_CW,1,3)
    C2_W  = SUBSTR(TMP_RTN_CW,4,3)
    C3_W  = SUBSTR(TMP_RTN_CW,7,3)
    C4_W  = SUBSTR(TMP_RTN_CW,10,3)
    C5_W  = SUBSTR(TMP_RTN_CW,13,3)
    C6_W  = SUBSTR(TMP_RTN_CW,16,3)
    C7_W  = SUBSTR(TMP_RTN_CW,19,3)
    C1 = VAL(C1_W)
    C2 = VAL(C2_W)
    C3 = VAL(C3_W)
    C4 = VAL(C4_W)
    C5 = VAL(C5_W)
    C6 = VAL(C6_W)
    C7 = VAL(C7_W)
    TMP_CW = C1_W + ',' + C2_W + ',' + C3_W  + ',' + C4_W + ;
            ',' + C5_W + ',' + C6_W + ',' + C7_W

CASE TMP_CC = 8
    C1_W  = SUBSTR(TMP_RTN_CW,1,3)
    C2_W  = SUBSTR(TMP_RTN_CW,4,3)
```

```
    C3_W   = SUBSTR(TMP_RTN_CW,7,3)
    C4_W   = SUBSTR(TMP_RTN_CW,10,3)
    C5_W   = SUBSTR(TMP_RTN_CW,13,3)
    C6_W   = SUBSTR(TMP_RTN_CW,16,3)
    C7_W   = SUBSTR(TMP_RTN_CW,19,3)
    C8_W   = SUBSTR(TMP_RTN_CW,22,3)
    C1 = VAL(C1_W)
    C2 = VAL(C2_W)
    C3 = VAL(C3_W)
    C4 = VAL(C4_W)
    C5 = VAL(C5_W)
    C6 = VAL(C6_W)
    C7 = VAL(C7_W)
    C8 = VAL(C8_W)
    TMP_CW = C1_W + ',' + C2_W + ',' + C3_W  + ',' + C4_W + ;
             ',' + C5_W + ',' + C6_W + ',' + C7_W  + ',' +   ;
             C8_W

CASE TMP_CC = 9
    C1_W   = SUBSTR(TMP_RTN_CW,1,3)
    C2_W   = SUBSTR(TMP_RTN_CW,4,3)
    C3_W   = SUBSTR(TMP_RTN_CW,7,3)
    C4_W   = SUBSTR(TMP_RTN_CW,10,3)
    C5_W   = SUBSTR(TMP_RTN_CW,13,3)
    C6_W   = SUBSTR(TMP_RTN_CW,16,3)
    C7_W   = SUBSTR(TMP_RTN_CW,19,3)
    C8_W   = SUBSTR(TMP_RTN_CW,22,3)
    C9_W   = SUBSTR(TMP_RTN_CW,25,3)
    C1 = VAL(C1_W)
    C2 = VAL(C2_W)
    C3 = VAL(C3_W)
    C4 = VAL(C4_W)
    C5 = VAL(C5_W)
    C6 = VAL(C6_W)
    C7 = VAL(C7_W)
    C8 = VAL(C8_W)
    C9 = VAL(C9_W)
    TMP_CW = C1_W + ',' + C2_W + ',' + C3_W  + ',' + C4_W + ;
             ',' + C5_W + ',' + C6_W + ',' + C7_W  + ',' +  ;
             C8_W + ',' + C9_W

  CASE TMP_CC = 10
    C1_W   = SUBSTR(TMP_RTN_CW,1,3)
    C2_W   = SUBSTR(TMP_RTN_CW,4,3)
    C3_W   = SUBSTR(TMP_RTN_CW,7,3)
    C4_W   = SUBSTR(TMP_RTN_CW,10,3)
    C5_W   = SUBSTR(TMP_RTN_CW,13,3)
    C6_W   = SUBSTR(TMP_RTN_CW,16,3)
    C7_W   = SUBSTR(TMP_RTN_CW,19,3)
    C8_W   = SUBSTR(TMP_RTN_CW,22,3)
```

```
    C9_W  = SUBSTR(TMP_RTN_CW,25,3)
    C10_W = SUBSTR(TMP_RTN_CW,28,3)
    C1 = VAL(C1_W)
    C2 = VAL(C2_W)
    C3 = VAL(C3_W)
    C4 = VAL(C4_W)
    C5 = VAL(C5_W)
    C6 = VAL(C6_W)
    C7 = VAL(C7_W)
    C8 = VAL(C8_W)
    C9 = VAL(C9_W)
    C10 = VAL(C10_W)
    TMP_CW = C1_W + ',' + C2_W + ',' + C3_W  + ',' + C4_W + ;
             ',' + C5_W + ',' + C6_W + ',' + C7_W  + ',' +  ;
             C8_W + ',' + C9_W + ',' + C10_W

 CASE TMP_CC = 11
    C1_W  = SUBSTR(TMP_RTN_CW,1,3)
    C2_W  = SUBSTR(TMP_RTN_CW,4,3)
    C3_W  = SUBSTR(TMP_RTN_CW,7,3)
    C4_W  = SUBSTR(TMP_RTN_CW,10,3)
    C5_W  = SUBSTR(TMP_RTN_CW,13,3)
    C6_W  = SUBSTR(TMP_RTN_CW,16,3)
    C7_W  = SUBSTR(TMP_RTN_CW,19,3)
    C8_W  = SUBSTR(TMP_RTN_CW,22,3)
    C9_W  = SUBSTR(TMP_RTN_CW,25,3)
    C10_W = SUBSTR(TMP_RTN_CW,28,3)
    C11_W = SUBSTR(TMP_RTN_CW,31,3)
    C1 = VAL(C1_W)
    C2 = VAL(C2_W)
    C3 = VAL(C3_W)
    C4 = VAL(C4_W)
    C5 = VAL(C5_W)
    C6 = VAL(C6_W)
    C7 = VAL(C7_W)
    C8 = VAL(C8_W)
    C9 = VAL(C9_W)
    C10 = VAL(C10_W)
    C11 = VAL(C11_W)
    TMP_CW = C1_W + ',' + C2_W + ',' + C3_W  + ',' + C4_W + ;
             ',' + C5_W + ',' + C6_W + ',' + C7_W  + ',' +  ;
             C8_W + ',' + C9_W + ',' + C10_W + ',' + C11_W

 CASE TMP_CC = 12
    C1_W  = SUBSTR(TMP_RTN_CW,1,3)
    C2_W  = SUBSTR(TMP_RTN_CW,4,3)
    C3_W  = SUBSTR(TMP_RTN_CW,7,3)
    C4_W  = SUBSTR(TMP_RTN_CW,10,3)
    C5_W  = SUBSTR(TMP_RTN_CW,13,3)
    C6_W  = SUBSTR(TMP_RTN_CW,16,3)
```

```
    C7_W  = SUBSTR(TMP_RTN_CW,19,3)
    C8_W  = SUBSTR(TMP_RTN_CW,22,3)
    C9_W  = SUBSTR(TMP_RTN_CW,25,3)
    C10_W = SUBSTR(TMP_RTN_CW,28,3)
    C11_W = SUBSTR(TMP_RTN_CW,31,3)
    C12_W = SUBSTR(TMP_RTN_CW,34,3)
    C1 = VAL(C1_W)
    C2 = VAL(C2_W)
    C3 = VAL(C3_W)
    C4 = VAL(C4_W)
    C5 = VAL(C5_W)
    C6 = VAL(C6_W)
    C7 = VAL(C7_W)
    C8 = VAL(C8_W)
    C9 = VAL(C9_W)
    C10 = VAL(C10_W)
    C11 = VAL(C11_W)
    C12 = VAL(C12_W)
    TMP_CW = C1_W + ',' + C2_W + ',' + C3_W  + ',' + C4_W + ;
             ',' + C5_W + ',' + C6_W + ',' + C7_W  + ',' +  ;
             C8_W + ',' + C9_W + ',' + C10_W + ',' + C11_W  ;
             + ',' + C12_W

CASE TMP_CC = 13
    C1_W  = SUBSTR(TMP_RTN_CW,1,3)
    C2_W  = SUBSTR(TMP_RTN_CW,4,3)
    C3_W  = SUBSTR(TMP_RTN_CW,7,3)
    C4_W  = SUBSTR(TMP_RTN_CW,10,3)
    C5_W  = SUBSTR(TMP_RTN_CW,13,3)
    C6_W  = SUBSTR(TMP_RTN_CW,16,3)
    C7_W  = SUBSTR(TMP_RTN_CW,19,3)
    C8_W  = SUBSTR(TMP_RTN_CW,22,3)
    C9_W  = SUBSTR(TMP_RTN_CW,25,3)
    C10_W = SUBSTR(TMP_RTN_CW,28,3)
    C11_W = SUBSTR(TMP_RTN_CW,31,3)
    C12_W = SUBSTR(TMP_RTN_CW,34,3)
    C13_W = SUBSTR(TMP_RTN_CW,37,3)
    C1 = VAL(C1_W)
    C2 = VAL(C2_W)
    C3 = VAL(C3_W)
    C4 = VAL(C4_W)
    C5 = VAL(C5_W)
    C6 = VAL(C6_W)
    C7 = VAL(C7_W)
    C8 = VAL(C8_W)
    C9 = VAL(C9_W)
    C10 = VAL(C10_W)
    C11 = VAL(C11_W)
    C12 = VAL(C12_W)
    C13 = VAL(C13_W)
```

```
     TMP_CW = C1_W + ',' + C2_W + ',' + C3_W  + ',' + C4_W + ;
              ',' + C5_W + ',' + C6_W + ',' + C7_W  + ',' +  ;
              C8_W + ',' + C9_W + ',' + C10_W + ',' + C11_W  ;
              + ',' + C12_W

  ENDCASE
  THISFORM.AO06_LIST_COLUMN_WIDTH(TMP_CW)
  THISFORM.B07_SETUP_LIST_COLUMN(C1,C2,C3,C4,C5,C6,C7,C8,C9,
                                 C10,C11,C12,C13)

ENDIF



*==============================================================*
* Procedure: B09_INDEX_USED                                    *
*                                                              *
*==============================================================*
LPARAMETERS TMP_INDEX_USED, TMP_WITH_SEARCH
LOCAL TMP_CC

 IF TMP_WITH_SEARCH = .F.

    DO CASE
    CASE TMP_INDEX_USED = 1
        THISFORM.AF03_VIEW_IDX1
    CASE TMP_INDEX_USED = 2
        THISFORM.AF04_VIEW_IDX2
    ENDCASE

 ELSE

    DO CASE
    CASE TMP_INDEX_USED = 1
       THISFORM.AF05_VIEW_SEARCH_IDX1
    CASE TMP_INDEX_USED = 2
       THISFORM.AF06_VIEW_SEARCH_IDX2
    ENDCASE

 ENDIF


 TMP_CC = THISFORM.AD05_LIST_COLUMN_COUNT()

 DO CASE
   CASE TMP_INDEX_USED = 1
      THISFORM.AO12_INIT_PB_COLOR_IDX1(TMP_CC)
      THISFORM.LABEL_IDX.CAPTION = "1"
   CASE TMP_INDEX_USED = 2
      THISFORM.AO13_INIT_PB_COLOR_IDX2(TMP_CC)
```

```
    THISFORM.LABEL_IDX.CAPTION = "2"
ENDCASE



*============================================================*
* Procedure: B20_SETUP_QUERY                                 *
*                                                            *
*============================================================*
LOCAL TMP_Q_PARMS

TMP_Q_PARMS = THISFORM.AD20_QTY_QRY_PARMS()

THISFORM.AOD_01_SET_DSP_QRY_CONTAINER

DO CASE
CASE TMP_Q_PARMS = 1

   THISFORM.AOD_03_QRY_TEXTBOX_RTN_INF("Q_TXTBOX_1", "",1)

CASE TMP_Q_PARMS = 2

   THISFORM.AOD_03_QRY_TEXTBOX_RTN_INF("Q_TXTBOX_1", "",1)
   THISFORM.AOD_03_QRY_TEXTBOX_RTN_INF("Q_TXTBOX_2", "",1)

CASE TMP_Q_PARMS = 3

   THISFORM.AOD_03_QRY_TEXTBOX_RTN_INF("Q_TXTBOX_1", "",1)
   THISFORM.AOD_03_QRY_TEXTBOX_RTN_INF("Q_TXTBOX_2", "",1)
   THISFORM.AOD_03_QRY_TEXTBOX_RTN_INF("Q_TXTBOX_3", "",1)

CASE TMP_Q_PARMS = 4

   THISFORM.AOD_03_QRY_TEXTBOX_RTN_INF("Q_TXTBOX_1", "",1)
   THISFORM.AOD_03_QRY_TEXTBOX_RTN_INF("Q_TXTBOX_2", "",1)
   THISFORM.AOD_03_QRY_TEXTBOX_RTN_INF("Q_TXTBOX_3", "",1)
   THISFORM.AOD_03_QRY_TEXTBOX_RTN_INF("Q_TXTBOX_4", "",1)

CASE TMP_Q_PARMS = 5

   THISFORM.AOD_03_QRY_TEXTBOX_RTN_INF("Q_TXTBOX_1", "",1)
   THISFORM.AOD_03_QRY_TEXTBOX_RTN_INF("Q_TXTBOX_2", "",1)
   THISFORM.AOD_03_QRY_TEXTBOX_RTN_INF("Q_TXTBOX_3", "",1)
   THISFORM.AOD_03_QRY_TEXTBOX_RTN_INF("Q_TXTBOX_4", "",1)
   THISFORM.AOD_03_QRY_TEXTBOX_RTN_INF("Q_TXTBOX_5", "",1)

ENDCASE
```

```
*==============================================================*
* Procedure: B21_QRY_PICKLIST_RUN                              *
*                                              See page 157.  *
*==============================================================*
 LPARAMETER TMP_TXTBOX_ID
 LOCAL TMP_RTN_PL, TMP_NA

 TMP_RTN_PL = THISFORM.AD21_QRY_PICKLIST_CALL(TMP_TXTBOX_ID)

 IF TMP_RTN_PL = "CANCEL"
 ELSE

   IF LEN(ALLTRIM(TMP_RTN_PL)) > 0
     THISFORM.AOD_02_QRY_CONTAIN_TEXT_VALUE(TMP_TXTBOX_ID, ;
                                          TMP_RTN_PL)
     TMP_NA = THISFORM.B22_QRY_TEXTBOX_VALIDATE( ;
                              TMP_TXTBOX_ID, TMP_RTN_PL)
   ENDIF

 ENDIF

 THISFORM.REFRESH




*==============================================================*
* Procedure: B22_QRY_TEXTBOX_VALIDATE                          *
*                                              See page 157.  *
*==============================================================*
 LPARAMETERS TMP_TXTBOX_ID, TMP_TEXTBOX_VAL

 LOCAL TMP_RTN

 Thisform.AF15_REFRESH_LIST

 TMP_RTN = THISFORM.AD22_QRY_TEXTBOX_VALIDATE( ;
                              TMP_TXTBOX_ID,TMP_TEXTBOX_VAL)

 THISFORM.REFRESH

 RETURN TMP_RTN
```

```
*==============================================================*
* Procedure: B82_PB_CHANGE                                     *
*                                                              *
*==============================================================*
 LOCAL TMP_L_VAL, TMP_IDX_NO

 TMP_L_VAL = THISFORM.A002_LIST_VALUE()

 IF LEN(TRIM(TMP_L_VAL)) > 0

    THISFORM.AD16_CALL_DATA_ENTRY_FORM("CHG", TMP_L_VAL)

    TMP_IDX_NO = VAL(THISFORM.LABEL_IDX.CAPTION)
    THISFORM.B09_INDEX_USED(TMP_IDX_NO, .F.)
    THISFORM.A001_LIST_REQUERY
    Thisform.Refresh

 ELSE
    WAIT WINDOW NOWAIT " Select a valid record. "

 ENDIF




*==============================================================*
* Procedure: B83_PB_COPY                                       *
*                                                              *
*==============================================================*
 LOCAL TMP_L_VAL, TMP_IDX_NO

 TMP_L_VAL = THISFORM.A002_LIST_VALUE()

 IF LEN(TRIM(TMP_L_VAL)) > 0

    THISFORM.AD16_CALL_DATA_ENTRY_FORM("CPY", TMP_L_VAL)

    TMP_IDX_NO = VAL(THISFORM.LABEL_IDX.CAPTION)
    THISFORM.B09_INDEX_USED(TMP_IDX_NO, .F.)
    THISFORM.A001_LIST_REQUERY
    Thisform.Refresh

 ELSE
    WAIT WINDOW NOWAIT " Select a valid record. "

 ENDIF
```

```
*=============================================================*
* Procedure: B84_PB_DELETE                                    *
*                                                             *
*=============================================================*
 LOCAL TMP_L_VAL, TMP_IDX_NO

 TMP_L_VAL = THISFORM.AO02_LIST_VALUE()


 IF LEN(TRIM(TMP_L_VAL)) > 0

     THISFORM.AD16_CALL_DATA_ENTRY_FORM("DEL", TMP_L_VAL)

     TMP_IDX_NO = VAL(THISFORM.LABEL_IDX.CAPTION)
     THISFORM.B09_INDEX_USED(TMP_IDX_NO, .F.)
     THISFORM.AO01_LIST_REQUERY
     Thisform.Refresh

 ELSE
     WAIT WINDOW NOWAIT " Select a valid record. "

 ENDIF



*=============================================================*
* Procedure: B85_PB_DISPLAY                                   *
*                                                             *
*=============================================================*
 LOCAL TMP_L_VAL, TMP_IDX_NO

 TMP_L_VAL = THISFORM.AO02_LIST_VALUE()

 IF LEN(TRIM(TMP_L_VAL)) > 0

    THISFORM.AD16_CALL_DATA_ENTRY_FORM("DSP", TMP_L_VAL)

    TMP_IDX_NO = VAL(THISFORM.LABEL_IDX.CAPTION)
    THISFORM.B09_INDEX_USED(TMP_IDX_NO, .F.)
    THISFORM.AO01_LIST_REQUERY
    THISFORM.Refresh

 ELSE
    WAIT WINDOW NOWAIT " Select a valid record. "

 ENDIF
```

```
*==============================================================*
* Procedure: B86_PB_ADD                                        *
*                                                              *
*==============================================================*
LOCAL TMP_IDX_NO

THISFORM.AD16_CALL_DATA_ENTRY_FORM("ADD", " ")

TMP_IDX_NO = VAL(THISFORM.LABEL_IDX.CAPTION)
THISFORM.B09_INDEX_USED(TMP_IDX_NO, .F.)
THISFORM.A001_LIST_REQUERY
THISFORM.Refresh




*==============================================================*
* Procedure: B87_PB_SAVE                                       *
*                                                              *
*==============================================================*




*==============================================================*
* Procedure: B88_PB_PRINT                                      *
*                                                              *
*==============================================================*




*==============================================================*
* Procedure: B90_PB_EXIT                                       *
*                                                              *
*==============================================================*

Thisform.AD17_CLEANUP

CLOSE DATABASES

THISFORM.RELEASE
```

```
*==============================================================*
* Procedure : AD01_FORMS_PROPERTIES                            *
*                                                              *
* Description: The following form properties are changed       *
*              using the Property Window:                      *
*                                                              *
*                ShowWindow  = 2 As Top Level Form             *
*                WindowType  = 1 Modal                         *
*                DataSession = 2 Private Data Session          *
*                                                              *
*                Height= 425, Width= 630, Top = 0, Left = 0    *
*                                                              *
*==============================================================*




*==============================================================*
* Procedure: AD03_FORM_CAPTION                                 *
*                                                              *
*==============================================================*

 Thisform.Caption = QR_FRM_CAPTION
                    *=============




*==============================================================*
* Procedure: AD04_WITH_SEARCH_WINDOW                           *
*                                                              *
*==============================================================*
 Lparameters na
 Local with_search


   with_search = QR_WITH_SEARCH   && .T. or .F.
                 *=============


 *-------------------------------
 * Do not the change code below.
 *-------------------------------
 IF with_search = .T.
   Return .T.
 ELSE
   Return .F.
 ENDIF
```

```
*==============================================================*
* Procedure: AD05_LIST_COLUMN_COUNT                             *
*                                                               *
*==============================================================*
 Local column_count


    column_count = QR_LIST_COL_COUNT
                  *=================


 RETURN column_count




*==============================================================*
* Procedure: AD06_LIST_COLUMN_WIDTH                             *
*                                                               *
*==============================================================*
 Lparameters cc
 Local c1,c2,c3,c4,c5,c6,c7,c8,c9,c10,c11,c12,c13
 Local cw, c1_w, c2_w ,c3_w, c4_w, c5_w, c6_w, c7_w
 Local c8_W ,c9_w, c10_w, c11_w, c12_w , c13_w

   *------------------
   * Column Width:
   *------------------
   c1  = QR_WIDTH_COL1
   c2  = QR_WIDTH_COL2
   c3  = QR_WIDTH_COL3
   c4  = QR_WIDTH_COL4
   c5  = QR_WIDTH_COL5
   c6  = QR_WIDTH_COL6
   c7  = QR_WIDTH_COL7
   c8  = QR_WIDTH_COL8
   c9  = QR_WIDTH_COL9
   c10 = QR_WIDTH_COL10
   c11 = QR_WIDTH_COL11
   c12 = QR_WIDTH_COL12
   c13 = QR_WIDTH_COL13
         *=============

 *------------------------------
 * Do not change the code below.
 *------------------------------

 DO CASE
 CASE CC = 1
```

```
    C1_W = ALLTRIM(STR(C1))
    CW   =  C1_W
 CASE CC = 2
    C1_W = ALLTRIM(STR(C1))
    C2_W = ALLTRIM(STR(C2))
    CW =  C1_W + ',' + C2_W
 CASE CC = 3
    C1_W = ALLTRIM(STR(C1))
    C2_W = ALLTRIM(STR(C2))
    C3_W = ALLTRIM(STR(C3))
    CW   = C1_W + ',' + C2_W + ',' + C3_W

 CASE CC = 4
    C1_W = ALLTRIM(STR(C1))
    C2_W = ALLTRIM(STR(C2))
    C3_W = ALLTRIM(STR(C3))
    C4_W = ALLTRIM(STR(C4))
    CW = C1_W + ',' + C2_W + ',' + C3_W  + ',' + C4_W

 CASE CC = 5
    C1_W = ALLTRIM(STR(C1))
    C2_W = ALLTRIM(STR(C2))
    C3_W = ALLTRIM(STR(C3))
    C4_W = ALLTRIM(STR(C4))
    C5_W = ALLTRIM(STR(C5))
    CW = C1_W + ',' + C2_W + ',' + C3_W  + ',' + C4_W  + ;
         ',' + C5_W

 CASE CC = 6
    C1_W = ALLTRIM(STR(C1))
    C2_W = ALLTRIM(STR(C2))
    C3_W = ALLTRIM(STR(C3))
    C4_W = ALLTRIM(STR(C4))
    C5_W = ALLTRIM(STR(C5))
    C6_W = ALLTRIM(STR(C6))

    CW = C1_W + ',' + C2_W + ',' + C3_W  + ',' + C4_W + ;
         ',' + C5_W + ',' + C6_W

 CASE CC = 7
    C1_W = ALLTRIM(STR(C1))
    C2_W = ALLTRIM(STR(C2))
    C3_W = ALLTRIM(STR(C3))
    C4_W = ALLTRIM(STR(C4))
    C5_W = ALLTRIM(STR(C5))
    C6_W = ALLTRIM(STR(C6))
    C7_W = ALLTRIM(STR(C7))
    CW = C1_W + ',' + C2_W + ',' + C3_W  + ',' + C4_W +  ;
         ',' + C5_W + ',' + C6_W + ',' + C7_W
```

```
CASE CC = 8
   C1_W = ALLTRIM(STR(C1))
   C2_W = ALLTRIM(STR(C2))
   C3_W = ALLTRIM(STR(C3))
   C4_W = ALLTRIM(STR(C4))
   C5_W = ALLTRIM(STR(C5))
   C6_W = ALLTRIM(STR(C6))
   C7_W = ALLTRIM(STR(C7))
   C8_W = ALLTRIM(STR(C8))

   CW = C1_W + ',' + C2_W + ',' + C3_W  + ',' + C4_W + ;
        ',' + C5_W + C6_W + ',' + C7_W  + ',' + C8_W

CASE CC = 9
   C1_W = ALLTRIM(STR(C1))
   C2_W = ALLTRIM(STR(C2))
   C3_W = ALLTRIM(STR(C3))
   C4_W = ALLTRIM(STR(C4))
   C5_W = ALLTRIM(STR(C5))
   C6_W = ALLTRIM(STR(C6))
   C7_W = ALLTRIM(STR(C7))
   C8_W = ALLTRIM(STR(C8))
   C9_W = ALLTRIM(STR(C9))

   CW = C1_W + ',' + C2_W + ',' + C3_W  + ',' + C4_W + ;
         ',' + C5_W + ',' + C6_W + ',' + C7_W  + ',' + ;
         C8_W + ',' + C9_W

CASE CC = 10

   C1_W = ALLTRIM(STR(C1))
   C2_W = ALLTRIM(STR(C2))
   C3_W = ALLTRIM(STR(C3))
   C4_W = ALLTRIM(STR(C4))
   C5_W = ALLTRIM(STR(C5))
   C6_W = ALLTRIM(STR(C6))
   C7_W = ALLTRIM(STR(C7))
   C8_W = ALLTRIM(STR(C8))
   C9_W = ALLTRIM(STR(C9))
   C10_W = ALLTRIM(STR(C10))

   CW = C1_W + ',' + C2_W + ',' + C3_W  + ',' + C4_W + ;
        ',' + C5_W + C6_W + ',' + C7_W  + ',' + C8_W + ;
        ',' + C9_W + C10_W

CASE CC = 11

   C1_W = ALLTRIM(STR(C1))
   C2_W = ALLTRIM(STR(C2))
   C3_W = ALLTRIM(STR(C3))
```

```
    C4_W = ALLTRIM(STR(C4))
    C5_W = ALLTRIM(STR(C5))
    C6_W = ALLTRIM(STR(C6))
    C7_W = ALLTRIM(STR(C7))
    C8_W = ALLTRIM(STR(C8))
    C9_W = ALLTRIM(STR(C9))
    C10_W = ALLTRIM(STR(C10))
    C11_W = ALLTRIM(STR(C11))

    CW = C1_W + ',' + C2_W + ',' + C3_W  + ',' + C4_W + ;
         ',' + C5_W + C6_W + ',' + C7_W  + ',' + C8_W + ;
         ',' + C9_W + C10_W + ',' + C11_W

 CASE CC = 12
    C1_W = ALLTRIM(STR(C1))
    C2_W = ALLTRIM(STR(C2))
    C3_W = ALLTRIM(STR(C3))
    C4_W = ALLTRIM(STR(C4))
    C5_W = ALLTRIM(STR(C5))
    C6_W = ALLTRIM(STR(C6))
    C7_W = ALLTRIM(STR(C7))
    C8_W = ALLTRIM(STR(C8))
    C9_W = ALLTRIM(STR(C9))
    C10_W = ALLTRIM(STR(C10))
    C11_W = ALLTRIM(STR(C11))
    C12_W = ALLTRIM(STR(C12))

    CW = C1_W + ',' + C2_W + ',' + C3_W  + ',' + C4_W + ;
         ',' + C5_W + C6_W + ',' + C7_W  + ',' + C8_W + ;
         ',' + C9_W + C10_W + ',' + C11_W  + ',' + C12_W

CASE CC = 13
    C1_W = ALLTRIM(STR(C1))
    C2_W = ALLTRIM(STR(C2))
    C3_W = ALLTRIM(STR(C3))
    C4_W = ALLTRIM(STR(C4))
    C5_W = ALLTRIM(STR(C5))
    C6_W = ALLTRIM(STR(C6))
    C7_W = ALLTRIM(STR(C7))
    C8_W = ALLTRIM(STR(C8))
    C9_W = ALLTRIM(STR(C9))
    C10_W = ALLTRIM(STR(C10))
    C11_W = ALLTRIM(STR(C11))
    C12_W = ALLTRIM(STR(C12))
    C13_W = ALLTRIM(STR(C13))

    CW = C1_W + ',' + C2_W + ',' + C3_W  + ',' + C4_W + ;
         ',' + C5_W + ',' + C6_W + ',' + C7_W  + ',' + ;
          C8_W + ',' + C9_W + ',' + C10_W + ',' + C11_W ;
          + ',' + C12_W + ',' + C13_W
```

```
ENDCASE

THISFORM.B07_SETUP_LIST_COLUMN(C1,C2,C3,C4,C5,C6,C7,C8, ;
                               C9,C10,C11,C12,C13)

RETURN CW  && Column Width



*==============================================================*
* Procedure  : AD07_LIST_PB_CAPTION                             *
*                                                               *
*==============================================================*
Lparameters cc

Local c1, c2, c3, c4, c5, c6, c7, c8, c9, c10, c11, c12, c13

    *------------------------
    * Column Name/ PB Caption
    *------------------------
    c1  =  QR_CAPTION_COL1
    c2  =  QR_CAPTION_COL2
    c3  =  QR_CAPTION_COL3
    c4  =  QR_CAPTION_COL4
    c5  =  QR_CAPTION_COL5
    c6  =  QR_CAPTION_COL6
    c7  =  QR_CAPTION_COL7
    c8  =  QR_CAPTION_COL8
    c9  =  QR_CAPTION_COL9
    c10 =  QR_CAPTION_COL10
    c11 =  QR_CAPTION_COL11
    c12 =  QR_CAPTION_COL12
    c13 =  QR_CAPTION_COL13
          *================


*------------------------------
* Do not change the code below.
*------------------------------

Thisform.ao07_list_pb_caption(cc,c1,c2,c3,c4,c5,c6,c7,;
                              c8,c9,c10,c11,c12,c13)
```

Source Code

```
*================================================================*
* Procedure   : AD09_LIST_ROW_SOURCE_TYPE                        *
*                                                                *
*  SourceType   Description    RowSource                         *
*  ----------   ------------   ---------------------------       *
*      6          Field        "USERS.user_id, user_name"        *
*================================================================*
 Lparameters na
 Local row_source_type

    row_source_type = 6       && Field
                    *==

 RETURN row_source_type




*================================================================*
* Procedure: AD11_LIST_FONT                                      *
*                                                                *
*================================================================*
 Local font_name, font_size


    font_name = "Arial"    &&
    font_size = 8          && 9
             *=======

 *-------------------------------
 * Do not change the code below.
 *-------------------------------

 Thisform.ao11_list_font(font_name,font_size)



*================================================================*
* Procedure   : AD12_LIST_BOUND_COLUMN                           *
* Description: Determines which column is bound to the           *
*              Value Property.                                   *
*================================================================*
 Local bound_column


     bound_column = 1
                  *==

 RETURN bound_column
```

```
*==============================================================*
* Procedure   : AD13_INIT_INDEX                                *
* Description: Selects initial index (1) or (2). Also,         *
*              selects initial color of command buttons.       *
*==============================================================*
 Lparameters na
 Local index_used


     index_used  = 1      && Select index: 1 or 2
                 *===

 RETURN index_used



*==============================================================*
* Procedure: AD05_BEFORE_INIT                                  *
*                                                              *
*==============================================================*

 * Public RTV_???_CODE  && View Parameter: Region Code Field
                        && For view       : V_REG_RTV_DSP
                        && To retrieve    : Region Description
 * Public RTV_???_CODE  &&
 * Public RTV_???_CODE  &&
          *===========


 * RTV_???_CODE = " "   &&  (CHR.)
 * RTV_???_CODE = " "
 * RTV_???_CODE = " "
 * RTV_VND_CODE = 0


*==============================================================*
* Procedure: AD14_BEFORE_INIT                                  *
*                                                              *
*==============================================================*

 * Public RTV_???_CODE  && View Parameter: Region Code Field
                        && For view       : V_REG_RTV_DSP
                        && To retrieve    : Region Description
 * Public RTV_???_CODE  &&
 * Public RTV_???_CODE  &&
          *===========
 * RTV_???_CODE = " "   &&  (CHR.)
 * RTV_???_CODE = " "
 * RTV_???_CODE = " "
 * RTV_VND_CODE = 0
```

```
*-------------------------------
* Do not change the code below.
*-------------------------------

* ================================================================
* Parameterized View Parameters for Views:
*             V_???_qsrc1, V_???_qidx2, ....
*            (View Parameters for columns 1 and 2.)
* ================================================================
 Public QRY_COL_1        && Column #1: CUS_CODE
 Public QRY_COL_2        && Column #2: CUS_DESC


 DO CASE
 CASE qr_type_col1 = "CHR"
                             QRY_COL_1 = " "
 CASE qr_type_col1 = "NUM"
                             QRY_COL_1 = 0
 CASE qr_type_col1 = "DATE"
                             QRY_COL_1 = CTOD("00/00/00")
 ENDCASE

 DO CASE
 CASE qr_type_col2 = "CHR"
                             QRY_COL_2 = " "
 CASE qr_type_col2 = "NUM"
                             QRY_COL_2 = 0
 CASE qr_type_col2 = "DATE"
                             QRY_COL_2 = CTOD("00/00/00")
 ENDCASE
*------------------------------------------------------------
*  Example: Field Name: QR_PARM_1 = QRY_CUS_REGION
*------------------------------------------------------------
IF QR_QTY_QRY_PARMS >= 1
   DO CASE
   CASE qr_type_parm1 = "CHR"
                             &QR_PARM_1 = " "
   CASE qr_type_parm1 = "NUM"
                             &QR_PARM_1 = 0
   CASE qr_type_parm1 = "DATE"
                             &QR_PARM_1 = CTOD("00/00/00")
   ENDCASE
ENDIF

IF QR_QTY_QRY_PARMS >= 2

   DO CASE
   CASE qr_type_parm2 = "CHR"
```

```
                                        &QR_PARM_2 = " "
   CASE qr_type_parm2 = "NUM"
                                        &QR_PARM_2 = 0
   CASE qr_type_parm2 = "DATE"
                                        &QR_PARM_2 = CTOD("00/00/00")
   ENDCASE
ENDIF


IF QR_QTY_QRY_PARMS >= 3

   DO CASE
   CASE qr_type_parm3 = "CHR"
                                        &QR_PARM_3 = " "
   CASE qr_type_parm3 = "NUM"
                                        &QR_PARM_3 = 0
   CASE qr_type_parm3 = "DATE"
                                        &QR_PARM_3 = CTOD("00/00/00")
   ENDCASE
ENDIF


IF QR_QTY_QRY_PARMS >= 4

   DO CASE
   CASE qr_type_parm4 = "CHR"
                                        &QR_PARM_4 = " "
   CASE qr_type_parm4 = "NUM"
                                        &QR_PARM_4 = 0
   CASE qr_type_parm4 = "DATE"
                                        &QR_PARM_4 = CTOD("00/00/00")
   ENDCASE
ENDIF


IF QR_QTY_QRY_PARMS >= 5
   DO CASE
   CASE qr_type_parm5 = "CHR"
                                        &QR_PARM_5 = " "
   CASE qr_type_parm5 = "NUM"
                                        &QR_PARM_5 = 0
   CASE qr_type_parm5 = "DATE"
                                        &QR_PARM_5 = CTOD("00/00/00")
   ENDCASE
ENDIF
```

```
*=================================================================*
* Procedure: AD15_AFTER_INIT                                      *
*                                                                 *
*=================================================================*



*=================================================================*
* Procedure: AD16_CALL_DATA_ENTRY_FORM                            *
*                                                                 *
*=================================================================*
Lparameters maint_mode, sel_rec

   *   DO FORM ________.SCX with maint_mode, sel_rec
          *========
```

```
*==============================================================*
* Procedure   : AD17_CLEANUP                                   *
* Description: Used to erase, "Pack", deleted records.         *
*==============================================================*

CLOSE DATABASES

DO FORM t_pack.scx WITH li_database, li_table
                        *==========  ========
***                     First parameter  = Database
***                     Second parameter = Table Name
***                                          (Not View)




*==============================================================*
* Procedure: AD20_QTY_QRY_PARMS                                *
*                                                              *
*==============================================================*
 Lparameters na
 Local qty_qry_parms

        qty_qry_parms = QR_QTY_QRY_PARMS
                         *===============


RETURN qty_qry_parms



*==============================================================*
* Procedure: AD21_QRY_PICKLIST_CALL                            *
*                                                              *
*==============================================================*
 Lparameters textbox_id
 Local rtn_pl

 DO CASE
 CASE textbox_id = "Q_TXTBOX_1"
   *  DO FORM REG_PLST.SCX  WITH " " TO rtn_pl
              *===========

 CASE textbox_id = "Q_TXTBOX_2"
   *  DO FORM ???_PLST.SCX  WITH " " TO rtn_pl
              *============

 CASE textbox_id = "Q_TXTBOX_3"
  *   DO FORM _____PLST.SCX  WITH " " TO rtn_pl
              *============
```

```
 CASE textbox_id = "Q_TXTBOX_4"
   *  DO FORM _____PLST.SCX  WITH " " TO rtn_pl
              *============

 CASE textbox_id = "Q_TXTBOX_5"
  *   DO FORM _____PLST.SCX  WITH " " TO rtn_pl
              *============

 ENDCASE

 RETURN rtn_pl


*==============================================================*
* Procedure: AD22_QRY_TEXTBOX_VALIDATE                         *
*                                                              *
*==============================================================*
Lparameters textbox_id, textbox_val
Local p_val1, rtn, parm_view, rtv_value, fld_seq


DO CASE
CASE textbox_id = "Q_TXTBOX_1"     && ____ Code

   parm_view    = "V_???_RTV_DSP"  && Parameterized View
 * RTV_???_CODE = textbox_val      && View Parameter
   *============================   && Change to Numeric if...
                                   && Ex. = VAL(textbox_val)
   Select &parm_view
   Use
   Select 0
   Use &parm_view Alias &parm_view
   CursorSetProp('Buffering', 5)


   IF BOF() AND EOF()
     rtn       = .F.
     rtv_value = " "
     fld_seq   = 1
     Thisform.aod_03_qry_textbox_rtn_inf( ;
                             textbox_id, rtv_value, fld_seq)
   ELSE
     rtn       = .T.
   * rtv_value = V_???_RTV_DSP.???_DESC
                 *======================
     fld_seq   = 1
     Thisform.aod_03_qry_textbox_rtn_inf( ;
                             textbox_id, rtv_value, fld_seq)
   ENDIF
```

```
   RETURN rtn

*-------------------------------------------------------------------
CASE textbox_id = "Q_TXTBOX_2"      && ____ Code

   parm_view    = "V_???_RTV_DSP"  && Parameterized View
 * RTV_???_CODE = textbox_val      && View Parameter
   *=============================  && Change to Numeric if...
                                   && Ex. = VAL(textbox_val)

   Select &parm_view
   Use
   Select 0
   Use &parm_view Alias &parm_view
   CursorSetProp('Buffering', 5)


   IF BOF() AND EOF()
     rtn       = .F.
     rtv_value = " "
     fld_seq   = 1
     Thisform.aod_03_qry_textbox_rtn_inf( ;
                            textbox_id, rtv_value, fld_seq)
   ELSE
     rtn       = .T.
   * rtv_value = V_???_RTV_DSP.???_DESC
                 *=====================
     fld_seq   = 1
     Thisform.aod_03_qry_textbox_rtn_inf( ;
                            textbox_id, rtv_value, fld_seq)
   ENDIF

   RETURN rtn

*-------------------------------------------------------------------
CASE textbox_id = "Q_TXTBOX_3"      && ____ Code

   parm_view    = "V_???_RTV_DSP"  && Parameterized View
 * RTV_???_CODE = textbox_val      && View Parameter
   *=============================  && Change to Numeric if...
                                   && Ex. = VAL(textbox_val)

   Select &parm_view
   Use
   Select 0
   Use &parm_view Alias &parm_view
   CursorSetProp('Buffering', 5)

   IF BOF() AND EOF()
     rtn       = .F.
```

```
    rtv_value = " "
    fld_seq   = 1
    Thisform.aod_03_qry_textbox_rtn_inf( ;
                            textbox_id, rtv_value, fld_seq)
  ELSE
    rtn       = .T.
  * rtv_value = V_???_RTV_DSP.???_DESC
                *======================
    fld_seq   = 1
    Thisform.aod_03_qry_textbox_rtn_inf( ;
                            textbox_id, rtv_value, fld_seq)
  ENDIF
  RETURN rtn

*--------------------------------------------------------------
CASE textbox_id = "Q_TXTBOX_4"     && ____ Code

  parm_view    = "V_???_RTV_DSP"  && Parameterized View
 * RTV_???_CODE = textbox_val      && View Parameter
  *============================    && Change to Numeric if...
                                   && Ex. = VAL(textbox_val)
  Select &parm_view
  Use
  Select 0
  Use &parm_view Alias &parm_view
  CursorSetProp('Buffering', 5)
  IF BOF() AND EOF()
    rtn       = .F.
    rtv_value = " "
    fld_seq   = 1
    Thisform.aod_03_qry_textbox_rtn_inf( ;
                            textbox_id, rtv_value, fld_seq)
  ELSE
    rtn       = .T.
  * rtv_value = V_???_RTV_DSP.???_DESC
                *======================
    fld_seq   = 1
    Thisform.aod_03_qry_textbox_rtn_inf( ;
                            textbox_id, rtv_value, fld_seq)
  ENDIF

  RETURN rtn

*--------------------------------------------------------------
CASE textbox_id = "Q_TXTBOX_5"     && ____ Code

  parm_view    = "V_???_RTV_DSP"  && Parameterized View
 * RTV_???_CODE = textbox_val      && View Parameter
  *============================    && Change to Numeric if...
                                   && Ex. = VAL(textbox_val)
```

```
   Select &parm_view
   Use
   Select 0
   Use &parm_view Alias &parm_view
   CursorSetProp('Buffering', 5)

   IF BOF() AND EOF()
     rtn       = .F.
     rtv_value = " "
     fld_seq   = 1
     Thisform.aod_03_qry_textbox_rtn_inf( ;
                             textbox_id, rtv_value, fld_seq)
   ELSE
     rtn       = .T.
   * rtv_value = V_???_RTV_DSP.???_DESC
                 *=====================
     fld_seq   = 1
     Thisform.aod_03_qry_textbox_rtn_inf( ;
                             textbox_id, rtv_value, fld_seq)
   ENDIF

   RETURN rtn

ENDCASE



*==============================================================*
* Procedure: AF01_OPEN_DATABASE                                *
*                                                              *
*==============================================================*
 Local dbase1


    dbase1  = QR_DATABASE
              *==========



 *------------------------------
 * Do not change the code below.
 *------------------------------

 OPEN DATABASE &dbase1

 Nodefault    &&  Optional - (Just in case.)
```

```
*====================================================================*
* Procedure: AF02_OPEN_FILES_VIEWS                                   *
*                                                                    *
*====================================================================*
 Local file1 ,file2, file3, file4, file5  && file6, file7

 * ================================
 * Views to Retrieve Description:
 * ================================
 *  file5     = "V_???_RTV_DSP"     && Example: "V_REG_RTV_DSP"
 *  file6     = "V_???_RTV_DSP"
 *  file7     = "V_???_RTV_DSP"
 *  file8     = "V_???_RTV_DSP"
 *  file9     = "V_???_RTV_DSP"


 * ================================
 * Views for the Query:
 * ================================
   file1     = QR_VIEW1             && Do not change.
   file2     = QR_VIEW2             &&      "
   file3     = QR_VIEW3             &&      "
   file4     = QR_VIEW4             &&      "
 * ================================



 *-------------------------------------------------------------------
 SELECT 0
 USE &FILE1 ALIAS &FILE1  NODATA
 CURSORSETPROP('BUFFERING', 5)  && Optimistic Table Buffering
 *-------------------------------------------------------------------
 *-------------------------------------------------------------------
 SELECT 0
 USE &FILE2 ALIAS &FILE2  NODATA
 CURSORSETPROP('BUFFERING', 5)  && Optimistic Table Buffering
 *-------------------------------------------------------------------
 *-------------------------------------------------------------------
 SELECT 0
 USE &FILE3 ALIAS &FILE3  NODATA
 CURSORSETPROP('BUFFERING', 5)  && Optimistic Table Buffering
 *-------------------------------------------------------------------
 *-------------------------------------------------------------------
 SELECT 0
 USE &FILE4 ALIAS &FILE4  NODATA
 CURSORSETPROP('BUFFERING', 5)  && Optimistic Table Buffering
 *-------------------------------------------------------------------
 *-------------------------------------------------------------------
 * SELECT 0
 * USE &FILE5 ALIAS &FILE5  NODATA
```

```
* CURSORSETPROP('BUFFERING', 5) && Optimistic Table Buff.
*-----------------------------------------------------------
*-----------------------------------------------------------
* SELECT 0
* USE &FILE6 ALIAS &FILE6  NODATA
* CURSORSETPROP('BUFFERING', 5)  && Optimistic Table Buff.
*-----------------------------------------------------------
*-----------------------------------------------------------
* SELECT 0
* USE &FILE7 ALIAS &FILE7  NODATA
* CURSORSETPROP('BUFFERING', 5)  && Optimistic Table Buff.
*-----------------------------------------------------------

Nodefault


*============================================================*
* Procedure   : AF03_VIEW_IDX1                               *
* Description: Opens the view with sort order 1,             *
*              and sets the row source.                      *
*============================================================*
Local parm_view, row_source, qp, q_error, no_err
Local qry_chr1, qry_chr2, qry_chr3, qry_chr4, qry_chr5


 parm_view  = QR_VIEW1
 row_source = QR_ROW_SOURCE_1
              *==============


qp = Thisform.ad20_qty_qry_parms()

IF qp >= 1
    qry_chr1 = Thisform.aod_05_qry_rtn_textbox_value( ;
                                              "Q_TXTBOX_1")
    If Len(Alltrim(qry_chr1)) = 0
       DO CASE
       CASE qr_type_parm1 = "CHR"
                                 &QR_PARM_1 = " "
       CASE qr_type_parm1 = "NUM"
                                 &QR_PARM_1 = 0
       CASE qr_type_parm1 = "DATE"
                            &QR_PARM_1 = CTOD("00/00/00")
       ENDCASE

    Else

       DO CASE
       CASE qr_type_parm1 = "CHR"
```

```
                                    &QR_PARM_1 = qry_chr1
        CASE qr_type_parm1 = "NUM"
                                &QR_PARM_1 = VAL(qry_chr1)
        CASE qr_type_parm1 = "DATE"
                               &QR_PARM_1 = CTOD(qry_chr1)
        ENDCASE

     Endif

  ENDIF

  *---------------------------------------------------------------
  IF qp >= 2
     qry_chr2 = Thisform.aod_05_qry_rtn_textbox_value( ;
                                                  "Q_TXTBOX_2")
     If Len(Alltrim(qry_chr2)) = 0
        DO CASE
        CASE qr_type_parm2 = "CHR"
                                    &QR_PARM_2 = " "
        CASE qr_type_parm2 = "NUM"
                                    &QR_PARM_2 = 0
        CASE qr_type_parm2 = "DATE"
                               &QR_PARM_2 = CTOD("00/00/00")
        ENDCASE

     Else

        DO CASE
        CASE qr_type_parm2 = "CHR"
                                    &QR_PARM_2 = qry_chr2
        CASE qr_type_parm2 = "NUM"
                                &QR_PARM_2 = VAL(qry_chr2)
        CASE qr_type_parm2 = "DATE"
                               &QR_PARM_2 = CTOD(qry_chr2)
        ENDCASE

     Endif
  ENDIF
  *---------------------------------------------------------------
  IF qp >= 3
     qry_chr3 = Thisform.aod_05_qry_rtn_textbox_value( ;
                                                  "Q_TXTBOX_3")

     If Len(Alltrim(qry_chr3)) = 0
        DO CASE
        CASE qr_type_parm3 = "CHR"
                                    &QR_PARM_3 = " "
        CASE qr_type_parm3 = "NUM"
                                    &QR_PARM_3 = 0
        CASE qr_type_parm3 = "DATE"
```

```
                              &QR_PARM_3 = CTOD("00/00/00")
      ENDCASE

   Else

      DO CASE
      CASE qr_type_parm3 = "CHR"
                                  &QR_PARM_3 = qry_chr3
      CASE qr_type_parm3 = "NUM"
                              &QR_PARM_3 = VAL(qry_chr3)
      CASE qr_type_parm3 = "DATE"
                             &QR_PARM_3 = CTOD(qry_chr3)
      ENDCASE
   Endif
ENDIF
*------------------------------------------------------------
*------------------------------------------------------------
IF qp >= 4
   qry_chr4 = Thisform.aod_05_qry_rtn_textbox_value(;
                                             "Q_TXTBOX_4")

   If Len(Alltrim(qry_chr4)) = 0
      DO CASE
      CASE qr_type_parm4 = "CHR"
                                  &QR_PARM_4 = " "
      CASE qr_type_parm4 = "NUM"
                                  &QR_PARM_4 = 0
      CASE qr_type_parm4 = "DATE"
                              &QR_PARM_4 = CTOD("00/00/00")
      ENDCASE

   Else

      DO CASE
      CASE qr_type_parm4 = "CHR"
                                  &QR_PARM_4 = qry_chr4
      CASE qr_type_parm4 = "NUM"
                              &QR_PARM_4 = VAL(qry_chr4)
      CASE qr_type_parm4 = "DATE"
                             &QR_PARM_4 = CTOD(qry_chr4)
      ENDCASE
   Endif
ENDIF
*------------------------------------------------------------
IF qp >= 5
   qry_chr5 = Thisform.aod_05_qry_rtn_textbox_value( ;
                                             "Q_TXTBOX_5")

   If Len(Alltrim(qry_chr5)) = 0
      DO CASE
```

```
        CASE qr_type_parm5 = "CHR"
                                    &QR_PARM_5 = " "
        CASE qr_type_parm5 = "NUM"
                                    &QR_PARM_5 = 0
        CASE qr_type_parm5 = "DATE"
                                &QR_PARM_5 = CTOD("00/00/00")
        ENDCASE
     Else

        DO CASE
        CASE qr_type_parm5 = "CHR"
                                    &QR_PARM_5 = qry_chr5
        CASE qr_type_parm5 = "NUM"
                                &QR_PARM_5 = VAL(qry_chr5)
        CASE qr_type_parm5 = "DATE"
                               &QR_PARM_5 = CTOD(qry_chr5)
        ENDCASE

     Endif

  ENDIF

*------------------------------------------------------------

*------------------------------
* Do not change the code below.
*------------------------------
 Select &parm_view
 Use
 Select 0
 Use &parm_view Alias &parm_view
 CursorSetProp('Buffering', 5)

 no_err = .T.
 no_err = Thisform.ao10_list_row_source(row_source)

 If no_err = .f.
   Thisform.ao01_list_requery
   Thisform.Refresh
   no_err = Thisform.ao10_list_row_source(row_source)
 Endif

 On Error

 Thisform.ao15_list_reset_value
```

```
*===========================================================*
* Procedure   : AF04_VIEW_IDX2                              *
* Description: Opens the view with sort order 2,            *
*              and sets the row source.                     *
*===========================================================*
 Local parm_view, row_source, qp, q_error, no_err
 Local qry_chr1, qry_chr2, qry_chr3, qry_chr4, qry_chr5

  parm_view  = QR_VIEW2
  row_source = QR_ROW_SOURCE_2
               *===============


qp = Thisform.ad20_qty_qry_parms()

 IF qp >= 1
     qry_chr1 = Thisform.aod_05_qry_rtn_textbox_value( ;
                                            "Q_TXTBOX_1")
     If Len(Alltrim(qry_chr1)) = 0
        DO CASE
        CASE qr_type_parm1 = "CHR"
                                &QR_PARM_1 = " "
        CASE qr_type_parm1 = "NUM"
                                &QR_PARM_1 = 0
        CASE qr_type_parm1 = "DATE"
                           &QR_PARM_1 = CTOD("00/00/00")
        ENDCASE

     Else

        DO CASE
        CASE qr_type_parm1 = "CHR"
                                &QR_PARM_1 = qry_chr1
        CASE qr_type_parm1 = "NUM"
                            &QR_PARM_1 = VAL(qry_chr1)
        CASE qr_type_parm1 = "DATE"
                           &QR_PARM_1 = CTOD(qry_chr1)
        ENDCASE

     Endif

  ENDIF
  *---------------------------------------------------------
  IF qp >= 2
     qry_chr2 = Thisform.aod_05_qry_rtn_textbox_value( ;
                                             "Q_TXTBOX_2")
     If Len(Alltrim(qry_chr2)) = 0
        DO CASE
        CASE qr_type_parm2 = "CHR"
                                &QR_PARM_2 = " "
```

```
      CASE qr_type_parm2 = "NUM"
                                 &QR_PARM_2 = 0
      CASE qr_type_parm2 = "DATE"
                            &QR_PARM_2 = CTOD("00/00/00")
      ENDCASE

   Else

      DO CASE
      CASE qr_type_parm2 = "CHR"
                                 &QR_PARM_2 = qry_chr2
      CASE qr_type_parm2 = "NUM"
                             &QR_PARM_2 = VAL(qry_chr2)
      CASE qr_type_parm2 = "DATE"
                            &QR_PARM_2 = CTOD(qry_chr2)
      ENDCASE

   Endif
ENDIF
*------------------------------------------------------------
IF qp >= 3
   qry_chr3 = Thisform.aod_05_qry_rtn_textbox_value( ;
                                             "Q_TXTBOX_3")

   If Len(Alltrim(qry_chr3)) = 0
      DO CASE
      CASE qr_type_parm3 = "CHR"
                                 &QR_PARM_3 = " "
      CASE qr_type_parm3 = "NUM"
                                 &QR_PARM_3 = 0
      CASE qr_type_parm3 = "DATE"
                             &QR_PARM_3 = CTOD("00/00/00")
      ENDCASE

   Else

      DO CASE
      CASE qr_type_parm3 = "CHR"
                                 &QR_PARM_3 = qry_chr3
      CASE qr_type_parm3 = "NUM"
                             &QR_PARM_3 = VAL(qry_chr3)

      CASE qr_type_parm3 = "DATE"
                            &QR_PARM_3 = CTOD(qry_chr3)
      ENDCASE
   Endif
ENDIF
*------------------------------------------------------------
*------------------------------------------------------------
```

```
IF qp >= 4
   qry_chr4 = Thisform.aod_05_qry_rtn_textbox_value(;
                                                     "Q_TXTBOX_4")

   If Len(Alltrim(qry_chr4)) = 0
      DO CASE
      CASE qr_type_parm4 = "CHR"
                                        &QR_PARM_4 = " "
      CASE qr_type_parm4 = "NUM"
                                        &QR_PARM_4 = 0
      CASE qr_type_parm4 = "DATE"
                                    &QR_PARM_4 = CTOD("00/00/00")
      ENDCASE

   Else

      DO CASE
      CASE qr_type_parm4 = "CHR"
                                        &QR_PARM_4 = qry_chr4
      CASE qr_type_parm4 = "NUM"
                                    &QR_PARM_4 = VAL(qry_chr4)
      CASE qr_type_parm4 = "DATE"
                                   &QR_PARM_4 = CTOD(qry_chr4)
      ENDCASE
   Endif
ENDIF
*-------------------------------------------------------------
IF qp >= 5
   qry_chr5 = Thisform.aod_05_qry_rtn_textbox_value( ;
                                                     "Q_TXTBOX_5")

   If Len(Alltrim(qry_chr5)) = 0
      DO CASE
      CASE qr_type_parm5 = "CHR"
                                        &QR_PARM_5 = " "
      CASE qr_type_parm5 = "NUM"
                                        &QR_PARM_5 = 0
      CASE qr_type_parm5 = "DATE"
                                    &QR_PARM_5 = CTOD("00/00/00")
      ENDCASE
   Else

      DO CASE
      CASE qr_type_parm5 = "CHR"
                                        &QR_PARM_5 = qry_chr5
      CASE qr_type_parm5 = "NUM"
                                    &QR_PARM_5 = VAL(qry_chr5)
      CASE qr_type_parm5 = "DATE"
                                   &QR_PARM_5 = CTOD(qry_chr5)
      ENDCASE
```

```
    Endif

 ENDIF

*-------------------------------------------------------------

*------------------------------
* Do not change the code below.
*------------------------------
 Select &parm_view
 Use
 Select 0
 Use &parm_view Alias &parm_view
 CursorSetProp('Buffering', 5)

 no_err = .T.
 no_err = Thisform.ao10_list_row_source(row_source)

 If no_err = .f.
   Thisform.ao01_list_requery
   Thisform.Refresh
   no_err = Thisform.ao10_list_row_source(row_source)
 Endif

 On Error

 Thisform.ao15_list_reset_value


*==============================================================*
* Procedure  : AF05_VIEW_SEARCH_IDX1                           *
* Description: Opens the view with sort order 1, and           *
*              sets the row source. (Using Search Window.)     *
*==============================================================*
Local parm_view, row_source, qp, q_error, no_err
Local f_caption, input_mask, parm1
Local qry_chr1, qry_chr2, qry_chr3, qry_chr4, qry_chr5
 parm_view  = QR_VIEW3
 row_source = QR_ROW_SOURCE_3
             *===============

 *--------------------------------------------------------
 * For Search Window:                                     *
 *--------------------------------------------------------
 f_caption  = QR_C1_SW_Caption
 input_mask = QR_C1_SW_Input_Mask
             *==================

 DO FORM t_search.scx WITH input_mask, f_caption TO parm1
```

```
 DO CASE
 CASE qr_type_col1 = "CHR"
                            QRY_COL_1 = ALLTRIM(parm1)
 CASE qr_type_col1 = "NUM"
                            QRY_COL_1 = VAL(ALLTRIM(parm1))
 CASE qr_type_col1 = "DATE"
                            QRY_COL_1 = CTOD(ALLTRIM(parm1))
 ENDCASE

*---------------------------------------------------------------

qp = Thisform.ad20_qty_qry_parms()

 IF qp >= 1
     qry_chr1 = Thisform.aod_05_qry_rtn_textbox_value( ;
                                                "Q_TXTBOX_1")
     If Len(Alltrim(qry_chr1)) = 0
        DO CASE
        CASE qr_type_parm1 = "CHR"
                                  &QR_PARM_1 = " "
        CASE qr_type_parm1 = "NUM"
                                  &QR_PARM_1 = 0
        CASE qr_type_parm1 = "DATE"
                             &QR_PARM_1 = CTOD("00/00/00")
        ENDCASE
     Else
        DO CASE
        CASE qr_type_parm1 = "CHR"
                                  &QR_PARM_1 = qry_chr1
        CASE qr_type_parm1 = "NUM"
                              &QR_PARM_1 = VAL(qry_chr1)
        CASE qr_type_parm1 = "DATE"
                             &QR_PARM_1 = CTOD(qry_chr1)
        ENDCASE
     Endif
  ENDIF
  *-------------------------------------------------------------
  IF qp >= 2
     qry_chr2 = Thisform.aod_05_qry_rtn_textbox_value( ;
                                                 "Q_TXTBOX_2")
     If Len(Alltrim(qry_chr2)) = 0
        DO CASE
        CASE qr_type_parm2 = "CHR"
                                  &QR_PARM_2 = " "
        CASE qr_type_parm2 = "NUM"
                                  &QR_PARM_2 = 0
        CASE qr_type_parm2 = "DATE"
                             &QR_PARM_2 = CTOD("00/00/00")
        ENDCASE
```

```
    Else

        DO CASE
        CASE qr_type_parm2 = "CHR"
                                   &QR_PARM_2 = qry_chr2
        CASE qr_type_parm2 = "NUM"
                               &QR_PARM_2 = VAL(qry_chr2)
        CASE qr_type_parm2 = "DATE"
                              &QR_PARM_2 = CTOD(qry_chr2)
        ENDCASE

    Endif
ENDIF
*-------------------------------------------------------------
IF qp >= 3
    qry_chr3 = Thisform.aod_05_qry_rtn_textbox_value( ;
                                                 "Q_TXTBOX_3")

    If Len(Alltrim(qry_chr3)) = 0
        DO CASE
        CASE qr_type_parm3 = "CHR"
                                   &QR_PARM_3 = " "
        CASE qr_type_parm3 = "NUM"
                                   &QR_PARM_3 = 0
        CASE qr_type_parm3 = "DATE"
                               &QR_PARM_3 = CTOD("00/00/00")
        ENDCASE

    Else

        DO CASE
        CASE qr_type_parm3 = "CHR"
                                   &QR_PARM_3 = qry_chr3
        CASE qr_type_parm3 = "NUM"
                               &QR_PARM_3 = VAL(qry_chr3)
        CASE qr_type_parm3 = "DATE"
                              &QR_PARM_3 = CTOD(qry_chr3)
        ENDCASE
    Endif
ENDIF
*-------------------------------------------------------------
*-------------------------------------------------------------
IF qp >= 4
    qry_chr4 = Thisform.aod_05_qry_rtn_textbox_value(;
                                                 "Q_TXTBOX_4")

    If Len(Alltrim(qry_chr4)) = 0
        DO CASE
        CASE qr_type_parm4 = "CHR"
```

```
                                        &QR_PARM_4 = " "
      CASE qr_type_parm4 = "NUM"
                                        &QR_PARM_4 = 0
      CASE qr_type_parm4 = "DATE"
                                    &QR_PARM_4 = CTOD("00/00/00")
      ENDCASE

   Else

      DO CASE
      CASE qr_type_parm4 = "CHR"
                                        &QR_PARM_4 = qry_chr4
      CASE qr_type_parm4 = "NUM"
                                    &QR_PARM_4 = VAL(qry_chr4)
      CASE qr_type_parm4 = "DATE"
                                   &QR_PARM_4 = CTOD(qry_chr4)
      ENDCASE
   Endif
ENDIF
*-----------------------------------------------------------
IF qp >= 5
   qry_chr5 = Thisform.aod_05_qry_rtn_textbox_value( ;
                                                "Q_TXTBOX_5")

   If Len(Alltrim(qry_chr5)) = 0
      DO CASE
      CASE qr_type_parm5 = "CHR"
                                        &QR_PARM_5 = " "
      CASE qr_type_parm5 = "NUM"
                                        &QR_PARM_5 = 0
      CASE qr_type_parm5 = "DATE"
                                    &QR_PARM_5 = CTOD("00/00/00")
      ENDCASE
   Else

      DO CASE
      CASE qr_type_parm5 = "CHR"
                                        &QR_PARM_5 = qry_chr5
      CASE qr_type_parm5 = "NUM"
                                    &QR_PARM_5 = VAL(qry_chr5)
      CASE qr_type_parm5 = "DATE"
                                   &QR_PARM_5 = CTOD(qry_chr5)
      ENDCASE

   Endif

ENDIF

*-----------------------------------------------------------
```

```
*------------------------------
* Do not change the code below.
*------------------------------
 Select &parm_view
 Use
 Select 0
 Use &parm_view Alias &parm_view
 CursorSetProp('Buffering', 5)

 no_err = .T.
 no_err = Thisform.ao10_list_row_source(row_source)

 If no_err = .f.
   Thisform.ao01_list_requery
   Thisform.Refresh
   no_err = Thisform.ao10_list_row_source(row_source)
 Endif

 On Error
 Thisform.ao15_list_reset_value



*==========================================================*
* Procedure  : AF06_VIEW_SEARCH_IDX2                       *
* Description: Opens the view with sort order 2, and       *
*              sets the row source. (Using Search Window.) *
*==========================================================*
Local parm_view, row_source, qp, q_error, no_err
Local f_caption, input_mask, parm1
Local qry_chr1, qry_chr2, qry_chr3, qry_chr4, qry_chr5
  parm_view  = QR_VIEW4
  row_source = QR_ROW_SOURCE_4
               *===============

 *---------------------------------------------------------
 * For Search Window:                                     *
 *---------------------------------------------------------
 f_caption  = QR_C2_SW_Caption
 input_mask = QR_C2_SW_Input_Mask
              *===================

 DO FORM t_search.scx WITH input_mask, f_caption TO parm1

 DO CASE
 CASE qr_type_col2 = "CHR"
                             QRY_COL_2 = ALLTRIM(parm1)
 CASE qr_type_col2 = "NUM"
                             QRY_COL_2 = VAL(ALLTRIM(parm1))
```

```
CASE qr_type_col2 = "DATE"
                              QRY_COL_2 = CTOD(ALLTRIM(parm1))
ENDCASE

*-----------------------------------------------------------

qp = Thisform.ad20_qty_qry_parms()

IF qp >= 1
    qry_chr1 = Thisform.aod_05_qry_rtn_textbox_value( ;
                                          "Q_TXTBOX_1")
    If Len(Alltrim(qry_chr1)) = 0
       DO CASE
       CASE qr_type_parm1 = "CHR"
                              &QR_PARM_1 = " "
       CASE qr_type_parm1 = "NUM"
                              &QR_PARM_1 = 0
       CASE qr_type_parm1 = "DATE"
                         &QR_PARM_1 = CTOD("00/00/00")
       ENDCASE
    Else
       DO CASE
       CASE qr_type_parm1 = "CHR"
                              &QR_PARM_1 = qry_chr1
       CASE qr_type_parm1 = "NUM"
                          &QR_PARM_1 = VAL(qry_chr1)
       CASE qr_type_parm1 = "DATE"
                         &QR_PARM_1 = CTOD(qry_chr1)
       ENDCASE
    Endif
ENDIF
*-----------------------------------------------------------
IF qp >= 2
    qry_chr2 = Thisform.aod_05_qry_rtn_textbox_value( ;
                                          "Q_TXTBOX_2")
    If Len(Alltrim(qry_chr2)) = 0
       DO CASE
       CASE qr_type_parm2 = "CHR"
                              &QR_PARM_2 = " "
       CASE qr_type_parm2 = "NUM"
                              &QR_PARM_2 = 0
       CASE qr_type_parm2 = "DATE"
                         &QR_PARM_2 = CTOD("00/00/00")
       ENDCASE

    Else

       DO CASE
       CASE qr_type_parm2 = "CHR"
                              &QR_PARM_2 = qry_chr2
```

```
      CASE qr_type_parm2 = "NUM"
                                     &QR_PARM_2 = VAL(qry_chr2)
      CASE qr_type_parm2 = "DATE"
                                    &QR_PARM_2 = CTOD(qry_chr2)
      ENDCASE

   Endif
ENDIF
*------------------------------------------------------------
IF qp >= 3
   qry_chr3 = Thisform.aod_05_qry_rtn_textbox_value( ;
                                                 "Q_TXTBOX_3")

   If Len(Alltrim(qry_chr3)) = 0
      DO CASE
      CASE qr_type_parm3 = "CHR"
                                         &QR_PARM_3 = " "
      CASE qr_type_parm3 = "NUM"
                                         &QR_PARM_3 = 0
      CASE qr_type_parm3 = "DATE"
                                     &QR_PARM_3 = CTOD("00/00/00")
      ENDCASE

   Else

      DO CASE
      CASE qr_type_parm3 = "CHR"
                                         &QR_PARM_3 = qry_chr3
      CASE qr_type_parm3 = "NUM"
                                     &QR_PARM_3 = VAL(qry_chr3)
      CASE qr_type_parm3 = "DATE"
                                    &QR_PARM_3 = CTOD(qry_chr3)
      ENDCASE
   Endif
ENDIF
*------------------------------------------------------------
*------------------------------------------------------------
IF qp >= 4
   qry_chr4 = Thisform.aod_05_qry_rtn_textbox_value(;
                                                 "Q_TXTBOX_4")

   If Len(Alltrim(qry_chr4)) = 0
      DO CASE
      CASE qr_type_parm4 = "CHR"
                                         &QR_PARM_4 = " "
      CASE qr_type_parm4 = "NUM"
                                         &QR_PARM_4 = 0
      CASE qr_type_parm4 = "DATE"
                                     &QR_PARM_4 = CTOD("00/00/00")
      ENDCASE
```

```
   Else

      DO CASE
      CASE qr_type_parm4 = "CHR"
                                    &QR_PARM_4 = qry_chr4
      CASE qr_type_parm4 = "NUM"
                                &QR_PARM_4 = VAL(qry_chr4)
      CASE qr_type_parm4 = "DATE"
                               &QR_PARM_4 = CTOD(qry_chr4)
      ENDCASE
   Endif
ENDIF
*------------------------------------------------------------
IF qp >= 5
   qry_chr5 = Thisform.aod_05_qry_rtn_textbox_value( ;
                                              "Q_TXTBOX_5")

   If Len(Alltrim(qry_chr5)) = 0
      DO CASE
      CASE qr_type_parm5 = "CHR"
                                    &QR_PARM_5 = " "
      CASE qr_type_parm5 = "NUM"
                                    &QR_PARM_5 = 0
      CASE qr_type_parm5 = "DATE"
                                &QR_PARM_5 = CTOD("00/00/00")
      ENDCASE
   Else

      DO CASE
      CASE qr_type_parm5 = "CHR"
                                    &QR_PARM_5 = qry_chr5
      CASE qr_type_parm5 = "NUM"
                                &QR_PARM_5 = VAL(qry_chr5)
      CASE qr_type_parm5 = "DATE"
                               &QR_PARM_5 = CTOD(qry_chr5)
      ENDCASE

   Endif

ENDIF

*------------------------------------------------------------

*-------------------------------
* Do not change the code below.
*-------------------------------
Select &parm_view
Use
Select 0
```

```
 Use &parm_view Alias &parm_view
 CursorSetProp('Buffering', 5)

 no_err = .T.
 no_err = Thisform.ao10_list_row_source(row_source)

 If no_err = .f.
   Thisform.ao01_list_requery
   Thisform.Refresh
   no_err = Thisform.ao10_list_row_source(row_source)
 Endif

 On Error
 Thisform.ao15_list_reset_value


*===============================================================*
* Procedure: AF15_REFRESH_LIST                                  *
*                                                               *
*===============================================================*
Local parm_view, row_source

parm_view  = QR_VIEW3
row_source = QR_ROW_SOURCE_3  && List Row Source
             *===============



*===========================================================
* Parameterized View Parameters for columns 1 and 2.
*===========================================================
DO CASE
CASE qr_type_col1 = "CHR"
                             QRY_COL_1 = " "
CASE qr_type_col1 = "NUM"
                             QRY_COL_1 = 0
CASE qr_type_col1 = "DATE"
                             QRY_COL_1 = CTOD("00/00/00")
ENDCASE

DO CASE
CASE qr_type_col2 = "CHR"
                             QRY_COL_2 = " "
CASE qr_type_col2 = "NUM"
                             QRY_COL_2 = 0
CASE qr_type_col2 = "DATE"
                             QRY_COL_2 = CTOD("00/00/00")
ENDCASE
```

```
*------------------------------------------------------------
*  Field Name: QR_PARM_1 = QRY_P_CATEGORY
*------------------------------------------------------------
IF QR_QTY_QRY_PARMS >= 1
   DO CASE
   CASE qr_type_parm1 = "CHR"
                                    &QR_PARM_1 = " "
   CASE qr_type_parm1 = "NUM"
                                    &QR_PARM_1 = 0
   CASE qr_type_parm1 = "DATE"
                                    &QR_PARM_1 = CTOD("00/00/00")
   ENDCASE
ENDIF

IF QR_QTY_QRY_PARMS >= 2
   DO CASE
   CASE qr_type_parm2 = "CHR"
                                    &QR_PARM_2 = " "
   CASE qr_type_parm2 = "NUM"
                                    &QR_PARM_2 = 0
   CASE qr_type_parm2 = "DATE"
                                    &QR_PARM_2 = CTOD("00/00/00")
   ENDCASE
ENDIF
IF QR_QTY_QRY_PARMS >= 3
   DO CASE
   CASE qr_type_parm3 = "CHR"
                                    &QR_PARM_3 = " "
   CASE qr_type_parm3 = "NUM"
                                    &QR_PARM_3 = 0
   CASE qr_type_parm3 = "DATE"
                                    &QR_PARM_3 = CTOD("00/00/00")
  ENDCASE
ENDIF

IF QR_QTY_QRY_PARMS >= 4
   DO CASE
   CASE qr_type_parm4 = "CHR"
                                    &QR_PARM_4 = " "
   CASE qr_type_parm4 = "NUM"
                                    &QR_PARM_4 = 0
   CASE qr_type_parm4 = "DATE"
                                    &QR_PARM_4 = CTOD("00/00/00")
   ENDCASE
ENDIF

IF QR_QTY_QRY_PARMS >= 5
   DO CASE
   CASE qr_type_parm5 = "CHR"
                                    &QR_PARM_5 = " "
```

```
   CASE qr_type_parm5 = "NUM"
                                  &QR_PARM_5 = 0
   CASE qr_type_parm5 = "DATE"
                                  &QR_PARM_5 = CTOD("00/00/00")
   ENDCASE
 ENDIF

 *------------------------------------------------------------

 SELECT &parm_view
 USE
 SELECT 0
 USE &parm_view ALIAS &parm_view NODATA
 CURSORSETPROP('BUFFERING', 5)
 THISFORM.ao10_list_row_source(row_source)

 THISFORM.REFRESH


*==============================================================*
* Procedure: AO01_LIST_REQUERY                                 *
*                                                              *
*==============================================================*

Thisform.CONTAIN_LIST_021.List1.Requery
        *=================



*==============================================================*
* Procedure: AO02_LIST_VALUE                                   *
*                                                              *
*==============================================================*
Lparameters na
Local  lst_val


       lst_val = Thisform.CONTAIN_LIST_021.List1.Value
                                 *=================

RETURN lst_val



*==============================================================*
* Procedure: AO03_RETURN_LIST_LEFT                             *
*                                                              *
*==============================================================*
Lparameters na
```

```
Local  ll

       ll = Thisform.CONTAIN_LIST_021.List1.Left
                      *=================

RETURN ll


*==============================================================*
* Procedure: A004_RETURN_LIST_WIDTH                            *
*                                                              *
*==============================================================*
Lparameters na
Local  lw

       lw = Thisform.CONTAIN_LIST_021.List1.Width
                      *=================

RETURN lw



*==============================================================*
* Procedure: A005_LIST_COLUMN_COUNT                            *
*                                                              *
*==============================================================*
Lparameters cc

     Thisform.CONTAIN_LIST_021.List1.ColumnCount = cc
             *=================



*==============================================================*
* Procedure: A006_LIST_COLUMN_WIDTH                            *
*                                                              *
*==============================================================*
Lparameters cw

     Thisform.CONTAIN_LIST_021.List1.ColumnWidths = cw
             *=================


*==============================================================*
* Procedure: A007_LIST_PB_CAPTION                              *
*                                                              *
*==============================================================*
Lparameters cc,c1,c2,c3,c4,c5,c6,c7,c8,c9,c10,c11,c12,c13

 If cc >= 1
```

```
       Thisform.CONTAIN_LIST_021.Command1.Caption  = c1
 Endif        && =================
 If cc >= 2
       Thisform.CONTAIN_LIST_021.Command2.Caption  = c2
 Endif        && =================
 If cc >= 3
       THISFORM.CONTAIN_LIST_021.Command3.Caption  = c3
 Endif        && =================
 If cc >= 4
       Thisform.CONTAIN_LIST_021.Command4.Caption  = c4
 Endif        && =================
 If cc >= 5
       Thisform.CONTAIN_LIST_021.Command5.Caption  = c5
 Endif        && =================
 If cc >= 6
       THISFORM.CONTAIN_LIST_021.Command6.Caption  = c6
 Endif        && =================
 If cc >= 7
       Thisform.CONTAIN_LIST_021.Command7.Caption  = c7
 Endif        && =================
If cc >= 8
       Thisform.CONTAIN_LIST_021.Command8.Caption  = c8
 Endif        && =================
 If cc >= 9
       THISFORM.CONTAIN_LIST_021.Command9.Caption  = c9
 Endif        && =================
 If cc >= 10
       Thisform.CONTAIN_LIST_021.Command10.Caption = c10
 Endif        && =================
 If cc >= 11
       Thisform.CONTAIN_LIST_021.Command11.Caption = c11
 Endif        && =================
 If cc >= 12
       THISFORM.CONTAIN_LIST_021.Command12.Caption = c12
 Endif        && =================
 If cc >= 13
       THISFORM.CONTAIN_LIST_021.Command13.Caption = c13
 Endif        && =================


*============================================================*
* Procedure: A008_LIST_COLUMN_PB_WIDTH                       *
*                                                            *
*============================================================*
Lparameters cc,pb1_l, pb1_w, pb2_l, pb2_w, pb3_l, pb3_w,    ;
   pb4_l, pb4_w, pb5_l, pb5_w, pb6_l, pb6_w, pb7_l, pb7_w, ;
   pb8_l, pb8_w, pb9_l, pb9_w, pb10_l, pb10_w, pb11_l,     ;
   pb11_w, pb12_l, pb12_w, pb13_l, pb13_w
```

```
 IF cc >= 1
     On Error Return
     With Thisform.CONTAIN_LIST_021.Command1
                     *=================
        .Left  = pb1_l
        .Width = pb1_w
     Endwith
 ENDIF

 IF cc >= 2
     On Error Return
     With Thisform.CONTAIN_LIST_021.Command2
                     *=================
        .Left  = pb2_l
        .Width = pb2_w
     Endwith
 ENDIF

IF cc >= 3
     On Error Return
     With Thisform.CONTAIN_LIST_021.Command3
                     *=================
        .Left  = pb3_l
        .Width = pb3_w
     Endwith
 ENDIF

 IF cc >= 4
     On error Return
     With Thisform.CONTAIN_LIST_021.Command4
                     *=================
        .Left  = pb4_l
        .Width = pb4_w
     Endwith
 ENDIF

 IF cc >= 5
     On Error Return
     With Thisform.CONTAIN_LIST_021.Command5
                     *=================
        .Left  = pb5_l
        .Width = pb5_w
     Endwith
 ENDIF

 IF cc >= 6
     On Error Return
     With Thisform.CONTAIN_LIST_021.Command6
                     *=================
```

```
        .Left  = pb6_l
        .Width = pb6_w
    Endwith
ENDIF

IF cc >= 7
    On error Return
    With Thisform.CONTAIN_LIST_021.Command7
                  *=================
        .Left  = pb7_l
        .Width = pb7_w
    Endwith
ENDIF

IF cc >= 8
    On Error Return
    With Thisform.CONTAIN_LIST_021.Command8
                  *=================
        .Left  = pb8_l
        .Width = pb8_w
    Endwith
ENDIF

IF cc >= 9
    On Error Return
    With Thisform.CONTAIN_LIST_021.Command9
                  *=================
        .Left  = pb9_l
        .Width = pb9_w
    Endwith
ENDIF

IF cc >= 10
    On Error Return
    With Thisform.CONTAIN_LIST_021.Command10
                  *=================
        .Left  = pb10_l
        .Width = pb10_w
    Endwith
ENDIF

IF cc >= 11
    On Error Return
    With Thisform.CONTAIN_LIST_021.Command11
                  *=================
        .Left  = pb11_l
        .Width = pb11_w
    Endwith
ENDIF
```

```
 IF cc >= 12
     On error Return
     With Thisform.CONTAIN_LIST_021.Command12
                    *================
       .Left  = pb12_l
       .Width = pb12_w
     Endwith
 ENDIF

 IF cc >= 13
     On Error Return
     With Thisform.CONTAIN_LIST_021.Command13
                    *================
       .Left  = pb13_l
       .Width = pb13_w
     Endwith
 ENDIF


*==============================================================*
* Procedure: A009_LIST_ROW_SOURCE_TYPE                         *
*                                                              *
*==============================================================*
Lparameters row_source_type

Thisform.CONTAIN_LIST_021.List1.RowSourceType =row_source_type
        *================


*==============================================================*
* Procedure: A010_LIST_ROW_SOURCE                              *
*                                                              *
*==============================================================*
Lparameters row_source

On Error Return .F.


     Thisform.CONTAIN_LIST_021.List1.RowSource  = row_source
             *================

RETURN .T.


*==============================================================*
* Procedure: A011_LIST_FONT                                    *
*                                                              *
*==============================================================*
Lparameters font_name, font_size
```

```
  Thisform.CONTAIN_LIST_021.List1.FontName  = font_name
  Thisform.CONTAIN_LIST_021.List1.FontSize  = font_size
          *=================


*==================================================================*
* Procedure: AO12_INIT_PB_COLOR_IDX1                               *
*                                                                  *
*==================================================================*
Lparameters cc

  Thisform.CONTAIN_LIST_021.Command1.Forecolor = RGB(64,0,128)
          *=================                     && Blue

If cc > 1
  Thisform.CONTAIN_LIST_021.Command2.Forecolor = RGB(0,0,0)
          *=================                     && Black
Endif



*==================================================================*
* Procedure: AO13_INIT_PB_COLOR_IDX2                               *
*                                                                  *
*==================================================================*
Lparameters cc

 Thisform.CONTAIN_LIST_021.Command1.Forecolor = RGB(0,0,0)
         *=================                     && Black

If cc > 1
  Thisform.CONTAIN_LIST_021.Command2.Forecolor = RGB(64,0,128)
            *=================                   && Blue
Endif



*==================================================================*
* Procedure: AO14_INIT_SET_FOCUS                                   *
*                                                                  *
*==================================================================*

 Thisform.CONTAIN_LIST_021.List1.SetFocus()
         *=================
```

```
*==============================================================*
* Procedure: AO15_LIST_RESET_VALUE                             *
*                                                              *
*==============================================================*

 Thisform.CONTAIN_LIST_021.List1.Value = ""
        *================



*==============================================================*
* Procedure: AO16_LIST_BOUND_COLUMN                            *
*                                                              *
*==============================================================*
Lparameters bc

Thisform.CONTAIN_LIST_021.list1.BoundColumn  = bc
       *================



*==============================================================*
* Procedure: AOD_01_SET_DSP                                    *
*                                                              *
*==============================================================*
* Thisform.CONTAIN_QRY_11.command1.Caption     = "REGION"
* Thisform.CONTAIN_QRY_11.qry_txt_1.InputMask = "XXXXX"
* Thisform.CONTAIN_QRY_11.text1.Format         = "KR"

* Thisform.CONTAIN_QRY_11.command2.Caption     = "________"
* Thisform.CONTAIN_QRY_11.text2.InputMask      = "XXX"
* Thisform.CONTAIN_QRY_11.text2.Format         = "KR"

* Thisform.CONTAIN_QRY_11.command3.Caption     = "_______"
* Thisform.CONTAIN_QRY_11.text3.InputMask      = "9999"
* Thisform.CONTAIN_QRY_11.text3.Format         = "K"
         *==============



*==============================================================*
* Procedure: AOD_02_QRY_CONTAIN_TEXT_VALUE                     *
*                                                              *
*==============================================================*
 Lparameters textbox_id, txt_value

 DO CASE
 CASE textbox_id = "Q_TXTBOX_1"
    Thisform.CONTAIN_QRY_11.qry_txt_1.Value = txt_value
           *==============
```

```
 CASE textbox_id = "Q_TXTBOX_2"
    Thisform.CONTAIN_QRY_11.qry_txt_2.Value = txt_value
            *===============

 CASE textbox_id = "Q_TXTBOX_3"
    Thisform.CONTAIN_QRY_11.qry_txt_3.Value = txt_value
            *===============

  CASE textbox_id = "Q_TXTBOX_4"
    Thisform.CONTAIN_QRY_11.qry_txt_4.Value = txt_value
            *===============

 CASE textbox_id = "Q_TXTBOX_5"
    Thisform.CONTAIN_QRY_11.qry_txt_5.Value = txt_value
            *===============

 ENDCASE


*============================================================*
* Procedure: AOD_03_QRY_TEXTBOX_RTN_INF                      *
*                                                            *
*============================================================*
Lparameters textbox_id, txt_value, fld_seq


 DO CASE
 CASE textbox_id = "Q_TXTBOX_1"
     Thisform.CONTAIN_QRY_11.qry_txt_rtv_1.Value = txt_value
             *===============

 CASE textbox_id = "Q_TXTBOX_2"
     Thisform.CONTAIN_QRY_11.qry_txt_rtv_2.Value = txt_value
             *===============

 CASE textbox_id = "Q_TXTBOX_3"
     Thisform.CONTAIN_QRY_11.qry_txt_rtv_3.Value = txt_value
             *===============

 CASE textbox_id = "Q_TXTBOX_4"
     Thisform.CONTAIN_QRY_11.qry_txt_rtv_4.Value = txt_value
             *===============

 CASE textbox_id = "Q_TXTBOX_5"
     Thisform.CONTAIN_QRY_11.qry_txt_rtv_5.Value = txt_value
             *===============
 ENDCASE
```

```
*==============================================================*
* Procedure: AOD_04_QRY_CONTAIN_TXT_SETFOCUS                   *
*                                                              *
*==============================================================*
Lparameters textbox_id

 DO CASE
 CASE textbox_id = "Q_TXTBOX_1"
     Thisform.CONTAIN_QRY_11.qry_txt_1.SetFocus()
             *===============

 CASE textbox_id = "Q_TXTBOX_2"
     Thisform.CONTAIN_QRY_11.qry_txt_2.SetFocus()
             *===============

 CASE textbox_id = "Q_TXTBOX_3"
     Thisform.CONTAIN_QRY_11.qry_txt_3.SetFocus()
             *===============

 CASE textbox_id = "Q_TXTBOX_4"
     Thisform.CONTAIN_QRY_11.qry_txt_4.SetFocus()
             *===============

 CASE textbox_id = "Q_TXTBOX_5"
     Thisform.CONTAIN_QRY_11.qry_txt_5.SetFocus()
             *===============
 ENDCASE




*==============================================================*
* Procedure: AOD_05_QRY_RTN_TEXTBOX_VALUE                      *
*                                                              *
*==============================================================*
Lparameters textbox_id
Local qry_chr1, qry_chr2, qry_chr3, qry_chr4, qry_chr5

 DO CASE
 CASE textbox_id = "Q_TXTBOX_1"
      qry_chr1 = Thisform.CONTAIN_QRY_11.qry_txt_1.Value
                          *===============
      Return qry_chr1

 CASE textbox_id = "Q_TXTBOX_2"
      qry_chr2 = Thisform.CONTAIN_QRY_11.qry_txt_2.Value
                          *===============
      Return qry_chr2
```

```
CASE textbox_id = "Q_TXTBOX_3"
     qry_chr3 = Thisform.CONTAIN_QRY_11.qry_txt_3.Value
                        *===============
     Return qry_chr3

CASE textbox_id = "Q_TXTBOX_4"
     qry_chr4 = Thisform.CONTAIN_QRY_11.qry_txt_4.Value
                        *===============
     Return qry_chr4

CASE textbox_id = "Q_TXTBOX_5"
     qry_chr4 = Thisform.CONTAIN_QRY_11.qry_txt_5.Value
                        *===============
     Return qry_chr5

ENDCASE


*==============================================================*
* Procedure: B02_COMMAND_GROUP_CLICK                           *
*                                                              *
* Options/Methods:                                             *
*                                                              *
*   B80_PB_CANCEL     B85_PB_DISPLAY      B90_PB_PROCESS       *
*   B81_PB_OK         B86_PB_ADD                               *
*   B82_PB_CHANGE     B87_PB_SAVE                              *
*   B83_PB_COPY       B88_PB_PRINT                             *
*   B84_PB_DELETE     B89_PB_EXIT                              *
*                                                              *
*==============================================================*
 LPARAMETERS TMP_OPT

 DO CASE
 CASE TMP_OPT = 1                  && OK : DISPLAY
    THISFORM.B85_PB_DISPLAY

 CASE TMP_OPT = 2                  && EXIT
    THISFORM.B89_PB_EXIT

 ENDCASE

NODEFAULT  && Do not run parent class method.
```

Source Code Example for the Contain_qry_1 Control

```
*=====================================================================*
* Class           : Contain_qry_1                                     *
* Object/Procedure: Command1 / Click                                  *
*=====================================================================*
 LOCAL TEXTBOX_ID
 TEXTBOX_ID = "Q_TXTBOX_1"
 THISFORM.B21_QRY_PICKLIST_RUN(TEXTBOX_ID)

*=====================================================================*
* Class           : Contain_qry_1                                     *
* Object/Procedure: QRY_TXT_1 / DblClick                              *
*=====================================================================*
 LOCAL TEXTBOX_ID
 TEXTBOX_ID = "Q_TXTBOX_1"
 THISFORM.B21_QRY_PICKLIST_RUN(TEXTBOX_ID)

*=====================================================================*
* Class      : Contain_qry_1                                          *
* Object/Procedure: QRY_TXT_1 / Valid                                 *
*=====================================================================*
 LOCAL TEXTBOX_ID, TEXBOX_VAL, RTN
 TEXTBOX_ID = "Q_TXTBOX_1"
 TEXTBOX_VAL = THIS.VALUE
 RTN = THISFORM.B22_QRY_TEXTBOX_VALIDATE(TEXTBOX_ID, TEXTBOX_VAL)
 IF RTN = .F.
     THISFORM.B21_QRY_PICKLIST_RUN(TEXTBOX_ID)
 ELSE
     RETURN .T.
 ENDIF
```

Source Code Example for the Pbg_list_1 and Pbg_search_sort Control

```
*================================================================*
* Object    : Pbg_list_01                                        *
* Procedure: Click                                               *
*================================================================*
LOCAL CMD_G
CMD_G = THIS.VALUE
Thisform.B02_COMMAND_GROUP_CLICK(CMD_G)

*================================================================*
* Class           : Pbg_search_sort                              *
* Object/Procedure: Command1 / Click                             *
*================================================================*
THISFORM.B04_LIST_COLUMN_PB_CLICK(1)
THISFORM.SETALL('FORECOLOR',RGB(0,0,0),'CommandButton')
THIS.ForeColor = RGB(64,0,128)
```

Data Entry Form

```
*==============================================================*
* Form         : DE_20.scx           (Created from DE_20.scx) *
* Procedure    : Init                                          *
* Description  : ________ Master File - Data Entry,            *
*                                      File Maintenance        *
* Programmer   : E. Aleu                                       *
* Date created: 8/10/05                                        *
* Date revised:                                                *
*--------------------------------------------------------------*
* To add Pick-Lists and retrieve information from other        *
* database tables, see the following methods:                  *
*                                                              *
*        1.) AD03_CALL_PICKLIST_FORM                           *
*        2.) AF04_OPEN_OTHER_FILES_VIEWS                       *
*        3.) AD05_BEFORE_INIT                                  *
*        4.) AD04_TEXT_VALID_RTN_VALUE                         *
*        5.) AOD_01_SET_DSP                                    *
*        6.) AOD_02_GET_VAL                                    *
*        7.) AOD_06_TEXTBOX_VALUE                              *
*        8.) AOD_07_TEXTBOX_VAL_RTN_INF                        *
*                                                              *
* To add validation for text boxes, see the following          *
* method:    AOD_04_VALIDATE                                   *
*                                                              *
*==============================================================*
LPARAMETERS tmp_mode, tmp_sel_rec
SET TALK OFF
SET ECHO OFF
Public DE_QTY_TXTFLDS
Public DE_FRM_CAPTION_ADD_MODE, DE_FRM_CAPTION_CHG_MODE
Public DE_FRM_CAPTION_DSP_MODE, DE_FRM_CAPTION_DEL_MODE
Public DE_FRM_CAPTION_CPY_MODE, DE_DATABASE, DE_VIEW_ADD
Public DE_VIEW_CHG, DE_VIEW_DSP, DE_VIEW_DEL
Public DE_VIEW_SORT_A, DE_VIEW_SORT_D

Public DE_TABLE_FLD_NAME_1, DE_TABLE_FLD_NAME_2
Public DE_TABLE_FLD_NAME_3, DE_TABLE_FLD_NAME_4
Public DE_TABLE_FLD_NAME_5, DE_TABLE_FLD_NAME_6
Public DE_TABLE_FLD_NAME_7, DE_TABLE_FLD_NAME_8
Public DE_TABLE_FLD_NAME_9, DE_TABLE_FLD_NAME_10
Public DE_TABLE_FLD_NAME_11, DE_TABLE_FLD_NAME_12
Public DE_TABLE_FLD_NAME_13, DE_TABLE_FLD_NAME_14
Public DE_TABLE_FLD_NAME_15, DE_TABLE_FLD_NAME_16
Public DE_TABLE_FLD_NAME_17, DE_TABLE_FLD_NAME_18
Public DE_TABLE_FLD_NAME_19, DE_TABLE_FLD_NAME_20
Public DE_TABLE_FLD1_TYPE, DE_TABLE_FLD2_TYPE
```

```
Public DE_TABLE_FLD3_TYPE, DE_TABLE_FLD4_TYPE
Public DE_TABLE_FLD5_TYPE, DE_TABLE_FLD6_TYPE
Public DE_TABLE_FLD7_TYPE, DE_TABLE_FLD8_TYPE
Public DE_TABLE_FLD9_TYPE, DE_TABLE_FLD10_TYPE
Public DE_TABLE_FLD11_TYPE, DE_TABLE_FLD12_TYPE
Public DE_TABLE_FLD13_TYPE, DE_TABLE_FLD14_TYPE
Public DE_TABLE_FLD15_TYPE, DE_TABLE_FLD16_TYPE
Public DE_TABLE_FLD17_TYPE, DE_TABLE_FLD18_TYPE
Public DE_TABLE_FLD19_TYPE, DE_TABLE_FLD20_TYPE

Public DE_NUM_FLD1_WIDTH, DE_NUM_FLD1_DECIMALS
Public DE_NUM_FLD2_WIDTH, DE_NUM_FLD2_DECIMALS
Public DE_NUM_FLD3_WIDTH, DE_NUM_FLD3_DECIMALS
Public DE_NUM_FLD4_WIDTH, DE_NUM_FLD4_DECIMALS
Public DE_NUM_FLD5_WIDTH, DE_NUM_FLD5_DECIMALS
Public DE_NUM_FLD6_WIDTH, DE_NUM_FLD6_DECIMALS
Public DE_NUM_FLD7_WIDTH, DE_NUM_FLD7_DECIMALS
Public DE_NUM_FLD8_WIDTH, DE_NUM_FLD8_DECIMALS
Public DE_NUM_FLD9_WIDTH, DE_NUM_FLD9_DECIMALS
Public DE_NUM_FLD10_WIDTH, DE_NUM_FLD10_DECIMALS
Public DE_NUM_FLD11_WIDTH, DE_NUM_FLD11_DECIMALS
Public DE_NUM_FLD12_WIDTH, DE_NUM_FLD12_DECIMALS
Public DE_NUM_FLD13_WIDTH, DE_NUM_FLD13_DECIMALS
Public DE_NUM_FLD14_WIDTH, DE_NUM_FLD14_DECIMALS
Public DE_NUM_FLD15_WIDTH, DE_NUM_FLD15_DECIMALS
Public DE_NUM_FLD16_WIDTH, DE_NUM_FLD16_DECIMALS
Public DE_NUM_FLD17_WIDTH, DE_NUM_FLD17_DECIMALS
Public DE_NUM_FLD18_WIDTH, DE_NUM_FLD18_DECIMALS
Public DE_NUM_FLD19_WIDTH, DE_NUM_FLD19_DECIMALS
Public DE_NUM_FLD20_WIDTH, DE_NUM_FLD20_DECIMALS

Public DE_QTY_ADD_TXTFLDS, DE_QTY_ADD_LABELS

*==============================================================*
* Quantity of Fields,(Text Boxes), and Form Caption:           *
*                                                              *
* Note: For quantity of Text Fields,                           *
*       see the following views:  V_???_DSP, V_???_CHG         *
*                                                              *
*==============================================================*

 DE_QTY_TXTFLDS          = 0  && Qty. Fields. See views above.


 DE_FRM_CAPTION_ADD_MODE = "File: ________ Master File " + ;
                           "                            " + ;
                           "                            " + ;
                           "                  Mode: Add"
DE_FRM_CAPTION_CHG_MODE = "File: ________ Master File " + ;
                           "                            " + ;
```

```
                               "                                " + ;
                               "                         Mode: Change"

 DE_FRM_CAPTION_DSP_MODE = "File: _______ Master File " + ;
                               "                                " + ;
                               "                                " + ;
                               "                         Mode: Display"

 DE_FRM_CAPTION_DEL_MODE = "File: ________ Master File " + ;
                               "                                " + ;
                               "                                " + ;
                               "                         Mode: Delete"

 DE_FRM_CAPTION_CPY_MODE = "File: ________ Master File " + ;
                               "                                " + ;
                               "                                " + ;
                               "                         Mode: Copy"


*============================================================*
* Database, Views and Fields Information (Type, Width, Dec.) *
*                    ( See chapter 4. )                      *
*============================================================*

 DE_DATABASE             = "C:\TMP2000\DATA\_______"

*-------------------------------------
* Views:
*-------------------------------------
 DE_VIEW_ADD             = "V_???_CHG"
 DE_VIEW_CHG             = "V_???_CHG"
 DE_VIEW_DSP             = "V_???_DSP"
 DE_VIEW_DEL             = "V_???_CHG"

 DE_VIEW_SORT_A          = "V_???_SRC_1"
 DE_VIEW_SORT_D          = "V_???_SRC_1D"


*-------------------------------------
* Table/Views Field Names:
*-------------------------------------
 DE_TABLE_FLD_NAME_1     = "???_CODE"
 DE_TABLE_FLD_NAME_2     = "???_NAME"
 DE_TABLE_FLD_NAME_3     = "_________"
 DE_TABLE_FLD_NAME_4     = " "
 DE_TABLE_FLD_NAME_5     = " "
 DE_TABLE_FLD_NAME_6     = " "
DE_TABLE_FLD_NAME_7     = " "
 DE_TABLE_FLD_NAME_8     = " "
 DE_TABLE_FLD_NAME_9     = " "
```

```
 DE_TABLE_FLD_NAME_10  = " "
 DE_TABLE_FLD_NAME_11  = " "
 DE_TABLE_FLD_NAME_12  = " "
 DE_TABLE_FLD_NAME_13  = " "
 DE_TABLE_FLD_NAME_14  = " "
 DE_TABLE_FLD_NAME_15  = " "
 DE_TABLE_FLD_NAME_16  = " "
 DE_TABLE_FLD_NAME_17  = " "
 DE_TABLE_FLD_NAME_18  = " "
 DE_TABLE_FLD_NAME_19  = " "
 DE_TABLE_FLD_NAME_20  = " "
*-------------------------------------
* Field Type, Width, Decimals:
*-------------------------------------
 DE_TABLE_FLD1_TYPE     = "CHR"  && "CHR", "NUM" or "DATE"
   * If Numeric:
   DE_NUM_FLD1_WIDTH    = 0      && Applies if Numeric.
   DE_NUM_FLD1_DECIMALS = 0      && Applies if Numeric.

 DE_TABLE_FLD2_TYPE     = "CHR"  && "CHR", "NUM" or "DATE"
   DE_NUM_FLD2_WIDTH    = 0
   DE_NUM_FLD2_DECIMALS = 0

 DE_TABLE_FLD3_TYPE     = "CHR"  && "CHR", "NUM" or "DATE"
   DE_NUM_FLD3_WIDTH    = 0
   DE_NUM_FLD3_DECIMALS = 0

 DE_TABLE_FLD4_TYPE     = "CHR"  && "CHR", "NUM" or "DATE"
   DE_NUM_FLD4_WIDTH    = 0
   DE_NUM_FLD4_DECIMALS = 0

 DE_TABLE_FLD5_TYPE     = "CHR"  && "CHR", "NUM" or "DATE"
   DE_NUM_FLD5_WIDTH    = 0
   DE_NUM_FLD5_DECIMALS = 0

 DE_TABLE_FLD6_TYPE     = "CHR"  && "CHR", "NUM" or "DATE"
   DE_NUM_FLD6_WIDTH    = 0
   DE_NUM_FLD6_DECIMALS = 0

 DE_TABLE_FLD7_TYPE     = "CHR"  && "CHR", "NUM" or "DATE"
   DE_NUM_FLD7_WIDTH    = 0
   DE_NUM_FLD7_DECIMALS = 0

 DE_TABLE_FLD8_TYPE     = "CHR"  && "CHR", "NUM" or "DATE"
   DE_NUM_FLD8_WIDTH    = 0
   DE_NUM_FLD8_DECIMALS = 0

 DE_TABLE_FLD9_TYPE     = "CHR"  && "CHR", "NUM" or "DATE"
   DE_NUM_FLD9_WIDTH    = 0
   DE_NUM_FLD9_DECIMALS = 0
```

```
DE_TABLE_FLD10_TYPE    = "CHR"  && "CHR", "NUM" or "DATE"
  DE_NUM_FLD10_WIDTH    = 0
  DE_NUM_FLD10_DECIMALS = 0

DE_TABLE_FLD11_TYPE    = "CHR"  && "CHR", "NUM" or "DATE"
  DE_NUM_FLD11_WIDTH    = 0
  DE_NUM_FLD11_DECIMALS = 0

DE_TABLE_FLD12_TYPE    = "CHR"  && "CHR", "NUM" or "DATE"
  DE_NUM_FLD12_WIDTH    = 0
  DE_NUM_FLD12_DECIMALS = 0

DE_TABLE_FLD13_TYPE    = "CHR"  && "CHR", "NUM" or "DATE"
  DE_NUM_FLD13_WIDTH    = 0
  DE_NUM_FLD13_DECIMALS = 0

DE_TABLE_FLD14_TYPE    = "CHR"  && "CHR", "NUM" or "DATE"
  DE_NUM_FLD14_WIDTH    = 0
  DE_NUM_FLD14_DECIMALS = 0

DE_TABLE_FLD15_TYPE    = "CHR"  && "CHR", "NUM" or "DATE"
  DE_NUM_FLD15_WIDTH    = 0
  DE_NUM_FLD15_DECIMALS = 0

DE_TABLE_FLD16_TYPE    = "CHR"  && "CHR", "NUM" or "DATE"
  DE_NUM_FLD16_WIDTH    = 0
  DE_NUM_FLD16_DECIMALS = 0

DE_TABLE_FLD17_TYPE    = "CHR"  && "CHR", "NUM" or "DATE"
  DE_NUM_FLD17_WIDTH    = 0
  DE_NUM_FLD17_DECIMALS = 0

DE_TABLE_FLD18_TYPE    = "CHR"  && "CHR", "NUM" or "DATE"
  DE_NUM_FLD18_WIDTH    = 0
  DE_NUM_FLD18_DECIMALS = 0

DE_TABLE_FLD19_TYPE    = "CHR"  && "CHR", "NUM" or "DATE"
  DE_NUM_FLD19_WIDTH    = 0
  DE_NUM_FLD19_DECIMALS = 0

DE_TABLE_FLD20_TYPE    = "CHR"  && "CHR", "NUM" or "DATE"
  DE_NUM_FLD20_WIDTH    = 0
  DE_NUM_FLD20_DECIMALS = 0


*==============================================================*
*           Setting Screen Labels and Text Boxes               *
*                                                              *
*==============================================================*
```

```
*--------------------------------------------------------------
* Quantity Additional Text Boxes to Retrieve Information:
*                           && Pick-List for Text Box #__.
* -------------------------------------------------------------
DE_QTY_ADD_TXTFLDS  = 0     && Text21 - ______ Description
                     *=     &&

*----------------------------
* Quantity Additional Labels:
* ---------------------------
DE_QTY_ADD_LABELS   = 0     && Label21 -
                     *=     &&

* Note: The Visible Property for Text Boxes and Labels
*       not used, will be set to False (.F.).

*=============================================================*
* Text Boxes, Labels and Containers Properties:               *
*                                                             *
* Note: These properties can also be changed using the        *
*       Property Window.                                      *
*=============================================================*
Local set_properties
set_properties    = "Y" && If "N", use other method, explained
                 *=== && above.


IF set_properties = "Y"
*-------------------------------------------------------------
* Caption for Labels:
*-------------------------------------------------------------
 Thisform.CONTAIN_TXTLBL_201.label1.Caption   = "_______"
 Thisform.CONTAIN_TXTLBL_201.label2.Caption   = "_______"
 Thisform.CONTAIN_TXTLBL_201.label3.Caption   = "_______"
 Thisform.CONTAIN_TXTLBL_201.label4.Caption   = "_______"
 Thisform.CONTAIN_TXTLBL_201.label5.Caption   = "_______"
 Thisform.CONTAIN_TXTLBL_201.label6.Caption   = "_______"
 Thisform.CONTAIN_TXTLBL_201.label7.Caption   = "_______"
 Thisform.CONTAIN_TXTLBL_201.label8.Caption   = "_______"
 Thisform.CONTAIN_TXTLBL_201.label9.Caption   = "_______"
 Thisform.CONTAIN_TXTLBL_201.label10.Caption  = "_______"
 * Not used:
 Thisform.CONTAIN_TXTLBL_201.label11.Caption  = " "
 Thisform.CONTAIN_TXTLBL_201.label12.Caption  = " "
 Thisform.CONTAIN_TXTLBL_201.label13.Caption  = " "
 Thisform.CONTAIN_TXTLBL_201.label14.Caption  = " "
 Thisform.CONTAIN_TXTLBL_201.label15.Caption  = " "
 Thisform.CONTAIN_TXTLBL_201.label16.Caption  = " "
 Thisform.CONTAIN_TXTLBL_201.label17.Caption  = " "
 Thisform.CONTAIN_TXTLBL_201.label18.Caption  = " "
```

```
 Thisform.CONTAIN_TXTLBL_201.label19.Caption  = " "
 Thisform.CONTAIN_TXTLBL_201.label20.Caption  = " "

*-------------------------------------------------------------
* Input Mask for Text Boxes:
*-------------------------------------------------------------
 Thisform.CONTAIN_TXTLBL_201.text1.InputMask  = "XXX"
 Thisform.CONTAIN_TXTLBL_201.text2.InputMask  = "XXX"
 Thisform.CONTAIN_TXTLBL_201.text3.InputMask  = "XXX"
 Thisform.CONTAIN_TXTLBL_201.text4.InputMask  = "XXX"
 Thisform.CONTAIN_TXTLBL_201.text5.InputMask  = "XXX"
 Thisform.CONTAIN_TXTLBL_201.text6.InputMask  = "999"
 Thisform.CONTAIN_TXTLBL_201.text7.InputMask  = "99.99"
 Thisform.CONTAIN_TXTLBL_201.text8.InputMask  = " "
 Thisform.CONTAIN_TXTLBL_201.text9.InputMask  = " "
 Thisform.CONTAIN_TXTLBL_201.text10.InputMask = " "
 * Not used:
 Thisform.CONTAIN_TXTLBL_201.text11.InputMask = ""
 Thisform.CONTAIN_TXTLBL_201.text12.InputMask = ""
 Thisform.CONTAIN_TXTLBL_201.text13.InputMask = ""
 Thisform.CONTAIN_TXTLBL_201.text14.InputMask = ""
 Thisform.CONTAIN_TXTLBL_201.text15.InputMask = ""
 Thisform.CONTAIN_TXTLBL_201.text16.InputMask = ""
 Thisform.CONTAIN_TXTLBL_201.text17.InputMask = ""
 Thisform.CONTAIN_TXTLBL_201.text18.InputMask = ""
 Thisform.CONTAIN_TXTLBL_201.text19.InputMask = ""
 Thisform.CONTAIN_TXTLBL_201.text20.InputMask = ""

*-------------------------------------------------------------
* Text Boxes - Width:
*-------------------------------------------------------------
 Thisform.CONTAIN_TXTLBL_201.text1.Width      =  42  &&   42
 Thisform.CONTAIN_TXTLBL_201.text2.Width      =  42  &&   42
 Thisform.CONTAIN_TXTLBL_201.text3.Width      =  42  &&    .
 Thisform.CONTAIN_TXTLBL_201.text4.Width      =  42  &&    .
 Thisform.CONTAIN_TXTLBL_201.text5.Width      =  42  &&    .
 Thisform.CONTAIN_TXTLBL_201.text6.Width      =  42  &&
 Thisform.CONTAIN_TXTLBL_201.text7.Width      =  42  &&
 Thisform.CONTAIN_TXTLBL_201.text8.Width      =  42  &&
 Thisform.CONTAIN_TXTLBL_201.text9.Width      =  42  &&
 Thisform.CONTAIN_TXTLBL_201.text10.Width     =  42  &&
 * Not used:
 Thisform.CONTAIN_TXTLBL_201.text11.Width     = 42   &&    .
 Thisform.CONTAIN_TXTLBL_201.text12.Width     = 42   &&
 Thisform.CONTAIN_TXTLBL_201.text13.Width     = 42   &&
 Thisform.CONTAIN_TXTLBL_201.text14.Width     = 42   &&
 Thisform.CONTAIN_TXTLBL_201.text15.Width     = 42   &&
 Thisform.CONTAIN_TXTLBL_201.text16.Width     = 42   &&
 Thisform.CONTAIN_TXTLBL_201.text17.Width     = 42   &&
 Thisform.CONTAIN_TXTLBL_201.text18.Width     = 42   &&
```

```
 Thisform.CONTAIN_TXTLBL_201.text19.Width     = 42    &&
 Thisform.CONTAIN_TXTLBL_201.text20.Width     = 42    &&

*---------------------------------------------------------------
* Text Boxes - Top:
*---------------------------------------------------------------
 Thisform.CONTAIN_TXTLBL_201.text1.Top        =  12   &&
 Thisform.CONTAIN_TXTLBL_201.text2.Top        =  40   &&
 Thisform.CONTAIN_TXTLBL_201.text3.Top        =  68   &&
 Thisform.CONTAIN_TXTLBL_201.text4.Top        =  96   &&
 Thisform.CONTAIN_TXTLBL_201.text5.Top        = 124   &&
 Thisform.CONTAIN_TXTLBL_201.text6.Top        = 152   &&
 Thisform.CONTAIN_TXTLBL_201.text7.Top        = 180   &&
 Thisform.CONTAIN_TXTLBL_201.text8.Top        = 208   &&
 Thisform.CONTAIN_TXTLBL_201.text9.Top        = 236   &&
 Thisform.CONTAIN_TXTLBL_201.text10.Top       = 264   &&
 * Not used:
 Thisform.CONTAIN_TXTLBL_201.text11.Top       =  12   &&
 Thisform.CONTAIN_TXTLBL_201.text12.Top       =  40   &&
 Thisform.CONTAIN_TXTLBL_201.text13.Top       =  68   &&
 Thisform.CONTAIN_TXTLBL_201.text14.Top       =  96   &&
 Thisform.CONTAIN_TXTLBL_201.text15.Top       = 124   &&
 Thisform.CONTAIN_TXTLBL_201.text16.Top       = 152   &&
 Thisform.CONTAIN_TXTLBL_201.text17.Top       = 180   &&
 Thisform.CONTAIN_TXTLBL_201.text18.Top       = 208   &&
 Thisform.CONTAIN_TXTLBL_201.text19.Top       = 236   &&
 Thisform.CONTAIN_TXTLBL_201.text20.Top       = 264   &&

*---------------------------------------------------------------
* Text Boxes - Left:
*---------------------------------------------------------------
 Thisform.CONTAIN_TXTLBL_201.text1.Left       = 172   &&   172
 Thisform.CONTAIN_TXTLBL_201.text2.Left       = 172   &&   172
 Thisform.CONTAIN_TXTLBL_201.text3.Left       = 172   &&    .
 Thisform.CONTAIN_TXTLBL_201.text4.Left       = 172   &&    .
 Thisform.CONTAIN_TXTLBL_201.text5.Left       = 172   &&    .
 Thisform.CONTAIN_TXTLBL_201.text6.Left       = 172   &&    .
 Thisform.CONTAIN_TXTLBL_201.text7.Left       = 172   &&    .
 Thisform.CONTAIN_TXTLBL_201.text8.Left       = 172   &&    .
 Thisform.CONTAIN_TXTLBL_201.text9.Left       = 172   &&    .
 Thisform.CONTAIN_TXTLBL_201.text10.Left      = 172   &&   383
 * Not used:
 Thisform.CONTAIN_TXTLBL_201.text11.Left      = 383   &&

 Thisform.CONTAIN_TXTLBL_201.text12.Left      = 383   &&
 Thisform.CONTAIN_TXTLBL_201.text13.Left      = 383   &&
 Thisform.CONTAIN_TXTLBL_201.text14.Left      = 383   &&
 Thisform.CONTAIN_TXTLBL_201.text15.Left      = 383   &&
 Thisform.CONTAIN_TXTLBL_201.text16.Left      = 383   &&
 Thisform.CONTAIN_TXTLBL_201.text17.Left      = 383   &&
```

```
 Thisform.CONTAIN_TXTLBL_201.text18.Left       = 383  &&
 Thisform.CONTAIN_TXTLBL_201.text19.Left       = 383  &&
 Thisform.CONTAIN_TXTLBL_201.text20.Left       = 383  &&


*-------------------------------------------------------------
* Text Boxes - Format (Output):
* This property was already set in the
* text boxes. ("K" = Format is the same
*                    as the Input Mask.)
*-------------------------------------------------------------
* Thisform.CONTAIN_TXTLBL_201.text1.Format     = "K"  &&
* Thisform.CONTAIN_TXTLBL_201.text2.Format     = "K"  &&
* Thisform.CONTAIN_TXTLBL_201.text3.Format     = "K"  &&


*-------------------------------------------------------------
* Labels - Top:
*-------------------------------------------------------------
 Thisform.CONTAIN_TXTLBL_201.label1.Top        =  16  &&    16
 Thisform.CONTAIN_TXTLBL_201.label2.Top        =  44  &&    44
 Thisform.CONTAIN_TXTLBL_201.label3.Top        =  72  &&
 Thisform.CONTAIN_TXTLBL_201.label4.Top        = 100  &&
 Thisform.CONTAIN_TXTLBL_201.label5.Top        = 128  &&
 Thisform.CONTAIN_TXTLBL_201.label6.Top        = 156  &&
 Thisform.CONTAIN_TXTLBL_201.label7.Top        = 184  &&
 Thisform.CONTAIN_TXTLBL_201.label8.Top        = 212  &&
 Thisform.CONTAIN_TXTLBL_201.label9.Top        = 240  &&
 Thisform.CONTAIN_TXTLBL_201.label10.Top       = 268  &&
 * Not used:
 Thisform.CONTAIN_TXTLBL_201.label11.Top       =  16  &&
 Thisform.CONTAIN_TXTLBL_201.label12.Top       =  44  &&
 Thisform.CONTAIN_TXTLBL_201.label13.Top       =  72  &&
 Thisform.CONTAIN_TXTLBL_201.label14.Top       = 100  &&
 Thisform.CONTAIN_TXTLBL_201.label15.Top       = 128  &&
 Thisform.CONTAIN_TXTLBL_201.label16.Top       = 156  &&
 Thisform.CONTAIN_TXTLBL_201.label17.Top       = 184  &&
 Thisform.CONTAIN_TXTLBL_201.label18.Top       = 212  &&
 Thisform.CONTAIN_TXTLBL_201.label19.Top       = 240  &&
 Thisform.CONTAIN_TXTLBL_201.label20.Top       = 268  &&

*-------------------------------------------------------------
* Labels - Left:
*-------------------------------------------------------------
 Thisform.CONTAIN_TXTLBL_201.label1.Left       = 20   &&
 Thisform.CONTAIN_TXTLBL_201.label2.Left       = 20   &&
 Thisform.CONTAIN_TXTLBL_201.label3.Left       = 20   &&
 Thisform.CONTAIN_TXTLBL_201.label4.Left       = 20   &&
 Thisform.CONTAIN_TXTLBL_201.label5.Left       = 20   &&
 Thisform.CONTAIN_TXTLBL_201.label6.Left       = 20   &&
```

```
 Thisform.CONTAIN_TXTLBL_201.label7.Left       = 20    &&
 Thisform.CONTAIN_TXTLBL_201.label8.Left       = 20    &&
 Thisform.CONTAIN_TXTLBL_201.label9.Left       = 20    &&
 Thisform.CONTAIN_TXTLBL_201.label10.Left      = 20    &&
 * Not used:
 Thisform.CONTAIN_TXTLBL_201.label11.Left      = 231
 Thisform.CONTAIN_TXTLBL_201.label12.Left      = 231
 Thisform.CONTAIN_TXTLBL_201.label13.Left      = 231
 Thisform.CONTAIN_TXTLBL_201.label14.Left      = 231
 Thisform.CONTAIN_TXTLBL_201.label15.Left      = 231
 Thisform.CONTAIN_TXTLBL_201.label16.Left      = 231
 Thisform.CONTAIN_TXTLBL_201.label17.Left      = 231
 Thisform.CONTAIN_TXTLBL_201.label18.Left      = 231
 Thisform.CONTAIN_TXTLBL_201.label19.Left      = 231
 Thisform.CONTAIN_TXTLBL_201.label20.Left      = 231

*-------------------------------------------------------------
* Labels - Width:
*-------------------------------------------------------------
 Thisform.CONTAIN_TXTLBL_201.label1.Width      = 135   &&   135
 Thisform.CONTAIN_TXTLBL_201.label2.Width      = 135
 Thisform.CONTAIN_TXTLBL_201.label3.Width      = 135
 Thisform.CONTAIN_TXTLBL_201.label4.Width      = 135
 Thisform.CONTAIN_TXTLBL_201.label5.Width      = 135
 Thisform.CONTAIN_TXTLBL_201.label6.Width      = 135
 Thisform.CONTAIN_TXTLBL_201.label7.Width      = 135
 Thisform.CONTAIN_TXTLBL_201.label8.Width      = 135
 Thisform.CONTAIN_TXTLBL_201.label9.Width      = 135
 Thisform.CONTAIN_TXTLBL_201.label10.Width     = 135
 * Not used:
 Thisform.CONTAIN_TXTLBL_201.label11.Width     = 135
 Thisform.CONTAIN_TXTLBL_201.label12.Width     = 135
 Thisform.CONTAIN_TXTLBL_201.label13.Width     = 135
 Thisform.CONTAIN_TXTLBL_201.label14.Width     = 135
 Thisform.CONTAIN_TXTLBL_201.label15.Width     = 135
 Thisform.CONTAIN_TXTLBL_201.label16.Width     = 135
 Thisform.CONTAIN_TXTLBL_201.label17.Width     = 135
 Thisform.CONTAIN_TXTLBL_201.label18.Width     = 135
 Thisform.CONTAIN_TXTLBL_201.label19.Width     = 135
 Thisform.CONTAIN_TXTLBL_201.label20.Width     = 135

*-------------------------------------------------------------
* Containers for Labels - Top:
* Note: Container #2 is for Label #1.
*-------------------------------------------------------------
 Thisform.CONTAIN_TXTLBL_201.Container2.Top    =  12   &&    12
 Thisform.CONTAIN_TXTLBL_201.Container3.Top    =  40   &&    40
 Thisform.CONTAIN_TXTLBL_201.Container4.Top    =  68   &&    68
 Thisform.CONTAIN_TXTLBL_201.Container5.Top    =  96   &&    96
 Thisform.CONTAIN_TXTLBL_201.Container6.Top    = 124   &&   124
```

```
 Thisform.CONTAIN_TXTLBL_201.Container7.Top   = 152  &&   152
 Thisform.CONTAIN_TXTLBL_201.Container8.Top   = 180  &&   180
 Thisform.CONTAIN_TXTLBL_201.Container9.Top   = 208  &&   208
 Thisform.CONTAIN_TXTLBL_201.Container10.Top  = 236  &&   236
 Thisform.CONTAIN_TXTLBL_201.Container11.Top  = 264  &&   264
* Not used:
 Thisform.CONTAIN_TXTLBL_201.Container12.Top  =  12
 Thisform.CONTAIN_TXTLBL_201.Container13.Top  =  40
 Thisform.CONTAIN_TXTLBL_201.Container14.Top  =  68  &&
 Thisform.CONTAIN_TXTLBL_201.Container15.Top  =  96  &&
 Thisform.CONTAIN_TXTLBL_201.Container16.Top  = 124  &&
 Thisform.CONTAIN_TXTLBL_201.Container17.Top  = 152  &&
 Thisform.CONTAIN_TXTLBL_201.Container18.Top  = 180  &&
 Thisform.CONTAIN_TXTLBL_201.Container19.Top  = 208  &&
 Thisform.CONTAIN_TXTLBL_201.Container20.Top  = 236  &&
 Thisform.CONTAIN_TXTLBL_201.Container21.Top  = 264  &&

*-------------------------------------------------------------
* Container for Labels - Left:
* Note: Container #2 is for Label #1.
*-------------------------------------------------------------
 Thisform.CONTAIN_TXTLBL_201.Container2.Left  =  12
 Thisform.CONTAIN_TXTLBL_201.Container3.Left  =  12
 Thisform.CONTAIN_TXTLBL_201.Container4.Left  =  12
 Thisform.CONTAIN_TXTLBL_201.Container5.Left  =  12
 Thisform.CONTAIN_TXTLBL_201.Container6.Left  =  12
 Thisform.CONTAIN_TXTLBL_201.Container7.Left  =  12
 Thisform.CONTAIN_TXTLBL_201.Container8.Left  =  12
 Thisform.CONTAIN_TXTLBL_201.Container9.Left  =  12
 Thisform.CONTAIN_TXTLBL_201.Container10.Left =  12    &&  12
 Thisform.CONTAIN_TXTLBL_201.Container11.Left =  12    &&  12
* Not used:
 Thisform.CONTAIN_TXTLBL_201.Container12.Left =  223
 Thisform.CONTAIN_TXTLBL_201.Container13.Left =  223
 Thisform.CONTAIN_TXTLBL_201.Container14.Left =  223
 Thisform.CONTAIN_TXTLBL_201.Container15.Left =  223
 Thisform.CONTAIN_TXTLBL_201.Container16.Left =  223
 Thisform.CONTAIN_TXTLBL_201.Container17.Left =  223
 Thisform.CONTAIN_TXTLBL_201.Container18.Left =  223
 Thisform.CONTAIN_TXTLBL_201.Container19.Left =  223
 Thisform.CONTAIN_TXTLBL_201.Container20.Left =  223
 Thisform.CONTAIN_TXTLBL_201.Container21.Left =  223

*-------------------------------------------------------------
* Container for Labels - Width:
* Note: Container #2 is for Label #1.
*-------------------------------------------------------------
 Thisform.CONTAIN_TXTLBL_201.Container2.Width  = 147
 Thisform.CONTAIN_TXTLBL_201.Container3.Width  = 147
 Thisform.CONTAIN_TXTLBL_201.Container4.Width  = 147
```

```
 Thisform.CONTAIN_TXTLBL_201.Container5.Width  = 147
 Thisform.CONTAIN_TXTLBL_201.Container6.Width  = 147
 Thisform.CONTAIN_TXTLBL_201.Container7.Width  = 147
 Thisform.CONTAIN_TXTLBL_201.Container8.Width  = 147
 Thisform.CONTAIN_TXTLBL_201.Container9.Width  = 147
 Thisform.CONTAIN_TXTLBL_201.Container10.Width = 147
 Thisform.CONTAIN_TXTLBL_201.Container11.Width = 147
* Not used:
 Thisform.CONTAIN_TXTLBL_201.Container12.Width = 147
 Thisform.CONTAIN_TXTLBL_201.Container13.Width = 147
 Thisform.CONTAIN_TXTLBL_201.Container14.Width = 147
 Thisform.CONTAIN_TXTLBL_201.Container15.Width = 147
 Thisform.CONTAIN_TXTLBL_201.Container16.Width = 147
 Thisform.CONTAIN_TXTLBL_201.Container17.Width = 147
 Thisform.CONTAIN_TXTLBL_201.Container18.Width = 147
 Thisform.CONTAIN_TXTLBL_201.Container19.Width = 147
 Thisform.CONTAIN_TXTLBL_201.Container20.Width = 147
 Thisform.CONTAIN_TXTLBL_201.Container21.Width = 147

*==============================================================
*         Additional Text Boxes and Labels
*==============================================================
*--------------------------------------------------------------
* Additional Text Boxes - Top:
*--------------------------------------------------------------
 Thisform.CONTAIN_TXTLBL_201.text21.Top       =  12  &&    12
* Not used:
 Thisform.CONTAIN_TXTLBL_201.text22.Top       =  40  &&    40
 Thisform.CONTAIN_TXTLBL_201.text23.Top       =  68  &&    68
 Thisform.CONTAIN_TXTLBL_201.text24.Top       =  96  &&    96
 Thisform.CONTAIN_TXTLBL_201.text25.Top       = 124  &&   124
 Thisform.CONTAIN_TXTLBL_201.text26.Top       = 152
 Thisform.CONTAIN_TXTLBL_201.text27.Top       = 180
 Thisform.CONTAIN_TXTLBL_201.text28.Top       = 208
 Thisform.CONTAIN_TXTLBL_201.text29.Top       = 236
 Thisform.CONTAIN_TXTLBL_201.text30.Top       = 264

*--------------------------------------------------------------
* Additional Text Boxes - Left:
*--------------------------------------------------------------
 Thisform.CONTAIN_TXTLBL_201.text21.Left      = 432  &&   432
* Not used:
 Thisform.CONTAIN_TXTLBL_201.text22.Left      = 432
 Thisform.CONTAIN_TXTLBL_201.text23.Left      = 432
 Thisform.CONTAIN_TXTLBL_201.text24.Left      = 432
 Thisform.CONTAIN_TXTLBL_201.text25.Left      = 432
 Thisform.CONTAIN_TXTLBL_201.text26.Left      = 432
 Thisform.CONTAIN_TXTLBL_201.text27.Left      = 432
 Thisform.CONTAIN_TXTLBL_201.text28.Left      = 432
 Thisform.CONTAIN_TXTLBL_201.text29.Left      = 432
```

```
 Thisform.CONTAIN_TXTLBL_201.text30.Left        = 432

*---------------------------------------------------------------------
* Additional Text Boxes - Width:
*---------------------------------------------------------------------
 Thisform.CONTAIN_TXTLBL_201.text21.Width     =  43  &&  43
* Not used:
 Thisform.CONTAIN_TXTLBL_201.text22.Width     =  43
 Thisform.CONTAIN_TXTLBL_201.text23.Width     =  43
 Thisform.CONTAIN_TXTLBL_201.text24.Width     =  43
 Thisform.CONTAIN_TXTLBL_201.text25.Width     =  43
 Thisform.CONTAIN_TXTLBL_201.text26.Width     =  43
 Thisform.CONTAIN_TXTLBL_201.text27.Width     =  43
 Thisform.CONTAIN_TXTLBL_201.text28.Width     =  43
 Thisform.CONTAIN_TXTLBL_201.text29.Width     =  43
 Thisform.CONTAIN_TXTLBL_201.text30.Width     =  43

*---------------------------------------------------------------------
* Additional Labels - Caption:
*---------------------------------------------------------------------
 Thisform.CONTAIN_TXTLBL_201.label21.Caption = "_____"
 Thisform.CONTAIN_TXTLBL_201.label22.Caption = "_____"

*---------------------------------------------------------------------
* Additional Labels - Top:
*---------------------------------------------------------------------
 Thisform.CONTAIN_TXTLBL_201.label21.Top      =  16
 Thisform.CONTAIN_TXTLBL_201.label22.Top      =  44

*---------------------------------------------------------------------
* Additional Labels - Left:
*---------------------------------------------------------------------
 Thisform.CONTAIN_TXTLBL_201.label21.Left     = 536
 Thisform.CONTAIN_TXTLBL_201.label22.Left     = 536

*---------------------------------------------------------------------
* Additional Labels - Width:
*---------------------------------------------------------------------
 Thisform.CONTAIN_TXTLBL_201.label21.Width    = 105
 Thisform.CONTAIN_TXTLBL_201.label22.Width    = 105


*---------------------------------------------------------------------
* Additional Containers for Labels - Top:
* Note: Container #22 is for Label #21.
*---------------------------------------------------------------------
 Thisform.CONTAIN_TXTLBL_201.Container22.Top   =  12  &&   12
 Thisform.CONTAIN_TXTLBL_201.Container23.Top   =  40  &&   40
```

```
*-------------------------------------------------------------
* Additional Containers for Labels - Left:
* Note: Container #22 is for Label #21.
*-------------------------------------------------------------
 Thisform.CONTAIN_TXTLBL_201.Container22.Left  = 528  &&  528
 Thisform.CONTAIN_TXTLBL_201.Container23.Left  = 528  &&  528

*-------------------------------------------------------------
* Additional Containers for Labels - Width:
* Note: Container #22 is for Label #21.
*-------------------------------------------------------------
 Thisform.CONTAIN_TXTLBL_201.Container22.Width = 147
 Thisform.CONTAIN_TXTLBL_201.Container23.Width = 147

ENDIF

*==============================================================*
* Do not change the code below.                                *
*==============================================================*

*========================================================
* Labels: Setting all Labels' Visible Properties to .F.
*========================================================
 thisform.CONTAIN_TXTLBL_201.label1.visible     = .F.
 thisform.CONTAIN_TXTLBL_201.label2.visible     = .F.
 thisform.CONTAIN_TXTLBL_201.label3.visible     = .F.
 thisform.CONTAIN_TXTLBL_201.label4.visible     = .F.
 thisform.CONTAIN_TXTLBL_201.label5.visible     = .F.
 thisform.CONTAIN_TXTLBL_201.label6.visible     = .F.
 thisform.CONTAIN_TXTLBL_201.label7.visible     = .F.
 thisform.CONTAIN_TXTLBL_201.label8.visible     = .F.
 thisform.CONTAIN_TXTLBL_201.label9.visible     = .F.
 thisform.CONTAIN_TXTLBL_201.label10.visible    = .F.
 thisform.CONTAIN_TXTLBL_201.label11.visible    = .F.
 thisform.CONTAIN_TXTLBL_201.label12.visible    = .F.
 thisform.CONTAIN_TXTLBL_201.label13.visible    = .F.
 thisform.CONTAIN_TXTLBL_201.label14.visible    = .F.
 thisform.CONTAIN_TXTLBL_201.label15.visible    = .F.
 thisform.CONTAIN_TXTLBL_201.label16.visible    = .F.
 thisform.CONTAIN_TXTLBL_201.label17.visible    = .F.
 thisform.CONTAIN_TXTLBL_201.label18.visible    = .F.
 thisform.CONTAIN_TXTLBL_201.label19.visible    = .F.
 thisform.CONTAIN_TXTLBL_201.label20.visible    = .F.

 * Additional Labels:
 thisform.CONTAIN_TXTLBL_201.label21.visible    = .F.
 thisform.CONTAIN_TXTLBL_201.label22.visible    = .F.
 thisform.CONTAIN_TXTLBL_201.label23.visible    = .F.
 thisform.CONTAIN_TXTLBL_201.label24.visible    = .F.
 thisform.CONTAIN_TXTLBL_201.label25.visible    = .F.
```

```
 thisform.CONTAIN_TXTLBL_201.label26.visible    = .F.
 thisform.CONTAIN_TXTLBL_201.label27.visible    = .F.
 thisform.CONTAIN_TXTLBL_201.label28.visible    = .F.
 thisform.CONTAIN_TXTLBL_201.label29.visible    = .F.
 thisform.CONTAIN_TXTLBL_201.label30.visible    = .F.

*=====================================================
* Containers: (Container for Label #1 is Container #2.)
*=====================================================
 thisform.CONTAIN_TXTLBL_201.Container2.visible = .F.
 thisform.CONTAIN_TXTLBL_201.Container3.visible = .F.
 thisform.CONTAIN_TXTLBL_201.Container4.visible = .F.
 thisform.CONTAIN_TXTLBL_201.Container5.visible = .F.
 thisform.CONTAIN_TXTLBL_201.Container6.visible = .F.
 thisform.CONTAIN_TXTLBL_201.Container7.visible = .F.
 thisform.CONTAIN_TXTLBL_201.Container8.visible = .F.
 thisform.CONTAIN_TXTLBL_201.Container9.visible = .F.
 thisform.CONTAIN_TXTLBL_201.Container10.visible = .F.
 thisform.CONTAIN_TXTLBL_201.Container11.visible = .F.
 thisform.CONTAIN_TXTLBL_201.Container12.visible = .F.
 thisform.CONTAIN_TXTLBL_201.Container13.visible = .F.
 thisform.CONTAIN_TXTLBL_201.Container14.visible = .F.
 thisform.CONTAIN_TXTLBL_201.Container15.visible = .F.
 thisform.CONTAIN_TXTLBL_201.Container16.visible = .F.
 thisform.CONTAIN_TXTLBL_201.Container17.visible = .F.
 thisform.CONTAIN_TXTLBL_201.Container18.visible = .F.
 thisform.CONTAIN_TXTLBL_201.Container19.visible = .F.
 thisform.CONTAIN_TXTLBL_201.Container20.visible = .F.
 thisform.CONTAIN_TXTLBL_201.Container21.visible = .F.

 * Additional Containers:
 thisform.CONTAIN_TXTLBL_201.Container22.visible = .F.
 thisform.CONTAIN_TXTLBL_201.Container23.visible = .F.
 thisform.CONTAIN_TXTLBL_201.Container24.visible = .F.
 thisform.CONTAIN_TXTLBL_201.Container25.visible = .F.
 thisform.CONTAIN_TXTLBL_201.Container26.visible = .F.
 thisform.CONTAIN_TXTLBL_201.Container27.visible = .F.
 thisform.CONTAIN_TXTLBL_201.Container28.visible = .F.
 thisform.CONTAIN_TXTLBL_201.Container29.visible = .F.
 thisform.CONTAIN_TXTLBL_201.Container30.visible = .F.
 thisform.CONTAIN_TXTLBL_201.Container31.visible = .F.

*=====================================================
* Text Boxes: Setting the visible properties to .F.
*=====================================================
 thisform.CONTAIN_TXTLBL_201.text1.visible      = .F.
 thisform.CONTAIN_TXTLBL_201.text2.visible      = .F.
 thisform.CONTAIN_TXTLBL_201.text3.visible      = .F.
 thisform.CONTAIN_TXTLBL_201.text4.visible      = .F.
 thisform.CONTAIN_TXTLBL_201.text5.visible      = .F.
```

```
thisform.CONTAIN_TXTLBL_201.text6.visible      = .F.
thisform.CONTAIN_TXTLBL_201.text7.visible      = .F.
thisform.CONTAIN_TXTLBL_201.text8.visible      = .F.
thisform.CONTAIN_TXTLBL_201.text9.visible      = .F.
thisform.CONTAIN_TXTLBL_201.text10.visible     = .F.
thisform.CONTAIN_TXTLBL_201.text11.visible     = .F.
thisform.CONTAIN_TXTLBL_201.text12.visible     = .F.
thisform.CONTAIN_TXTLBL_201.text13.visible     = .F.
thisform.CONTAIN_TXTLBL_201.text14.visible     = .F.
thisform.CONTAIN_TXTLBL_201.text15.visible     = .F.
thisform.CONTAIN_TXTLBL_201.text16.visible     = .F.
thisform.CONTAIN_TXTLBL_201.text17.visible     = .F.
thisform.CONTAIN_TXTLBL_201.text18.visible     = .F.
thisform.CONTAIN_TXTLBL_201.text19.visible     = .F.
thisform.CONTAIN_TXTLBL_201.text20.visible     = .F.

* Additional Text Boxes:
* For values retrieved (Read Only Property = .T. )

thisform.CONTAIN_TXTLBL_201.text21.visible      = .F.
thisform.CONTAIN_TXTLBL_201.text22.visible      = .F.
thisform.CONTAIN_TXTLBL_201.text23.visible      = .F.
thisform.CONTAIN_TXTLBL_201.text24.visible      = .F.
thisform.CONTAIN_TXTLBL_201.text25.visible      = .F.
thisform.CONTAIN_TXTLBL_201.text26.visible      = .F.
thisform.CONTAIN_TXTLBL_201.text27.visible      = .F.
thisform.CONTAIN_TXTLBL_201.text28.visible      = .F.
thisform.CONTAIN_TXTLBL_201.text29.visible      = .F.
thisform.CONTAIN_TXTLBL_201.text30.visible      = .F.
thisform.CONTAIN_TXTLBL_201.text31.visible      = .F.
thisform.CONTAIN_TXTLBL_201.text32.visible      = .F.
thisform.CONTAIN_TXTLBL_201.text33.visible      = .F.
thisform.CONTAIN_TXTLBL_201.text34.visible      = .F.
thisform.CONTAIN_TXTLBL_201.text35.visible      = .F.
thisform.CONTAIN_TXTLBL_201.text36.visible      = .F.
thisform.CONTAIN_TXTLBL_201.text37.visible      = .F.
thisform.CONTAIN_TXTLBL_201.text38.visible      = .F.
thisform.CONTAIN_TXTLBL_201.text39.visible      = .F.
thisform.CONTAIN_TXTLBL_201.text40.visible      = .F.

*=============================================================
* Setting Text Boxes and Labels Visible:
* (Text boxes according to the view used.)
*=============================================================

If DE_QTY_TXTFLDS >= 1
 thisform.CONTAIN_TXTLBL_201.label1.visible     = .T.
 thisform.CONTAIN_TXTLBL_201.text1.visible      = .T.
 thisform.CONTAIN_TXTLBL_201.Container2.visible = .T.
Endif
```

```
If DE_QTY_TXTFLDS >= 2
 thisform.CONTAIN_TXTLBL_201.label2.visible     = .T.
 thisform.CONTAIN_TXTLBL_201.text2.visible      = .T.
 thisform.CONTAIN_TXTLBL_201.Container3.visible = .T.
Endif

If DE_QTY_TXTFLDS >= 3
 thisform.CONTAIN_TXTLBL_201.label3.visible     = .T.
 thisform.CONTAIN_TXTLBL_201.text3.visible      = .T.
 thisform.CONTAIN_TXTLBL_201.Container4.visible = .T.
Endif

If DE_QTY_TXTFLDS >= 4
 thisform.CONTAIN_TXTLBL_201.label4.visible     = .T.
 thisform.CONTAIN_TXTLBL_201.text4.visible      = .T.
 thisform.CONTAIN_TXTLBL_201.Container5.visible = .T.
Endif

If DE_QTY_TXTFLDS >= 5
 thisform.CONTAIN_TXTLBL_201.label5.visible     = .T.
 thisform.CONTAIN_TXTLBL_201.text5.visible      = .T.
 thisform.CONTAIN_TXTLBL_201.Container6.visible = .T.
Endif

If DE_QTY_TXTFLDS >= 6
 thisform.CONTAIN_TXTLBL_201.label6.visible     = .T.
 thisform.CONTAIN_TXTLBL_201.text6.visible      = .T.
 thisform.CONTAIN_TXTLBL_201.Container7.visible = .T.
Endif

If DE_QTY_TXTFLDS >= 7
 thisform.CONTAIN_TXTLBL_201.label7.visible     = .T.
 thisform.CONTAIN_TXTLBL_201.text7.visible      = .T.
 thisform.CONTAIN_TXTLBL_201.Container8.visible = .T.
Endif

If DE_QTY_TXTFLDS >= 8
 thisform.CONTAIN_TXTLBL_201.label8.visible     = .T.
 thisform.CONTAIN_TXTLBL_201.text8.visible      = .T.
 thisform.CONTAIN_TXTLBL_201.Container9.visible = .T.
Endif

 If DE_QTY_TXTFLDS >= 9
 thisform.CONTAIN_TXTLBL_201.label9.visible      = .T.
 thisform.CONTAIN_TXTLBL_201.text9.visible       = .T.
 thisform.CONTAIN_TXTLBL_201.Container10.visible = .T.
Endif

If DE_QTY_TXTFLDS >= 10
```

```
 thisform.CONTAIN_TXTLBL_201.label10.visible     = .T.
 thisform.CONTAIN_TXTLBL_201.text10.visible      = .T.
 thisform.CONTAIN_TXTLBL_201.Container11.visible = .T.
Endif

If DE_QTY_TXTFLDS >= 11
 thisform.CONTAIN_TXTLBL_201.label11.visible     = .T.
 thisform.CONTAIN_TXTLBL_201.text11.visible      = .T.
 thisform.CONTAIN_TXTLBL_201.Container12.visible = .T.
Endif

If DE_QTY_TXTFLDS >= 12
 thisform.CONTAIN_TXTLBL_201.label12.visible     = .T.
 thisform.CONTAIN_TXTLBL_201.text12.visible      = .T.
 thisform.CONTAIN_TXTLBL_201.Container13.visible = .T.
Endif

If DE_QTY_TXTFLDS >= 13
 thisform.CONTAIN_TXTLBL_201.label13.visible     = .T.
 thisform.CONTAIN_TXTLBL_201.text13.visible      = .T.
 thisform.CONTAIN_TXTLBL_201.Container14.visible = .T.
Endif

If DE_QTY_TXTFLDS >= 14
 thisform.CONTAIN_TXTLBL_201.label14.visible     = .T.
 thisform.CONTAIN_TXTLBL_201.text14.visible      = .T.
 thisform.CONTAIN_TXTLBL_201.Container15.visible = .T.
Endif

If DE_QTY_TXTFLDS >= 15
 thisform.CONTAIN_TXTLBL_201.label15.visible     = .T.
 thisform.CONTAIN_TXTLBL_201.text15.visible      = .T.
 thisform.CONTAIN_TXTLBL_201.Container16.visible = .T.
Endif

If DE_QTY_TXTFLDS >= 16
 thisform.CONTAIN_TXTLBL_201.label16.visible     = .T.
 thisform.CONTAIN_TXTLBL_201.text16.visible      = .T.
 thisform.CONTAIN_TXTLBL_201.Container17.visible = .T.
Endif

If DE_QTY_TXTFLDS >= 17
 thisform.CONTAIN_TXTLBL_201.label17.visible     = .T.
 thisform.CONTAIN_TXTLBL_201.text17.visible      = .T.
 thisform.CONTAIN_TXTLBL_201.Container18.visible = .T.
Endif

If DE_QTY_TXTFLDS >= 18
 thisform.CONTAIN_TXTLBL_201.label18.visible     = .T.
 thisform.CONTAIN_TXTLBL_201.text18.visible      = .T.
```

```
  thisform.CONTAIN_TXTLBL_201.Container19.visible = .T.
 Endif

  If DE_QTY_TXTFLDS >= 19
  thisform.CONTAIN_TXTLBL_201.label19.visible     = .T.
  thisform.CONTAIN_TXTLBL_201.text19.visible      = .T.
  thisform.CONTAIN_TXTLBL_201.Container20.visible = .T.
 Endif

 If DE_QTY_TXTFLDS >= 20
  thisform.CONTAIN_TXTLBL_201.label20.visible     = .T.
  thisform.CONTAIN_TXTLBL_201.text20.visible      = .T.
  thisform.CONTAIN_TXTLBL_201.Container21.visible = .T.
 Endif


*========================================================
* Setting Additionals Text Boxes Visible:
* (Text Boxes used in values retrived from database.)
*========================================================

 If DE_QTY_ADD_TXTFLDS >= 1
  thisform.CONTAIN_TXTLBL_201.text21.visible      = .T.
 Endif

 If DE_QTY_ADD_TXTFLDS >= 2
  thisform.CONTAIN_TXTLBL_201.text22.visible      = .T.
 Endif

 If DE_QTY_ADD_TXTFLDS >= 3
  thisform.CONTAIN_TXTLBL_201.text23.visible      = .T.
 Endif

 If DE_QTY_ADD_TXTFLDS >= 4
  thisform.CONTAIN_TXTLBL_201.text24.visible      = .T.
 Endif

 If DE_QTY_ADD_TXTFLDS >= 5
  thisform.CONTAIN_TXTLBL_201.text25.visible      = .T.
 Endif

 If DE_QTY_ADD_TXTFLDS >= 6
  thisform.CONTAIN_TXTLBL_201.text26.visible      = .T.
 Endif

 If DE_QTY_ADD_TXTFLDS >= 7
  thisform.CONTAIN_TXTLBL_201.text27.visible      = .T.
 Endif

 If DE_QTY_ADD_TXTFLDS >= 8
```

```
 thisform.CONTAIN_TXTLBL_201.text28.visible      = .T.
Endif

If DE_QTY_ADD_TXTFLDS >= 9
 thisform.CONTAIN_TXTLBL_201.text29.visible      = .T.
Endif

If DE_QTY_ADD_TXTFLDS >= 10
 thisform.CONTAIN_TXTLBL_201.text30.visible      = .T.
Endif

If DE_QTY_ADD_TXTFLDS >= 11
 thisform.CONTAIN_TXTLBL_201.text31.visible      = .T.
Endif

If DE_QTY_ADD_TXTFLDS >= 12
 thisform.CONTAIN_TXTLBL_201.text32.visible      = .T.
Endif

If DE_QTY_ADD_TXTFLDS >= 13
 thisform.CONTAIN_TXTLBL_201.text33.visible      = .T.
Endif

If DE_QTY_ADD_TXTFLDS >= 14
 thisform.CONTAIN_TXTLBL_201.text34.visible      = .T.
Endif

If DE_QTY_ADD_TXTFLDS >= 15
 thisform.CONTAIN_TXTLBL_201.text35.visible      = .T.
Endif

If DE_QTY_ADD_TXTFLDS >= 16
 thisform.CONTAIN_TXTLBL_201.text36.visible      = .T.
Endif

If DE_QTY_ADD_TXTFLDS >= 17
 thisform.CONTAIN_TXTLBL_201.text37.visible      = .T.
Endif

If DE_QTY_ADD_TXTFLDS >= 18
 thisform.CONTAIN_TXTLBL_201.text38.visible      = .T.
Endif

If DE_QTY_ADD_TXTFLDS >= 19
 thisform.CONTAIN_TXTLBL_201.text39.visible      = .T.
Endif

If DE_QTY_ADD_TXTFLDS >= 20
 thisform.CONTAIN_TXTLBL_201.text40.visible      = .T.
Endif
```

```
*===========================================================
* Setting Additionals Labels Visible:
* (For values retrived from database table. )
*===========================================================

 If DE_QTY_ADD_LABELS >= 1
  thisform.CONTAIN_TXTLBL_201.label21.visible     = .T.
  thisform.CONTAIN_TXTLBL_201.Container22.visible = .T.
 Endif

 If DE_QTY_ADD_LABELS >= 2
  thisform.CONTAIN_TXTLBL_201.label22.visible     = .T.
  thisform.CONTAIN_TXTLBL_201.Container23.visible = .T.
 Endif

 If DE_QTY_ADD_LABELS >= 3
  thisform.CONTAIN_TXTLBL_201.label23.visible     = .T.
  thisform.CONTAIN_TXTLBL_201.Container24.visible = .T.
 Endif

 If DE_QTY_ADD_LABELS >= 4
  thisform.CONTAIN_TXTLBL_201.label24.visible     = .T.
  thisform.CONTAIN_TXTLBL_201.Container25.visible = .T.
 Endif

 If DE_QTY_ADD_LABELS >= 5
  thisform.CONTAIN_TXTLBL_201.label25.visible     = .T.
  thisform.CONTAIN_TXTLBL_201.Container26.visible = .T.
 Endif

 If DE_QTY_ADD_LABELS >= 6
  thisform.CONTAIN_TXTLBL_201.label26.visible     = .T.
  thisform.CONTAIN_TXTLBL_201.Container27.visible = .T.
 Endif

 If DE_QTY_ADD_LABELS >= 7
  thisform.CONTAIN_TXTLBL_201.label27.visible     = .T.
  thisform.CONTAIN_TXTLBL_201.Container28.visible = .T.
 Endif

 If DE_QTY_ADD_LABELS >= 8
  thisform.CONTAIN_TXTLBL_201.label28.visible     = .T.
  thisform.CONTAIN_TXTLBL_201.Container29.visible = .T.
 Endif

 If DE_QTY_ADD_LABELS >= 9
  thisform.CONTAIN_TXTLBL_201.label29.visible     = .T.
  thisform.CONTAIN_TXTLBL_201.Container30.visible = .T.
 Endif
```

```
 If DE_QTY_ADD_LABELS >= 10
  thisform.CONTAIN_TXTLBL_201.label30.visible     = .T.
  thisform.CONTAIN_TXTLBL_201.Container31.visible = .T.
 Endif

*==============================================================*
* Do not change the code below.                                *
*==============================================================*
PUBLIC TMP_SREC
LOCAL TMP_CONTINUE
SET SYSMENU OFF
THISFORM.CLOSABLE = .F.
THISFORM.AD05_BEFORE_INIT
TMP_CONTINUE = .T.
  TMP_CONTINUE = THISFORM.B70_PROCESS_INIT(TMP_MODE, ;
                                           TMP_SEL_REC)
  THISFORM.showtips = .T.
  IF TMP_CONTINUE = .F.
    RETURN
  ENDIF

Nodefault

*==============================================================*
* Form        : C_DE                                           *
* Description : Data Entry Parent Class Form                   *
* Author      : E. Aleu                                        *
* Date created: 04/03/97                                       *
* Date revised: 05/28/97, 12/23/97, 12/01/98, 6/12/05          *
* Parameters  :                                                *
*              PARM1 ......:  "ADD" , "CHG" , "DSP"            *
*              PARM2 ......:  Selected Record                  *
*==============================================================*
LPARAMETERS TMP_MODE, TMP_SEL_REC

 SET TALK OFF      && 12/22/98
 SET ECHO OFF      && 12/22/98

 PUBLIC TMP_SREC
 LOCAL TMP_CONTINUE

 SET SYSMENU OFF
 THISFORM.CLOSABLE = .F.

 THISFORM.AD05_BEFORE_INIT

 TMP_CONTINUE = .T.
 TMP_CONTINUE = THISFORM.B70_PROCESS_INIT(TMP_MODE, ;
                                          TMP_SEL_REC)
 THISFORM.showtips = .T.
```

```
 IF TMP_CONTINUE = .F.
    RETURN
 ENDIF


*=============================================================*
* Procedure: LOAD                                             *
*                                                             *
*=============================================================*
 SET TALK OFF
 SET ECHO OFF


*=============================================================*
* Procedure: B01_OPEN_FILES                                   *
*                                                             *
*=============================================================*
LPARAMETERS TMP_MODE

 LOCAL TMP_RTN_1, TMP_ERR_F

 SET EXCLUSIVE OFF
 SET REPROCESS TO 0
 SET MULTILOCKS ON
 SET DELETED ON

 TMP_RTN_1 = .T.

 Thisform.Buffermode = 2     && Optimistic Table Buffering

 THISFORM.AF01_OPEN_DATABASE

 IF TMP_MODE = "ADD" OR TMP_MODE = "CPY"
 ELSE
      TMP_ERR_F = THISFORM.B12_OPEN_MAIN_FILE_VIEW(TMP_MODE)
      IF TMP_ERR_F = "NO_VIEWS_OPEN"
      ELSE
        IF BOF() AND EOF()
          TMP_RTN_1 = .F.
        ENDIF
      ENDIF
 ENDIF

 RETURN TMP_RTN_1
```

```
*==============================================================*
* Procedure: B02_COMMAND_GROUP_CLICK                           *
*                                                              *
* Options/Methods:                                             *
*                                                              *
*    B80_PB_CANCEL        B85_PB_DISPLAY      B90_PB_EXIT      *
*    B81_PB_OK            B86_PB_ADD                           *
*    B82_PB_CHANGE        B87_PB_SAVE                          *
*    B83_PB_COPY          B88_PB_PRINT                         *
*    B84_PB_DELETE        B89_PB_PROCESS                       *
*                                              See page 237.  *
*==============================================================*
 LPARAMETERS TMP_OPT
 LOCAL TMP_NAV, TMP_MODE, TMP_NAV

 TMP_NAV = .F.
 TMP_MODE = THISFORM.LABEL_MODE.CAPTION

 DO CASE
 CASE TMP_OPT = 1                     && SAVE
    THISFORM.B87_PB_SAVE(TMP_NAV)

 CASE TMP_OPT = 2                     && CANCEL
    THISFORM.B80_PB_CANCEL

 CASE TMP_OPT = 3                     && ADD
   IF TMP_MODE = "ADD"
    THISFORM.B86_PB_ADD(TMP_NAV)
   ENDIF

 CASE TMP_OPT = 4                     && COPY

   THISFORM.B79_PB_CHG_MODE_CPY

 CASE TMP_OPT = 5                     && PRINT
    THISFORM.B88_PB_PRINT

 ENDCASE
```

```
*=============================================================*
* Procedure: B02_PBG_NAVIGATION_CLICK                         *
*                                                             *
* Options/Methods:                                            *
*                B71_PB_TOP                                   *
*                B72_PB_PRIOR                                 *
*                B73_PB_NEXT                                  *
*                B74_PB_BOTTOM                                *
*                                              See page 237.  *
*=============================================================*
 LPARAMETERS TMP_OPT

 DO CASE
 CASE TMP_OPT = 1               && TOP
    THISFORM.B71_PB_TOP
 CASE TMP_OPT = 2               && PRIOR
    THISFORM.B72_PB_PRIOR
 CASE TMP_OPT = 3               && NEXT
    THISFORM.B73_PB_NEXT
 CASE TMP_OPT = 4               && BOTTOM
    THISFORM.B74_PB_BOTTOM
 ENDCASE



*=============================================================*
* Procedure: B03_VIEW_PROCESS_MODE                            *
*                                                             *
*=============================================================*
LPARAMETERS TMP_MODE

DO CASE
CASE TMP_MODE = "ADD"

    THISFORM.Caption = "   Mode: Add New Record. "
    Thisform.setall("Value", " " ,"TEXTBOX")
    Thisform.AOD_01_SET_DSP
    THISFORM.AO03_SET_PB_CHG_MODE
    Thisform.AOD_05_INIT_SET_FOCUS
    On error

CASE TMP_MODE = "CHG"

    THISFORM.Caption = "   Mode: Change "
    Thisform.AOD_01_SET_DSP
    Thisform.AOD_02_GET_VAL
    THISFORM.AO03_SET_PB_CHG_MODE
    Thisform.AOD_05_INIT_SET_FOCUS
    On error
```

```
CASE TMP_MODE = "DSP"   && DISPLAY

    THISFORM.Caption = "   Mode: Display "
    Thisform.AOD_01_SET_DSP
    Thisform.AOD_02_GET_VAL
    Thisform.setall("ReadOnly", .T. ,"TEXTBOX")
    THISFORM.AO01_SET_PB_DSP_MODE


CASE TMP_MODE = "DEL"   && DELETE

   THISFORM.Caption = "   Mode: Delete "
   Thisform.AOD_01_SET_DSP
   Thisform.AOD_02_GET_VAL
   Thisform.setall("ReadOnly", .T. ,"TEXTBOX")
   THISFORM.AO02_SET_PB_DEL_MODE

CASE TMP_MODE = "CPY"

    THISFORM.AOD_11_COPY_CLEAR_KEY
    THISFORM.Caption = "   Mode: Copy/Add New Record. "
    Thisform.AOD_01_SET_DSP
    THISFORM.AO03_SET_PB_CHG_MODE
    THISFORM.AOD_05_INIT_SET_FOCUS
    On Error
ENDCASE

THISFORM.AD08_FORM_CAPTION



*==============================================================*
* Procedure: B05_PICKLIST_RUN                                  *
*                                              See page 236.  *
*==============================================================*
 LPARAMETER TMP_TXTBOX_ID
 LOCAL TMP_RTN_PL

 TMP_RTN_PL = THISFORM.AD03_CALL_PICKLIST_FORM(TMP_TXTBOX_ID)

 IF TMP_RTN_PL = "CANCEL"
 ELSE
    IF LEN(ALLTRIM(TMP_RTN_PL)) > 0
     THISFORM.AOD_06_TEXTBOX_VALUE(TMP_TXTBOX_ID, TMP_RTN_PL)
     THISFORM.B06_TEXTBOX_VALID_RTN_VALUE(TMP_TXTBOX_ID, ;
                                         TMP_RTN_PL)
   ENDIF
 ENDIF
 THISFORM.REFRESH
```

```
*===============================================================*
* Procedure: B06_TEXTBOX_VALID_RTN_VALUE                        *
*                                              See page 236.   *
*===============================================================*
LPARAMETERS TMP_TXTBOX_ID, TMP_P_VALUE
LOCAL TMP_RTN

TMP_RTN = THISFORM.AD04_TEXT_VALID_RTN_VALUE(TMP_TXTBOX_ID, ;
                                             TMP_P_VALUE)

THISFORM.REFRESH

RETURN TMP_RTN




*===============================================================*
* Procedure: B12_OPEN_MAIN_FILE_VIEW                            *
*                                                               *
*===============================================================*
 LPARAMETERS TMP_MODE
 LOCAL TMP_MAIN_FV

 TMP_MAIN_FV = THISFORM.AF02_MAIN_FILE_VIEW_NAME(TMP_MODE)

 IF TMP_MAIN_FV = "N"
  RETURN "NO_VIEWS_OPEN"
 ELSE

  IF USED(TMP_MAIN_FV)
    SELECT &TMP_MAIN_FV
    USE
  ENDIF

  DO CASE
  CASE TMP_MODE = "ADD"  or TMP_MODE = "CPY"
     SELECT 0
     USE &TMP_MAIN_FV ALIAS &TMP_MAIN_FV
     CURSORSETPROP('BUFFERING', 5)
     RETURN "OK"

  CASE TMP_MODE = "CHG"
     SELECT 0
     USE &TMP_MAIN_FV ALIAS &TMP_MAIN_FV
     CURSORSETPROP('BUFFERING', 3) && Optimistic Row Buff.
     RETURN "OK"
  CASE TMP_MODE = "DSP"
     SELECT 0
     USE &TMP_MAIN_FV ALIAS &TMP_MAIN_FV
```

```
        CURSORSETPROP('BUFFERING', 3)  && Optimistic Row Buff.
        RETURN "OK"

     CASE TMP_MODE = "DEL"
        SELECT 0
        USE &TMP_MAIN_FV ALIAS &TMP_MAIN_FV
        CURSORSETPROP('BUFFERING', 5)  && Optimistic Table Buf.
        RETURN "OK"

     ENDCASE

  ENDIF




*=============================================================*
* Procedure: B13_SELECT_MAIN_FILE_VIEW                        *
*                                                             *
*=============================================================*
 LPARAMETERS TMP_MODE
 LOCAL TMP_MAIN_FV

 TMP_MAIN_FV = THISFORM.AF02_MAIN_FILE_VIEW_NAME(TMP_MODE)

 IF TMP_MAIN_FV = "N"
 ELSE

   SELECT &TMP_MAIN_FV

 ENDIF


*=============================================================*
* Procedure: B14_MAIN_VIEW_TABLE_UPDATE                       *
*                                                             *
*=============================================================*
 LPARAMETERS TMP_MODE
 LOCAL TMP_MAIN_FV, TMP_RTN

 TMP_MAIN_FV = THISFORM.AF02_MAIN_FILE_VIEW_NAME(TMP_MODE)

 DO CASE
 CASE TMP_MODE = "ADD" OR TMP_MODE = "CPY"
    IF TABLEUPDATE(1,.F.,TMP_MAIN_FV)
       TMP_RTN =  .T.
       TMP_RTN = THISFORM.AF06_TABLE_UPDATE()
    ELSE
       TMP_RTN = .F.
    ENDIF
```

```
 CASE TMP_MODE = "CHG"
    IF TABLEUPDATE(0,.F.,TMP_MAIN_FV)
       TMP_RTN =  .T.
       TMP_RTN = THISFORM.AF06_TABLE_UPDATE()
    ELSE
       TMP_RTN = .F.
    ENDIF

 CASE TMP_MODE = "DSP"
   TMP_RTN = .F.

 CASE TMP_MODE = "DEL"

    IF TABLEUPDATE(1,.F.,TMP_MAIN_FV)
       TMP_RTN =  .T.
       TMP_RTN = THISFORM.AF06_TABLE_UPDATE()
    ELSE
       TMP_RTN = .F.
    ENDIF

 ENDCASE

 RETURN TMP_RTN


*==============================================================*
* Procedure: B15_MAIN_VIEW_TABLE_REVERT                        *
*                                                              *
*==============================================================*
 LPARAMETERS  TMP_MODE
 LOCAL TMP_MAIN_FV

 TMP_MAIN_FV = THISFORM.AF02_MAIN_FILE_VIEW_NAME(TMP_MODE)

 TABLEREVERT(.F.,TMP_MAIN_FV)


*==============================================================*
* Procedure: B16_SAVE_WITH_ADD                                 *
*                                                              *
*==============================================================*
LPARAMETERS TMP_NAV

LOCAL TMP_MODE, TMP_MAIN_FV

LOCAL TMP_REC_KEY, TMP_Success, TMP_ERR, TMP_ERR_MSG
LOCAL TMP_MTEXT, TMP_MSG, TMP_OVR_1
LOCAL TMP_VAL1, TMP_VAL2, TMP_VAL3, TMP_NTYPE, TMP_CTITLE, ;
      TMP_RSP
```

```
TMP_MODE = THISFORM.LABEL_MODE.CAPTION

TMP_OVR_1 = .T.
TMP_REC_KEY = THISFORM.AOD_08_KEY_FLD_TXT_VALUE(TMP_OVR_1)
TMP_SREC = THISFORM.AF03_MAIN_FILE_VIEW_KEY_VALUE(TMP_REC_KEY)

TMP_MAIN_FV = THISFORM.AF02_MAIN_FILE_VIEW_NAME(TMP_MODE)

IF TMP_MAIN_FV = "N"
   THISFORM.AD07_CLEANUP
   CLOSE DATABASES
   THISFORM.RELEASE
ELSE

   IF THISFORM.AOD_04_VALIDATE()

        TMP_MTEXT = " Confirm Save ? "
        TMP_MSG   = " RECORD SAVED. "
        TMP_VAL1  = 3                    && Yes, No  & CANCEL
        TMP_VAL2  = 32                   && Question Mark
        TMP_VAL3  = 0                    && First Push Button
        TMP_ntype = TMP_VAL1 + TMP_VAL2 + TMP_VAL3
        TMP_CTITLE = " "

        TMP_RSP = MESSAGEBOX(TMP_MTEXT,TMP_NTYPE,TMP_CTITLE)

        DO CASE
        CASE TMP_RSP = 6
           THISFORM.B12_OPEN_MAIN_FILE_VIEW(TMP_MODE)

           APPEND BLANK
           IF RLOCK()
              THISFORM.AOD_03_WRT_VAL

            BEGIN TRANSACTION
            TMP_Success = THISFORM.B14_MAIN_VIEW_TABLE_UPDATE(;
                                                    TMP_MODE)
            IF TMP_Success = .T.
               END TRANSACTION
               WAIT WINDOW NOWAIT TMP_MSG
            ELSE
               THISFORM.AF07_TABLE_REVERT
               ROLLBACK
               = AERROR(aErrors)
               TMP_ERR = STR(aErrors[1,1])
               TMP_ERR_MSG = ;
                   " RECORD NOT SAVED, ERROR NO.: " + TMP_ERR
               Messagebox(TMP_ERR_MSG)
            ENDIF
```

```
          IF ISRLOCKED()
            UNLOCK
          ENDIF

          IF ISFLOCKED()
            UNLOCK
          ENDIF

          THISFORM.AD07_CLEANUP

          IF TMP_NAV = .F.
            CLOSE DATABASES
            THISFORM.RELEASE
          ENDIF

         ELSE

           WAIT WINDOW " ;
                ERROR - UNABLE TO LOCK RECORD. TRY AGAIN. "
              IF ISRLOCKED()
                UNLOCK
              ENDIF

              IF ISFLOCKED()
                UNLOCK
              ENDIF
          ENDIF

      CASE TMP_RSP = 7
          IF TMP_NAV = .F.
            CLOSE DATABASES
            THISFORM.RELEASE
          ENDIF
      ENDCASE
   ENDIF
ENDIF


*============================================================*
* Procedure: B17_SAVE_WITH_CHG                               *
*                                                            *
*============================================================*
LPARAMETERS TMP_NAV

LOCAL TMP_MODE, TMP_MAIN_FV

LOCAL TMP_Success, TMP_ERR, TMP_ERR_MSG
LOCAL TMP_MTEXT, TMP_MSG, TMP_VAL1, TMP_VAL2, TMP_VAL3
```

```
LOCAL TMP_NTYPE, TMP_CTITLE, TMP_RSP
LOCAL TMP_REC_FOUND, TMP_OVR_1

TMP_REC_FOUND = " "

TMP_MODE = THISFORM.LABEL_MODE.CAPTION

TMP_OVR_1 = .T.
TMP_REC_KEY = THISFORM.AOD_08_KEY_FLD_TXT_VALUE(TMP_OVR_1)
TMP_SREC = THISFORM.AF03_MAIN_FILE_VIEW_KEY_VALUE(TMP_REC_KEY)

TMP_MAIN_FV = THISFORM.AF02_MAIN_FILE_VIEW_NAME(TMP_MODE)

IF TMP_MAIN_FV = "N"
    THISFORM.AD07_CLEANUP
    CLOSE DATABASES
    THISFORM.RELEASE
ELSE

   IF thisform.AOD_04_VALIDATE()
      TMP_MTEXT = " Confirm Save ? "
      TMP_MSG   = " RECORD SAVED. "
      TMP_VAL1  = 3                       && Yes, No  & CANCEL
      TMP_VAL2  = 32                      && Question Mark
      TMP_VAL3  = 0                       && First Push Button
      TMP_ntype = TMP_VAL1 + TMP_VAL2 + TMP_VAL3
      TMP_CTITLE = " "
      TMP_RSP = MESSAGEBOX(TMP_MTEXT,TMP_NTYPE,TMP_CTITLE)
      DO CASE
      CASE TMP_RSP = 6
        THISFORM.B13_SELECT_MAIN_FILE_VIEW(TMP_MODE)

        IF TMP_REC_FOUND = " " OR TMP_REC_FOUND = "Y"
         IF RLOCK()
          THISFORM.AOD_03_WRT_VAL
          BEGIN TRANSACTION
          TMP_Success = THISFORM.B14_MAIN_VIEW_TABLE_UPDATE(;
                                                        TMP_MODE)
          IF TMP_Success = .T.
             END TRANSACTION
             WAIT WINDOW NOWAIT TMP_MSG
          ELSE
             THISFORM.AF07_TABLE_REVERT
             ROLLBACK
             = AERROR(aErrors)
             TMP_ERR = STR(aErrors[1,1])
             TMP_ERR_MSG = ;
                 " RECORD NOT SAVED, ERROR NO.: " + TMP_ERR
             Messagebox(TMP_ERR_MSG)
          ENDIF
```

```
            THISFORM.AD07_CLEANUP

            IF ISRLOCKED()
               UNLOCK
            ENDIF

            IF ISFLOCKED()
               UNLOCK
            ENDIF

            IF TMP_NAV = .F.
               CLOSE DATABASES
               THISFORM.RELEASE
            ENDIF
         ELSE
            = MESSAGEBOX(" SOMEONE ELSE IS USING THIS RECORD.
TRY AGAIN. ")
            IF ISRLOCKED()
               UNLOCK
            ENDIF

            IF ISFLOCKED()
               UNLOCK
            ENDIF
         ENDIF
        ELSE
         = MESSAGEBOX(" ERROR IN PROGRAM. RECORD NOT FOUND. ")
        ENDIF

      CASE TMP_RSP = 7

        IF TMP_NAV = .F.
           CLOSE DATABASES
           THISFORM.RELEASE
        ENDIF

      ENDCASE

   ENDIF
 ENDIF


*==============================================================*
* Procedure: B18_SAVE_WITH_DEL                                 *
*                                                              *
*==============================================================*
LPARAMETERS TMP_NAV

LOCAL TMP_MODE, TMP_MAIN_FV
```

```
LOCAL TMP_Success, TMP_ERR, TMP_ERR_MSG
LOCAL TMP_MTEXT, TMP_MSG, TMP_VAL1, TMP_VAL2, TMP_VAL3
LOCAL TMP_NTYPE, TMP_CTITLE, TMP_RSP
LOCAL TMP_REC_FOUND, TMP_OVR_1

TMP_REC_FOUND = " "

TMP_MODE = THISFORM.LABEL_MODE.CAPTION

TMP_OVR_1 = .T.
TMP_REC_KEY = THISFORM.AOD_08_KEY_FLD_TXT_VALUE(TMP_OVR_1)
TMP_SREC = THISFORM.AF03_MAIN_FILE_VIEW_KEY_VALUE( ;
                                             TMP_REC_KEY)

TMP_MAIN_FV = THISFORM.AF02_MAIN_FILE_VIEW_NAME(TMP_MODE)

IF TMP_MAIN_FV = "N"
   WAIT WINDOW NOWAIT "NO VIEWS ARE OPENED."
ELSE

   *-----------------------------------------------
   * MESSAGE BOX
   *-----------------------------------------------
   TMP_MTEXT = " Confirm Delete ? "
   TMP_MSG   = " RECORD DELETED. "
   TMP_VAL1  = 3                   && Yes, No  & CANCEL
   TMP_VAL2  = 32                  && Question Mark
   TMP_VAL3  = 0                   && First Push Button
   TMP_ntype = TMP_VAL1 + TMP_VAL2 + TMP_VAL3
   TMP_CTITLE = " "

   TMP_RSP = MESSAGEBOX(TMP_MTEXT,TMP_NTYPE,TMP_CTITLE)
   *------------------------------------------------
  DO CASE
  CASE TMP_RSP = 6
     THISFORM.B13_SELECT_MAIN_FILE_VIEW(TMP_MODE)

      IF TMP_REC_FOUND = " " OR TMP_REC_FOUND = "Y"

       IF RLOCK()
        DELETE

        BEGIN TRANSACTION
        TMP_Success = THISFORM.B14_MAIN_VIEW_TABLE_UPDATE(;
                                                TMP_MODE)
        IF TMP_Success = .T.
            END TRANSACTION
            WAIT WINDOW NOWAIT TMP_MSG
        ELSE
           THISFORM.AF07_TABLE_REVERT
```

```
           ROLLBACK
           = AERROR(aErrors)
           TMP_ERR = STR(aErrors[1,1])
           TMP_ERR_MSG = ;
                " RECORD NOT SAVED, ERROR NO. : " + TMP_ERR
           Messagebox( "RECORD NOT DELETED." + TMP_ERR_MSG)
        ENDIF

          IF ISRLOCKED() OR ISFLOCKED()
            UNLOCK
          ENDIF

          THISFORM.AD07_CLEANUP

          IF TMP_NAV = .F.
            CLOSE DATABASES
            THISFORM.RELEASE
           ENDIF
       ELSE

         = MESSAGEBOX(" OPERATION NOT VALID. ")

         IF ISRLOCKED()
           UNLOCK
         ENDIF

         IF ISFLOCKED()
           UNLOCK
         ENDIF

       ENDIF

      ELSE
        = MESSAGEBOX(" ERROR IN PROGRAM. RECORD NOT FOUND. ")
      ENDIF

  CASE TMP_RSP = 7

     IF TMP_NAV = .F.
       CLOSE DATABASES
       THISFORM.RELEASE
     ENDIF

  ENDCASE

ENDIF
```

```
*===================================================================*
* Procedure: B20_VALIDATE_DUPLICATE_REC                             *
*                                                                   *
*===================================================================*
LPARAMETERS NA

 LOCAL TMP_MODE
 LOCAL TMP_RTN_1, TMP_ERR_F, TMP_REC_KEY, TMP_OVR_1

 TMP_RTN_1 = .F.

 *-------------------------------------------------------
 * RESET KEY VALUE. (PARAMETERIZED VIEW PARAMETER VALUE)
 *-------------------------------------------------------
 TMP_OVR_1 = .T.
 TMP_REC_KEY = THISFORM.AOD_08_KEY_FLD_TXT_VALUE(TMP_OVR_1)
 TMP_SREC = THISFORM.AF03_MAIN_FILE_VIEW_KEY_VALUE( ;
                                               TMP_REC_KEY)
 *-----------------------------------------------------
TMP_MODE = THISFORM.LABEL_MODE.CAPTION

 TMP_ERR_F = THISFORM.B12_OPEN_MAIN_FILE_VIEW(TMP_MODE)

 IF TMP_ERR_F = "NO_VIEWS_OPEN"
 ELSE
     IF BOF() AND EOF()
        TMP_RTN_1 = .T.
     ELSE
        TMP_RTN_1 = .F.
        WAIT WINDOW " ERROR - Record already exists. "
     ENDIF
  ENDIF

 RETURN TMP_RTN_1




*===================================================================*
* Procedure: B30_SETUP_GRID                                         *
*                                                                   *
*===================================================================*

 THISFORM.AOD_31_GRID_PROPERTIES
 THISFORM.AOD_32_GRID_COLUMN_PROP
 THISFORM.AOD_33_GRID_COL_HEADER_PROP

 THISFORM.REFRESH
```

```
*==============================================================*
* Procedure: B70_PROCESS_INIT                                  *
*                                                              *
*==============================================================*
LPARAMETERS TMP_MODE, TMP_SEL_REC
LOCAL FILE_NOT_EMPTY

FILE_NOT_EMPTY = .T.

TMP_SREC = THISFORM.AF03_MAIN_FILE_VIEW_KEY_VALUE(TMP_SEL_REC)

THISFORM.LABEL_MODE.CAPTION = TMP_MODE

FILE_NOT_EMPTY = thisform.B01_OPEN_FILES(TMP_MODE)

THISFORM.AF04_OPEN_OTHER_FILES_VIEWS

IF TMP_MODE = "ADD"  OR TMP_MODE = "CPY"
ELSE
   THISFORM.B13_SELECT_MAIN_FILE_VIEW(TMP_MODE)
ENDIF

Thisform.B03_VIEW_PROCESS_MODE(TMP_MODE)

THISFORM.B30_SETUP_GRID
THISFORM.AD06_AFTER_INIT

*----------------------------------

IF FILE_NOT_EMPTY = .F.
  IF TMP_MODE = "ADD" OR TMP_MODE = "CPY"
  ELSE
     MESSAGEBOX (" ERROR! RECORD NOT FOUND. ")
    CLOSE DATABASES
    RETURN .F.
  ENDIF
ENDIF


*==============================================================*
* Procedure: B71_PB_TOP                                        *
*                                                              *
*==============================================================*
LPARAMETERS TMP_NAV

 LOCAL TMP_MODE, TMP_MAIN_FV, TMP_REC_KEY, TMP_KEY_VAL

 TMP_NAV = .T.
```

```
TMP_MODE = THISFORM.LABEL_MODE.CAPTION

TMP_MAIN_FV = THISFORM.AF02_MAIN_FILE_VIEW_NAME(TMP_MODE)

IF TMP_MAIN_FV = "N"
  WAIT WINDOW NOWAIT " NO VIEWS ARE OPENED. "
ELSE

 DO CASE
 *----------------------------------------------------------
 CASE TMP_MODE = "DSP"
 *----------------------------------------------------------
   THISFORM.AF05_SELECT_NAVIGATION_IDX_VIEW("D") && D = DESC.
   GO BOTTOM

   TMP_KEY_VAL = THISFORM.AOD_09_KEY_VALUE()
   TMP_SREC = THISFORM.AF03_MAIN_FILE_VIEW_KEY_VALUE( ;
                                               TMP_KEY_VAL)

   FILE_NOT_EMPTY = thisform.B01_OPEN_FILES(TMP_MODE)

   THISFORM.B13_SELECT_MAIN_FILE_VIEW(TMP_MODE)

   Thisform.B03_VIEW_PROCESS_MODE(TMP_MODE)

   THISFORM.REFRESH

 *---------------------------------------------------------
 CASE TMP_MODE = "CHG"
 *---------------------------------------------------------
  THISFORM.B87_PB_SAVE(TMP_NAV)

  THISFORM.AF05_SELECT_NAVIGATION_IDX_VIEW("D") && D = DESC.
  GO BOTTOM

  TMP_KEY_VAL = THISFORM.AOD_09_KEY_VALUE()
  TMP_SREC = THISFORM.AF03_MAIN_FILE_VIEW_KEY_VALUE( ;
                                               TMP_KEY_VAL)

  FILE_NOT_EMPTY = thisform.B01_OPEN_FILES(TMP_MODE)

  THISFORM.B13_SELECT_MAIN_FILE_VIEW(TMP_MODE)

  THISFORM.B03_VIEW_PROCESS_MODE(TMP_MODE)

  THISFORM.REFRESH

   *----------------------------------------
 CASE TMP_MODE = "DEL"
    = MESSAGEBOX(" Delete-Prior Option, Not Available. ")
```

```
  OTHERWISE
     =MESSAGEBOX(  ;
  " Navigation only available with modes: 'DSP','CHG','DEL' ")
  ENDCASE

 ENDIF


*===============================================================*
* Procedure: B72_PB_PRIOR                                       *
*                                                               *
*===============================================================*
LPARAMETERS TMP_NAV

 LOCAL TMP_MODE, TMP_MAIN_FV, TMP_REC_KEY, TMP_KEY_VAL

TMP_NAV = .T.

 TMP_MODE = THISFORM.LABEL_MODE.CAPTION

 TMP_MAIN_FV = THISFORM.AF02_MAIN_FILE_VIEW_NAME(TMP_MODE)

 IF TMP_MAIN_FV = "N"
   WAIT WINDOW NOWAIT " NO VIEWS ARE OPENED. "
 ELSE

  DO CASE
  CASE TMP_MODE = "DSP"

    THISFORM.AF05_SELECT_NAVIGATION_IDX_VIEW("D") && D=DESC.

      IF NOT EOF( )
          SKIP 1
      ENDIF

      IF EOF( )
          GO BOTTOM
           = MESSAGEBOX(" BOF or EOF Encountered. ")
      ENDIF

    TMP_KEY_VAL = THISFORM.AOD_09_KEY_VALUE()
    TMP_SREC = THISFORM.AF03_MAIN_FILE_VIEW_KEY_VALUE(;
                                                   TMP_KEY_VAL)

    FILE_NOT_EMPTY = thisform.B01_OPEN_FILES(TMP_MODE)

    THISFORM.B13_SELECT_MAIN_FILE_VIEW(TMP_MODE)
    Thisform.B03_VIEW_PROCESS_MODE(TMP_MODE)
    THISFORM.REFRESH
```

```
 *--------------------------------------------------
 CASE TMP_MODE = "CHG"
 *--------------------------------------------------
   THISFORM.B87_PB_SAVE(TMP_NAV)

   THISFORM.AF05_SELECT_NAVIGATION_IDX_VIEW("D") && D=DESC.

     IF NOT EOF( )
          SKIP 1
     ENDIF

     IF EOF( )
         GO BOTTOM
          = MESSAGEBOX(" BOF or EOF Encountered. ")
     ENDIF

   TMP_KEY_VAL = THISFORM.AOD_09_KEY_VALUE()
   TMP_SREC = THISFORM.AF03_MAIN_FILE_VIEW_KEY_VALUE( ;
                                              TMP_KEY_VAL)

   FILE_NOT_EMPTY = thisform.B01_OPEN_FILES(TMP_MODE)

   THISFORM.B13_SELECT_MAIN_FILE_VIEW(TMP_MODE)

   Thisform.B03_VIEW_PROCESS_MODE(TMP_MODE)

   THISFORM.REFRESH

 *---------------------------------------
 CASE TMP_MODE = "DEL"
    = MESSAGEBOX(" Delete-Prior Option Not Available. ")
   OTHERWISE
    =MESSAGEBOX( ;
" Navigation only available with modes: 'DSP','CHG','DEL' ")
 ENDCASE

ENDIF



*==============================================================*
* Procedure: B73_PB_NEXT                                       *
*                                                              *
*==============================================================*
LPARAMETERS TMP_NAV

 LOCAL TMP_MODE, TMP_MAIN_FV

 LOCAL TMP_REC_KEY, TMP_KEY_VAL, TMP_OVR_1
```

```
TMP_NAV = .T.

TMP_MODE = THISFORM.LABEL_MODE.CAPTION

TMP_MAIN_FV = THISFORM.AF02_MAIN_FILE_VIEW_NAME(TMP_MODE)

IF TMP_MAIN_FV = "N"
   WAIT WINDOW NOWAIT " NO VIEWS ARE OPENED. "
ELSE

 DO CASE
 CASE TMP_MODE = "DSP"

    THISFORM.AF05_SELECT_NAVIGATION_IDX_VIEW("A") && A=ASC.
    IF NOT EOF( )
       SKIP 1
    ENDIF

    IF EOF( )
      GO BOTTOM
      = MESSAGEBOX(" End of File Encountered. ")
    ENDIF
   TMP_KEY_VAL = THISFORM.AOD_09_KEY_VALUE()
   TMP_SREC = THISFORM.AF03_MAIN_FILE_VIEW_KEY_VALUE( ;
                                                   TMP_KEY_VAL)
   FILE_NOT_EMPTY = thisform.B01_OPEN_FILES(TMP_MODE)

   THISFORM.B13_SELECT_MAIN_FILE_VIEW(TMP_MODE)

   Thisform.B03_VIEW_PROCESS_MODE(TMP_MODE)

   THISFORM.REFRESH

 *==============================================================
 CASE TMP_MODE = "CHG"  OR TMP_MODE = "DEL"

    THISFORM.B87_PB_SAVE(TMP_NAV)

    THISFORM.AF05_SELECT_NAVIGATION_IDX_VIEW("A") && A=ASC.

    IF NOT EOF( )
       SKIP 1
    ENDIF

    IF EOF( )
      GO BOTTOM
      IF TMP_MODE = "CHG"
         = MESSAGEBOX(" End of File Encountered. ")
      ENDIF
    ENDIF
```

```
    TMP_KEY_VAL = THISFORM.AOD_09_KEY_VALUE()
    TMP_SREC = THISFORM.AF03_MAIN_FILE_VIEW_KEY_VALUE( ;
                                           TMP_KEY_VAL)
    FILE_NOT_EMPTY = Thisform.B01_OPEN_FILES(TMP_MODE)

    THISFORM.B13_SELECT_MAIN_FILE_VIEW(TMP_MODE)

    Thisform.B03_VIEW_PROCESS_MODE(TMP_MODE)

    THISFORM.REFRESH
    OTHERWISE

  =MESSAGEBOX( ;
 " Navigation only available with modes: 'DSP','CHG','DEL'. ")

  ENDCASE

 ENDIF

*==============================================================*
* Procedure: B74_PB_BOTTOM                                     *
*                                                              *
*==============================================================*
LPARAMETERS TMP_NAV

 LOCAL TMP_MODE, TMP_MAIN_FV, TMP_REC_KEY, TMP_KEY_VAL

 TMP_NAV = .T.

 TMP_MODE = THISFORM.LABEL_MODE.CAPTION

 TMP_MAIN_FV = THISFORM.AF02_MAIN_FILE_VIEW_NAME(TMP_MODE)

 IF TMP_MAIN_FV = "N"
   WAIT WINDOW NOWAIT " NO VIEWS ARE OPENED. "
 ELSE

  DO CASE
  CASE TMP_MODE = "DSP"

    THISFORM.AF05_SELECT_NAVIGATION_IDX_VIEW("A") && A=ASC.

    GO BOTTOM

    TMP_KEY_VAL = THISFORM.AOD_09_KEY_VALUE()
    TMP_SREC = THISFORM.AF03_MAIN_FILE_VIEW_KEY_VALUE( ;
                                           TMP_KEY_VAL)

    FILE_NOT_EMPTY = Thisform.B01_OPEN_FILES(TMP_MODE)
```

```
    THISFORM.B13_SELECT_MAIN_FILE_VIEW(TMP_MODE)

    Thisform.B03_VIEW_PROCESS_MODE(TMP_MODE)

    THISFORM.REFRESH

  *==============================================================
  CASE TMP_MODE = "CHG"  OR TMP_MODE = "DEL"

    THISFORM.B87_PB_SAVE(TMP_NAV)

    THISFORM.AF05_SELECT_NAVIGATION_IDX_VIEW("A")  && A=ASC.

    GO BOTTOM

    TMP_KEY_VAL = THISFORM.AOD_09_KEY_VALUE()
    TMP_SREC = THISFORM.AF03_MAIN_FILE_VIEW_KEY_VALUE( ;
                                                    TMP_KEY_VAL)
    FILE_NOT_EMPTY = Thisform.B01_OPEN_FILES(TMP_MODE)

    THISFORM.B13_SELECT_MAIN_FILE_VIEW(TMP_MODE)

    Thisform.B03_VIEW_PROCESS_MODE(TMP_MODE)

    THISFORM.REFRESH

  OTHERWISE
   =MESSAGEBOX( ;
" Navigation only available with modes: 'DSP','CHG','DEL'. ")

  ENDCASE

 ENDIF


*==============================================================*
* Procedure: B75_PB_CHG_MODE_DSP                               *
*                                              See page 237. *
*==============================================================*
 LOCAL TMP_KEY_VAL, TMP_MODE, TMP_NEW_MODE, TMP_NAV, ;
       TMP_CONTINUE
 TMP_MODE = THISFORM.LABEL_MODE.CAPTION

 IF TMP_MODE = "DSP"
 ELSE

   TMP_NAV = .T.
   THISFORM.B87_PB_SAVE(TMP_NAV)
```

```
   TMP_NEW_MODE = "DSP"
   THISFORM.LABEL_MODE.CAPTION = TMP_NEW_MODE

   TMP_SEL_REC = THISFORM.AOD_08_KEY_FLD_TXT_VALUE(.T.)
   CLOSE DATABASES
   TMP_CONTINUE = .T.
   TMP_CONTINUE = THISFORM.B70_PROCESS_INIT(TMP_NEW_MODE, ;
                                            TMP_SEL_REC)
   IF TMP_CONTINUE = .F.
     CLOSE DATABASES
     THISFORM.RELEASE
   ENDIF
ENDIF


*==============================================================*
* Procedure: B76_PB_CHG_MODE_ADD                               *
*                                              See page 237.   *
*==============================================================*
 LOCAL TMP_KEY_VAL,TMP_MODE, TMP_MAIN_FV

 LOCAL TMP_NAV, TMP_CONTINUE

 TMP_MODE = THISFORM.LABEL_MODE.CAPTION

 TMP_MAIN_FV = THISFORM.AF02_MAIN_FILE_VIEW_NAME(TMP_MODE)

 IF TMP_MAIN_FV = "N"
    WAIT WINDOW NOWAIT " NO VIEWS ARE OPENED. "
 ELSE

   IF TMP_MODE # "DSP"
       TMP_NAV = .T.
      THISFORM.B87_PB_SAVE(TMP_NAV)
   ENDIF

 ENDIF

 Thisform.setall("ReadOnly", .F. ,"TEXTBOX")
 TMP_NEW_MODE = "ADD"
 THISFORM.LABEL_MODE.CAPTION = TMP_NEW_MODE
 TMP_SEL_REC = THISFORM.AOD_08_KEY_FLD_TXT_VALUE()
 CLOSE DATABASES
 TMP_CONTINUE = .T.
 TMP_CONTINUE = THISFORM.B70_PROCESS_INIT(TMP_NEW_MODE, ;
                                          TMP_SEL_REC)

 IF TMP_CONTINUE = .F.
     CLOSE DATABASES
```

```
    THISFORM.RELEASE
ELSE
    THISFORM.REFRESH
ENDIF


*==============================================================*
* Procedure: B77_PB_CHG_MODE_CHG                               *
*                                                See page 237. *
*==============================================================*
LOCAL TMP_KEY_VAL, TMP_MODE, TMP_NEW_MODE, TMP_NAV, ;
      TMP_CONTINUE

TMP_MODE = THISFORM.LABEL_MODE.CAPTION

IF TMP_MODE = "CHG"
ELSE

  Thisform.setall("ReadOnly", .F. ,"TEXTBOX")

  IF TMP_MODE # "DSP"
     TMP_NAV = .T.
     THISFORM.B87_PB_SAVE(TMP_NAV)
  ENDIF

  TMP_NEW_MODE = "CHG"

  THISFORM.LABEL_MODE.CAPTION = TMP_NEW_MODE

  TMP_SEL_REC = THISFORM.AOD_08_KEY_FLD_TXT_VALUE(.T.)

  CLOSE DATABASES

  TMP_CONTINUE = .T.

  TMP_CONTINUE = THISFORM.B70_PROCESS_INIT(TMP_NEW_MODE, ;
                                           TMP_SEL_REC)

  IF TMP_CONTINUE = .F.
    CLOSE DATABASES
    THISFORM.RELEASE
  ENDIF

ENDIF


*==============================================================*
* Procedure: B78_PB_CHG_MODE_DEL                               *
*                                                See page 237. *
*==============================================================*
```

```
 LOCAL TMP_KEY_VAL, TMP_MODE, TMP_NEW_MODE, TMP_NAV, ;
       TMP_CONTINUE

 TMP_MODE = THISFORM.LABEL_MODE.CAPTION

 IF TMP_MODE = "DEL"
 ELSE

   IF TMP_MODE # "DSP"
      TMP_NAV = .T.
      THISFORM.B87_PB_SAVE(TMP_NAV)
   ENDIF

   TMP_NEW_MODE = "DEL"
   THISFORM.LABEL_MODE.CAPTION = TMP_NEW_MODE

   TMP_SEL_REC = THISFORM.AOD_08_KEY_FLD_TXT_VALUE(.T.)

   CLOSE DATABASES
   TMP_CONTINUE = .T.
   TMP_CONTINUE = THISFORM.B70_PROCESS_INIT(TMP_NEW_MODE, ;
                                         TMP_SEL_REC)

   IF TMP_CONTINUE = .F.
     CLOSE DATABASES
     THISFORM.RELEASE
   ENDIF

 ENDIF



*============================================================*
* Procedure: B79_PB_CHG_MODE_CPY                             *
*                                              See page 237. *
*============================================================*
 LOCAL TMP_MODE, TMP_MAIN_FV
 LOCAL TMP_REC_KEY, TMP_KEY_VAL, TMP_S_REC
 LOCAL TMP_NEW_MODE, TMP_NAV, TMP_CONTINUE

 TMP_NAV = .T.

 TMP_MODE = THISFORM.LABEL_MODE.CAPTION

 TMP_MAIN_FV = THISFORM.AF02_MAIN_FILE_VIEW_NAME(TMP_MODE)

IF TMP_MAIN_FV = "N"
    WAIT WINDOW NOWAIT " NO VIEWS ARE OPENED. "
 ELSE
   DO CASE
```

```
   CASE TMP_MODE = "CHG"
     THISFORM.B87_PB_SAVE(TMP_NAV)
   CASE TMP_MODE = "ADD"
     THISFORM.B87_PB_SAVE(TMP_NAV)
   CASE TMP_MODE = "CPY"
     THISFORM.B87_PB_SAVE(TMP_NAV)
   ENDCASE

ENDIF

 Thisform.setall("ReadOnly", .F. ,"TEXTBOX")
 TMP_NEW_MODE = "CPY"
 THISFORM.LABEL_MODE.CAPTION = TMP_NEW_MODE
 TMP_SEL_REC = THISFORM.AOD_08_KEY_FLD_TXT_VALUE()

 IF TMP_MODE = "ADD"  OR TMP_MODE = "CPY"
    TMP_MODE = TMP_NEW_MODE
    TMP_MAIN_FV = THISFORM.AF02_MAIN_FILE_VIEW_NAME(TMP_MODE)

    IF  TMP_MAIN_FV = "N"
    ELSE
       Thisform.B03_VIEW_PROCESS_MODE(TMP_MODE)
    ENDIF

 ELSE
   CLOSE DATABASES
   TMP_CONTINUE = .T.
   TMP_CONTINUE = THISFORM.B70_PROCESS_INIT(TMP_NEW_MODE, ;
                                          TMP_SEL_REC)
 ENDIF

 THISFORM.REFRESH


*==============================================================*
* Procedure: B80_PB_CANCEL                                     *
*                                                              *
*==============================================================*
 CLOSE DATABASES
 SET SYSMENU ON
 THISFORM.RELEASE


*==============================================================*
* Procedure: B83_PB_COPY                                       *
*                                                              *
*==============================================================*
 LPARAMETERS TMP_NAV

 THISFORM.B79_PB_CHG_MODE_CPY
```

```
*==============================================================*
* Procedure: B86_PB_ADD                                        *
*                                                              *
*==============================================================*
 LPARAMETERS TMP_NAV

 THISFORM.B76_PB_CHG_MODE_ADD



*==============================================================*
* Procedure: B87_PB_SAVE                                       *
*                                                              *
*==============================================================*
 LPARAMETERS TMP_NAV
 LOCAL TMP_MODE

 TMP_MODE = THISFORM.LABEL_MODE.CAPTION

 DO CASE
 CASE TMP_MODE = "ADD"  OR TMP_MODE = "CPY"
    THISFORM.B16_SAVE_WITH_ADD(TMP_NAV)

 CASE TMP_MODE = "CHG"
    THISFORM.B17_SAVE_WITH_CHG(TMP_NAV)

 CASE TMP_MODE = "DEL"
    THISFORM.B18_SAVE_WITH_DEL(TMP_NAV)

 ENDCASE

 SET SYSMENU ON


*==============================================================*
* Procedure: B88_PB_PRINT                                      *
*                                                              *
*==============================================================*
```

```
*=============================================================*
* Procedure : AD01_FORMS_PROPERTIES                           *
*                                                             *
* Description: The following form properties are changed     *
*              using the Property Window:                     *
*                                                             *
*                ShowWindow  = 1 In Top Level Form            *
*                WindowType  = 1 Modal                        *
*                DataSession = 2 Private Data Session         *
*                                                             *
*                Height= 419, Width= 620, Top = 0, Left = 0   *
*                                                             *
*=============================================================*



*=============================================================*
* Procedure: AD03_CALL_PICKLIST_FORM                          *
*                                                             *
*=============================================================*
 Lparameters textbox_id

 Local rtn_pl
 rtn_pl = "CANCEL"

 DO CASE
 CASE textbox_id = "TXTBOX_01"
   *    DO FORM ____PLST.SCX  WITH " " TO rtn_pl
             *===========
 CASE textbox_id = "TXTBOX_02"
   *    DO FORM ____PLST.SCX  WITH " " TO rtn_pl

 CASE textbox_id = "TXTBOX_03"
   *    DO FORM ____PLST.SCX  WITH " " TO rtn_pl

 CASE textbox_id = "TXTBOX_04"
   *    DO FORM ____PLST.SCX  WITH " " TO rtn_pl

 CASE textbox_id = "TXTBOX_05"
   *    DO FORM ____PLST.SCX  WITH " " TO rtn_pl

 CASE textbox_id = "TXTBOX_06"
   *    DO FORM ____PLST.SCX  WITH " " TO rtn_pl

 CASE textbox_id = "TXTBOX_07"
   *    DO FORM ____PLST.SCX  WITH " " TO rtn_pl

 CASE textbox_id = "TXTBOX_08"
   *    DO FORM ____PLST.SCX  WITH " " TO rtn_pl
```

```
CASE textbox_id = "TXTBOX_09"
  *     DO FORM ____PLST.SCX  WITH " " TO rtn_pl

CASE textbox_id = "TXTBOX_10"
  *     DO FORM ____PLST.SCX  WITH " " TO rtn_pl

CASE textbox_id = "TXTBOX_11"
  *     DO FORM ____PLST.SCX  WITH " " TO rtn_pl
           *===========
CASE textbox_id = "TXTBOX_12"
  *     DO FORM ____PLST.SCX  WITH " " TO rtn_pl

CASE textbox_id = "TXTBOX_13"
  *     DO FORM ____PLST.SCX  WITH " " TO rtn_pl

CASE textbox_id = "TXTBOX_14"
  *     DO FORM ____PLST.SCX  WITH " " TO rtn_pl

CASE textbox_id = "TXTBOX_15"
  *     DO FORM ____PLST.SCX  WITH " " TO rtn_pl

CASE textbox_id = "TXTBOX_16"
  *     DO FORM ____PLST.SCX  WITH " " TO rtn_pl

CASE textbox_id = "TXTBOX_17"
  *     DO FORM ____PLST.SCX  WITH " " TO rtn_pl

CASE textbox_id = "TXTBOX_18"
  *     DO FORM ____PLST.SCX  WITH " " TO rtn_pl

CASE textbox_id = "TXTBOX_19"
  *     DO FORM ____PLST.SCX  WITH " " TO rtn_pl

CASE textbox_id = "TXTBOX_20"
  *     DO FORM ____PLST.SCX  WITH " " TO rtn_pl

ENDCASE

RETURN rtn_pl


*============================================================*
* Procedure: AD04_TEXTBOX_VALID_RTN_VALUE                    *
*                                                            *
*============================================================*
Lparameters textbox_id, textbox_val
Local p_val1, rtn, parm_view, rtv_value, fld_seq
```

Source Code

```
DO CASE
CASE textbox_id = "TXTBOX_0?"       && ________ Code
                  *=========

  parm_view     = "V_???_RTV_DSP"  && Parameterized View
* RTV_???_CODE  = textbox_val      && View Parameter
  *============================    && Change to Numeric if...
                                   && Ex. = VAL(textbox_val)
  SELECT &parm_view
  USE
  SELECT 0
  USE &parm_view ALIAS &parm_view
  CursorSetProp('Buffering', 5)    && Optimistic Table Buff.


  IF BOF() and EOF()
   *
    rtn         = .F.
    fld_seq     = 1
    rtv_value   = " "
    Thisform.aod_07_textbox_val_rtn_inf(textbox_id, ;
                                    rtv_value, fld_seq)

  ELSE

    rtn         = .T.
    fld_seq     = 1
 *  rtv_value   = V_???_RTV_DSP.???_DESC
                  *=====================
    Thisform.aod_07_textbox_val_rtn_inf(textbox_id, ;
                                    rtv_value, fld_seq)
  ENDIF
  RETURN rtn

*---------------------------------------------------------------
*---------------------------------------------------------------

CASE textbox_id = "TXTBOX_0?"       && ____ Code
                  *=========

  parm_view     = "V_???_RTV_DSP"  && Parameterized View
* RTV_???_CODE  = textbox_val      && View Parameter
  *============================    && Change to Numeric if...
                                   && Ex. = VAL(textbox_val)
  SELECT &parm_view
  USE
  SELECT 0
  USE &parm_view ALIAS &parm_view
  CursorSetProp('Buffering', 5)
```

```
  IF BOF() and EOF()
    *
    rtn          = .F.
    fld_seq      = 1
    rtv_value    = " "
    Thisform.aod_07_textbox_val_rtn_inf(textbox_id, ;
                                        rtv_value, fld_seq)

  ELSE

    rtn          = .T.
    fld_seq      = 1
  * rtv_value    = V_???_RTV_DSP.???_DESC
                   *======================


    Thisform.aod_07_textbox_val_rtn_inf(textbox_id, ;
                                        rtv_value, fld_seq)

  ENDIF

  RETURN rtn

*---------------------------------------------------------------
*---------------------------------------------------------------

CASE textbox_id = "TXTBOX_0?"         && ____ Code
                  *==========

  parm_view     = "V_???_RTV_DSP"   && Parameterized View
* RTV_???_CODE  = VAL(textbox_val)  && View Parameter
  *=============================     && Change to Numeric if...
                                    && Ex. = VAL(textbox_val)

  SELECT &parm_view
  USE
  SELECT 0
  USE &parm_view ALIAS &parm_view
  CursorSetProp('buffering', 5)     && Optimistic Table Buf.

  IF BOF() and EOF()
    *
    rtn          = .F.
    fld_seq      = 1
    rtv_value    = " "

    Thisform.aod_07_textbox_val_rtn_inf(textbox_id, ;
                                        rtv_value, fld_seq)
    fld_seq      = 2
```

```
    rtv_value     = " "
    Thisform.aod_07_textbox_val_rtn_inf(textbox_id, ;
                                         rtv_value, fld_seq)

    fld_seq       = 3
    rtv_value     = " "
    Thisform.aod_07_textbox_val_rtn_inf(textbox_id, ;
                                         rtv_value, fld_seq)

  ELSE

    rtn           = .T.
    fld_seq       = 1
  * rtv_value     = V_???_RTV_DSP.???_NAME
                    *======================
    Thisform.aod_07_textbox_val_rtn_inf(textbox_id, ;
                                         rtv_value, fld_seq)

    fld_seq       = 2
  * rtv_value     = V_???_RTV_DSP.???_CONTAC
                    *========================
    Thisform.aod_07_textbox_val_rtn_inf(textbox_id, ;
                                         rtv_value, fld_seq)

    fld_seq       = 3
  * rtv_value     = V_???_RTV_DSP.???_PHONE
                    *=======================
    Thisform.aod_07_textbox_val_rtn_inf(textbox_id, ;
                                         rtv_value, fld_seq)

  ENDIF
  RETURN rtn

ENDCASE


*============================================================*
* Procedure: AD05_BEFORE_INIT                                *
*                                                            *
*============================================================*
 Public PVP_COL_1    && Parameterized View Parameter Main View
        *========

* Public RTV_REG_CODE  && View Parameter: Region Code Field
                       && For view       : V_REG_RTV_DSP
* Public RTV_???_CODE  && View Parameter: Pick-List #2 - _____
* Public RTV_???_CODE  && View Parameter: Pick-List #3 - _____
         *===========
```

```
*==============================================================*
* Procedure: AD06_AFTER_INIT                                   *
*                                                              *
*==============================================================*
 LOCAL MODE

 MODE = THISFORM.LABEL_MODE.CAPTION


 IF MODE = "ADD"
   THISFORM.PBG_SAVE_CANCEL_MORE1.COMMAND3.VISIBLE = .T.
 ELSE
   THISFORM.PBG_SAVE_CANCEL_MORE1.COMMAND3.VISIBLE = .F.
 ENDIF


 IF MODE = "DEL" OR MODE = "DSP" && Push Button: COPY
   THISFORM.PBG_SAVE_CANCEL_MORE1.COMMAND4.VISIBLE = .F.
 ELSE
   THISFORM.PBG_SAVE_CANCEL_MORE1.COMMAND4.VISIBLE = .T.
 ENDIF


 IF MODE = "ADD"  OR MODE = "CPY"
     THISFORM.PBG_NAVIGATION_H1.ENABLED = .F.
 ELSE
     THISFORM.PBG_NAVIGATION_H1.ENABLED = .T.
 ENDIF


*==============================================================*
* Procedure: AD07_CLEANUP                                      *
*                                                              *
*==============================================================*

*-----------------------------------------
*  Used With Grids:
*-----------------------------------------
*  LOCAL view_grid

*  view_grid = "V_???_CHG"

*   IF TableUpdate(2, .F., VIEW_GRID)
*      wait window nowait " Record Saved."
*   ELSE
*      TableRevert(.F., VIEW_GRID)
*      = messagebox("Record Not Saved.")
*   ENDIF
```

```
*=============================================================*
* Procedure: AD08_FORM_CAPTION                                *
*                                                             *
* Note : The application will execute a default procedure    *
*        if this method is left blank.                        *
*=============================================================*
 LOCAL MODE

 MODE = THISFORM.LABEL_MODE.CAPTION

 DO CASE
 CASE MODE = "ADD"
   THISFORM.Caption = DE_FRM_CAPTION_ADD_MODE

 CASE MODE = "CHG"
   THISFORM.Caption = DE_FRM_CAPTION_CHG_MODE

 CASE MODE = "DSP"
   THISFORM.Caption = DE_FRM_CAPTION_DSP_MODE

 CASE MODE = "DEL"
   THISFORM.Caption = DE_FRM_CAPTION_DEL_MODE

 CASE MODE = "CPY"
   THISFORM.Caption = DE_FRM_CAPTION_CPY_MODE

 ENDCASE


*=============================================================*
* Procedure: AF01_OPEN_DATABASE                               *
*                                                             *
*=============================================================*
LOCAL dbase1

     dbase1  = DE_DATABASE
              *===========
OPEN DATABASE &dbase1
Nodefault



*=============================================================*
* Procedure: AF02_MAIN_FILE_VIEW_NAME                         *
*                                                             *
*=============================================================*
LPARAMETERS mode
LOCAL view_add, view_chg, view_dsp, view_del, main_view
```

```
   view_add = DE_VIEW_ADD    && Parameterized View or "N"
   view_chg = DE_VIEW_CHG    &&    "
   view_dsp = DE_VIEW_DSP    &&    "
   view_del = DE_VIEW_DEL    &&    "
             *============


*----------------------------
* Do not change code below.
*----------------------------

DO CASE
CASE mode = "ADD"  or mode = "CPY"
   main_view = view_add

CASE mode = "CHG"
   main_view = view_chg

CASE mode = "DSP"
   main_view = view_dsp

CASE mode = "DEL"
   main_view = view_del

ENDCASE

RETURN main_view


*==============================================================*
* Procedure: AF03_MAIN_FILE_VIEW_KEY_VALUE                     *
*                                                              *
*==============================================================*
LPARAMETERS selected_rec

ON ERROR DO ERROR_PROC_01

DO CASE
CASE DE_TABLE_FLD1_TYPE = "CHR"
                            PVP_COL_1 = Alltrim(selected_rec)
CASE DE_TABLE_FLD1_TYPE = "NUM"
                            PVP_COL_1 = VAL(selected_rec)
CASE DE_TABLE_FLD1_TYPE = "DATE"
                            PVP_COL_1 = CTOD(selected_rec)
ENDCASE


RETURN PVP_COL_1
      *=========
```

```
*=============================================================*
* Procedure: AF04_OPEN_OTHER_FILES_VIEWS                       *
*                                                              *
*=============================================================*
 LOCAL nav_src_sort1_A, nav_src_sort1_d
 * LOCAL File1, File2, File3

 *----------------------------------
 * Views to Retrieve Information:
 *----------------------------------
 * File1           = "V_???_RTV_DSP"
 * File2           = "V_???_RTV_DSP"
 * File3           = "V_???_RTV_DSP"

 *----------------------------------
 * View for Navigation Push Buttons:
 *----------------------------------
 nav_src_sort1_a = DE_VIEW_SORT_A     && ASCENDING
 nav_src_sort1_d = DE_VIEW_SORT_D     && DESCENDING
                 *==============

 *=============================================================
 * FOR NAVIGATION PUSH BUTTONS
 *=============================================================
 SELECT 0
 USE &NAV_SRC_SORT1_A  ALIAS  &NAV_SRC_SORT1_A  NODATA
 CURSORSETPROP('BUFFERING', 5)  && Optimistic Table Buffering
*-------------------------------------------------------------
 SELECT 0
 USE &NAV_SRC_SORT1_D  ALIAS  &NAV_SRC_SORT1_D  NODATA
 CURSORSETPROP('BUFFERING', 5)  && Optimistic Table Buffering
 *-------------------------------------------------------------


 *=============================================================
 * To Retrieve Information:
 *=============================================================
 * SELECT 0
 * USE &File1 ALIAS &File1  NODATA
 * CURSORSETPROP('BUFFERING', 5)  && Optimistic Table Buff.
 *-------------------------------------------------------------
 *-------------------------------------------------------------
 * SELECT 0
 * USE &File2 ALIAS &File2 NODATA
 * CURSORSETPROP('BUFFERING', 5)  && Optimistic Table Buff.
 *-------------------------------------------------------------
 *-------------------------------------------------------------
 * SELECT 0
 * USE &File3 ALIAS &File3  NODATA
 * CURSORSETPROP('BUFFERING', 5)  && Optimistic Table Buff.
```

```
*-------------------------------------------------------------
NODEFAULT


*==============================================================*
* Procedure: AF05_SELECT_NAVIGATION_IDX_VIEW                   *
*                                                              *
*==============================================================*
Lparameters order_seq      && (A/D)

Local nav_view, sort_field
Local nav_src_sort1_a, nav_src_sort1_d
Local rec_key_1

*------------------------------------------
* Parameterized views used for navigation:
*------------------------------------------
nav_src_sort1_a = DE_VIEW_SORT_A  && Ascending
                  *==============

nav_src_sort1_d = DE_VIEW_SORT_D  && Descending
                  *==============
*----------------------------------------

rec_key_1 = Thisform.aod_08_key_fld_txt_value(.F.)

ON ERROR DO ERROR_PROC_01

DO CASE
CASE DE_TABLE_FLD1_TYPE = "CHR"
                          PVP_COL_1 = REC_KEY_1
CASE DE_TABLE_FLD1_TYPE = "NUM"
                          PVP_COL_1 = VAL(Alltrim(REC_KEY_1))
CASE DE_TABLE_FLD1_TYPE = "DATE"
                          PVP_COL_1 = CTOD(REC_KEY_1)
ENDCASE


DO CASE
CASE order_seq = "A"
                     nav_view = nav_src_sort1_a
CASE order_seq = "D"
                     nav_view = nav_src_sort1_d
ENDCASE

SELECT &nav_view
USE
SELECT 0
USE &nav_view ALIAS &nav_view
CursorSetProp('BUFFERING', 5)  && Optimistic Table Buff.
```

```
*==============================================================*
* Procedure: AF06_TABLE_UPDATE                                 *
*                                                              *
* Note: Use the AOD_04_VALIDATE Method to update files.       *
*==============================================================*
 LPARAMETERS NA
* LOCAL FILE1
* FILE1 = "__________"
         *==========

* BEGIN TRANSACTION
* IF TABLEUPDATE(.F.,.F.,FILE1)
*    END TRANSACTION
*    RETURN .T.
* ELSE
*    THISFORM.AF07_TABLE_REVERT
*    RETURN .F.
* ENDIF



*==============================================================*
* Procedure: AF07_TABLE_REVERT                                 *
*                                                              *
* For transactions, use ROLLBACK, otherwise use TableRevert.  *
*==============================================================*

 *-----------------------------------------------------
 * Using UPDATE with transactions:
 *-----------------------------------------------------
 * LOCAL ERR, ERR_MSG

 * ROLLBACK
 * = AERROR(aErrors)
 * ERR = STR(aErrors[1, 1])
 * ERR_MSG = "Error No.: " + ERR
 * = Messagebox( "Record Not Saved." + ERR_MSG)

 *-----------------------------------------------------
 * Using UPDATE without using transactions:
 *-----------------------------------------------------
 * LOCAL   FILE1

 * FILE1  = "_______ "
          *=======
 * TABLEREVERT(.F., FILE1)
```

```
*==========================================================*
* Procedure: AO01_SET_PB_DSP_MODE                          *
*                                                          *
*==========================================================*

Thisform.PBG_SAVE_CANCEL_MORE1.Command1.Visible  = .F. && Save
Thisform.PBG_SAVE_CANCEL_MORE1.TabIndex = 1 && Cancel-SetFocus
       *=====================



*==========================================================*
* Procedure: AO02_SET_PB_DEL_MODE                          *
*                                                          *
*==========================================================*

Thisform.PBG_SAVE_CANCEL_MORE1.Command1.Caption  = "DELETE"
Thisform.PBG_SAVE_CANCEL_MORE1.Command1.Visible  = .T.
Thisform.PBG_SAVE_CANCEL_MORE1.TabIndex = 1
       *=====================



*==========================================================*
* Procedure: AO03_SET_PB_CHG_MODE                          *
*                                                          *
*==========================================================*

Thisform.PBG_SAVE_CANCEL_MORE1.Command1.Caption  = "SAVE"
Thisform.PBG_SAVE_CANCEL_MORE1.Command1.Visible  = .T.
Thisform.PBG_SAVE_CANCEL_MORE1.TabIndex = 1
       *=====================



*==========================================================*
* Procedure: AOD_01_SET_DSP                                *
*                                                          *
*==========================================================*

 *---------------------------------------------------
 * Format for Text Box: Text21 - Region Description
 * Retrieved from View:  V_REG_RTV_DSP
 *---------------------------------------------------
 * Thisform.CONTAIN_TXTLBL_201.text21.FORMAT  = "XXXXXXXXXXXXXX
XXXXXXXXXXXXXXXXXXXXXXXXXX"

 *---------------------------------------------------
 * Format for Text Box: Text21 - Category Description
```

```
 * Retrieved from View:  V_CAT_RTV_DSP
 *-----------------------------------------------------------
 * Thisform.CONTAIN_TXTLBL_201.text21.FORMAT  = "XXXXXXXXXXXXXX
XXXXXXXXXXXXXXXXXXXXXXXXXX"

 *-----------------------------------------------------------
 * Format for Text Box: Text22 - Type Description
 * Retrieved from View:  V_TYP_RTV_DSP
 *-----------------------------------------------------------
 * Thisform.CONTAIN_TXTLBL_201.text22.FORMAT  = "XXXXXXXXXXXXXX
XXXXXXXXXXXXXXXXXXXXXXXXXX"

 *-----------------------------------------------------------
 * Format for Text Boxes: Text23, Text24, Text25 -
 *                         Name,   Contact, Phone
 * Retrieved from View:  V_VND_RTV_DSP
 *-----------------------------------------------------------
 * Thisform.CONTAIN_TXTLBL_201.text23.FORMAT  = "XXXXXXXXXXXXXX
XXXXXXXXXXXXXXXXXXXXXXXXXX"
 * Thisform.CONTAIN_TXTLBL_201.text24.FORMAT  = "XXXXXXXXXXXXXX
XXXXXXXXXXXXXXXXXXXXXXXXXX"



*===============================================================*
* Procedure   : AOD_02_Get_Val                                  *
* Description: Moves values from table to text boxes.           *
*             All values are changed to character string.       *
*             For example: text1.value= STR(vnd_code, 3, 0)     *
*===============================================================*
 LOCAL mode, na
 mode = Thisform.LABEL_MODE.Caption

 *-----------------------------------------------------------------
 * Get Description from View:
 *-----------------------------------------------------------------
 * LOCAL chr_reg   && Pick-List Text Box Value -Region Code
 * LOCAL chr_cat   && Pick-List Text Box Value -Category (CHR)
 * LOCAL chr_typ   && Pick-List Text Box Value -Type     (CHR)
 * LOCAL chr_vnd   && Pick-List Text Box Value -Vendor   (CHR)

 * chr_reg    = CUS_REGION  && Table Field Name (Customer Tab.)
                            && Converted to Character.
                            && Ex.: chr_??? =STR(cus_reg, 3, 0)

 * chr_cat  = P_CATEGORY
 * chr_typ  = P_TYPE
 * chr_vnd  = STR(P_VENDOR, 3, 0)  && Converted to Character!

* THISFORM.B13_SELECT_MAIN_FILE_VIEW(mode)
```

```
* na = THISFORM.AD04_TEXT_VALID_RTN_VALUE("TXTBOX_04", chr_cat)

* THISFORM.B13_SELECT_MAIN_FILE_VIEW(mode)
* na = THISFORM.AD04_TEXT_VALID_RTN_VALUE("TXTBOX_05", chr_typ)

* THISFORM.B13_SELECT_MAIN_FILE_VIEW(mode)
* na = THISFORM.AD04_TEXT_VALID_RTN_VALUE("TXTBOX_06", chr_vnd)

*==============================================================*
*
*==============================================================*
Local xWidth, xDec

xWidth = 0
xDec   = 0

Thisform.B13_SELECT_MAIN_FILE_VIEW(mode)

IF DE_QTY_TXTFLDS >= 1
 DO CASE
 CASE DE_TABLE_FLD1_TYPE = "CHR"
   Thisform.CONTAIN_TXTLBL_201.Text1.Value = &DE_TABLE_FLD_
NAME_1

 CASE DE_TABLE_FLD1_TYPE = "NUM"
                               xWidth = DE_NUM_FLD1_WIDTH
                               xDec   = DE_NUM_FLD1_DECIMALS
   Thisform.CONTAIN_TXTLBL_201.Text1.Value = STR( ;
                         &DE_TABLE_FLD_NAME_1, xWidth, xDec)
 CASE DE_TABLE_FLD1_TYPE = "DATE"
   Thisform.CONTAIN_TXTLBL_201.Text1.Value = DTOC( ;
                                       &DE_TABLE_FLD_NAME_1)
 ENDCASE
ENDIF

IF DE_QTY_TXTFLDS >= 2
 DO CASE
 CASE DE_TABLE_FLD2_TYPE = "CHR"
   Thisform.CONTAIN_TXTLBL_201.Text2.Value = ;
                                        &DE_TABLE_FLD_NAME_2
 CASE DE_TABLE_FLD2_TYPE = "NUM"
                               xWidth = DE_NUM_FLD2_WIDTH
                               xDec   = DE_NUM_FLD2_DECIMALS
   Thisform.CONTAIN_TXTLBL_201.Text2.Value = STR( ;
                         &DE_TABLE_FLD_NAME_2, xWidth, xDec)
 CASE DE_TABLE_FLD2_TYPE = "DATE"
   Thisform.CONTAIN_TXTLBL_201.Text2.Value = DTOC( ;
                                       &DE_TABLE_FLD_NAME_2)
 ENDCASE
ENDIF
```

```
If DE_QTY_TXTFLDS >= 3
 DO CASE
 CASE DE_TABLE_FLD3_TYPE = "CHR"
   Thisform.CONTAIN_TXTLBL_201.Text3.Value = ;
                                               &DE_TABLE_FLD_NAME_3
 CASE DE_TABLE_FLD3_TYPE = "NUM"
                               xWidth = DE_NUM_FLD3_WIDTH
                               xDec   = DE_NUM_FLD3_DECIMALS
   Thisform.CONTAIN_TXTLBL_201.Text3.Value = STR( ;
                         &DE_TABLE_FLD_NAME_3, xWidth, xDec)
 CASE DE_TABLE_FLD3_TYPE = "DATE"
   Thisform.CONTAIN_TXTLBL_201.Text3.Value = DTOC( ;
                                       &DE_TABLE_FLD_NAME_3)
 ENDCASE
Endif

If DE_QTY_TXTFLDS >= 4
 DO CASE
 CASE DE_TABLE_FLD4_TYPE = "CHR"
   Thisform.CONTAIN_TXTLBL_201.Text4.Value = ;
                                               &DE_TABLE_FLD_NAME_4

 CASE DE_TABLE_FLD4_TYPE = "NUM"
                               xWidth = DE_NUM_FLD4_WIDTH
                               xDec   = DE_NUM_FLD4_DECIMALS
   Thisform.CONTAIN_TXTLBL_201.Text4.Value = STR( ;
                         &DE_TABLE_FLD_NAME_4, xWidth, xDec)
 CASE DE_TABLE_FLD4_TYPE = "DATE"
   Thisform.CONTAIN_TXTLBL_201.Text4.Value = DTOC( ;
                                       &DE_TABLE_FLD_NAME_4)
 ENDCASE
Endif

If DE_QTY_TXTFLDS >= 5
 DO CASE
 CASE DE_TABLE_FLD5_TYPE = "CHR"
   Thisform.CONTAIN_TXTLBL_201.Text5.Value = ;
                                              &DE_TABLE_FLD_NAME_5
 CASE DE_TABLE_FLD5_TYPE = "NUM"
                               xWidth = DE_NUM_FLD5_WIDTH
                               xDec   = DE_NUM_FLD5_DECIMALS
   Thisform.CONTAIN_TXTLBL_201.Text5.Value = STR( ;
                         &DE_TABLE_FLD_NAME_5, xWidth, xDec)
 CASE DE_TABLE_FLD5_TYPE = "DATE"
   Thisform.CONTAIN_TXTLBL_201.Text5.Value = DTOC( ;
                                       &DE_TABLE_FLD_NAME_5)
 ENDCASE
Endif
```

```
If DE_QTY_TXTFLDS >= 6
 DO CASE
 CASE DE_TABLE_FLD6_TYPE = "CHR"
   Thisform.CONTAIN_TXTLBL_201.Text6.Value = ;
                                      &DE_TABLE_FLD_NAME_6
 CASE DE_TABLE_FLD6_TYPE = "NUM"
                              xWidth = DE_NUM_FLD6_WIDTH
                              xDec   = DE_NUM_FLD6_DECIMALS
   Thisform.CONTAIN_TXTLBL_201.Text6.Value = STR( ;
                         &DE_TABLE_FLD_NAME_6, xWidth, xDec)
 CASE DE_TABLE_FLD6_TYPE = "DATE"
   Thisform.CONTAIN_TXTLBL_201.Text6.Value = DTOC( ;
                                     &DE_TABLE_FLD_NAME_6)
 ENDCASE
Endif

If DE_QTY_TXTFLDS >= 7
 DO CASE
 CASE DE_TABLE_FLD7_TYPE = "CHR"
   Thisform.CONTAIN_TXTLBL_201.Text7.Value = ;
                                      &DE_TABLE_FLD_NAME_7


 CASE DE_TABLE_FLD7_TYPE = "NUM"
                              xWidth = DE_NUM_FLD7_WIDTH
                              xDec   = DE_NUM_FLD7_DECIMALS
   Thisform.CONTAIN_TXTLBL_201.Text7.Value = STR( ;
                         &DE_TABLE_FLD_NAME_7, xWidth, xDec)
 CASE DE_TABLE_FLD7_TYPE = "DATE"
   Thisform.CONTAIN_TXTLBL_201.Text7.Value = DTOC( ;
                                    &DE_TABLE_FLD_NAME_7)
 ENDCASE
Endif

If DE_QTY_TXTFLDS >= 8
 DO CASE
 CASE DE_TABLE_FLD8_TYPE = "CHR"
   Thisform.CONTAIN_TXTLBL_201.Text8.Value = ;
                                      &DE_TABLE_FLD_NAME_8
 CASE DE_TABLE_FLD8_TYPE = "NUM"
                              xWidth = DE_NUM_FLD8_WIDTH
                              xDec   = DE_NUM_FLD8_DECIMALS
   Thisform.CONTAIN_TXTLBL_201.Text8.Value = STR( ;
                         &DE_TABLE_FLD_NAME_8, xWidth, xDec)
 CASE DE_TABLE_FLD8_TYPE = "DATE"
   Thisform.CONTAIN_TXTLBL_201.Text8.Value = DTOC( ;
                                     &DE_TABLE_FLD_NAME_8)
 ENDCASE
Endif
```

```
If DE_QTY_TXTFLDS >= 9
 DO CASE
 CASE DE_TABLE_FLD9_TYPE = "CHR"
   Thisform.CONTAIN_TXTLBL_201.Text9.Value = ;
                                       &DE_TABLE_FLD_NAME_9
 CASE DE_TABLE_FLD9_TYPE = "NUM"
                              xWidth = DE_NUM_FLD9_WIDTH
                              xDec   = DE_NUM_FLD9_DECIMALS
   Thisform.CONTAIN_TXTLBL_201.Text9.Value = STR( ;
                         &DE_TABLE_FLD_NAME_9, xWidth, xDec)
 CASE DE_TABLE_FLD9_TYPE = "DATE"
   Thisform.CONTAIN_TXTLBL_201.Text9.Value = DTOC( ;
                                      &DE_TABLE_FLD_NAME_9)
 ENDCASE
Endif

If DE_QTY_TXTFLDS >= 10
 DO CASE
 CASE DE_TABLE_FLD10_TYPE = "CHR"
   Thisform.CONTAIN_TXTLBL_201.Text10.Value = ;
                                       &DE_TABLE_FLD_NAME_10

 CASE DE_TABLE_FLD10_TYPE = "NUM"
                              xWidth = DE_NUM_FLD10_WIDTH
                              xDec   = DE_NUM_FLD10_DECIMALS
   Thisform.CONTAIN_TXTLBL_201.Text10.Value = STR( ;
                         &DE_TABLE_FLD_NAME_10, xWidth, xDec)
 CASE DE_TABLE_FLD10_TYPE = "DATE"
   Thisform.CONTAIN_TXTLBL_201.Text10.Value = DTOC( ;
                                      &DE_TABLE_FLD_NAME_10)
 ENDCASE
Endif

IF DE_QTY_TXTFLDS >= 11
 DO CASE
 CASE DE_TABLE_FLD11_TYPE = "CHR"
   Thisform.CONTAIN_TXTLBL_201.Text11.Value = ;
                                       &DE_TABLE_FLD_NAME_11
 CASE DE_TABLE_FLD11_TYPE = "NUM"
                              xWidth = DE_NUM_FLD11_WIDTH
                              xDec   = DE_NUM_FLD11_DECIMALS
   Thisform.CONTAIN_TXTLBL_201.Text11.Value = STR( ;
                         &DE_TABLE_FLD_NAME_11, xWidth, xDec)
 CASE DE_TABLE_FLD11_TYPE = "DATE"
   Thisform.CONTAIN_TXTLBL_201.Text11.Value = DTOC( ;
                                      &DE_TABLE_FLD_NAME_11)
 ENDCASE
ENDIF

IF DE_QTY_TXTFLDS >= 12
```

```
 DO CASE
 CASE DE_TABLE_FLD12_TYPE = "CHR"
   Thisform.CONTAIN_TXTLBL_201.Text12.Value = ;
                                             &DE_TABLE_FLD_NAME_12
 CASE DE_TABLE_FLD12_TYPE = "NUM"
                              xWidth = DE_NUM_FLD12_WIDTH
                              xDec   = DE_NUM_FLD12_DECIMALS
   Thisform.CONTAIN_TXTLBL_201.Text12.Value = STR( ;
                        &DE_TABLE_FLD_NAME_12, xWidth, xDec)
 CASE DE_TABLE_FLD12_TYPE = "DATE"
   Thisform.CONTAIN_TXTLBL_201.Text12.Value = DTOC( ;
                                            &DE_TABLE_FLD_NAME_12)
 ENDCASE
ENDIF

If DE_QTY_TXTFLDS >= 13
 DO CASE
 CASE DE_TABLE_FLD13_TYPE = "CHR"
   Thisform.CONTAIN_TXTLBL_201.Text13.Value = ;
                                              &DE_TABLE_FLD_NAME_13

 CASE DE_TABLE_FLD13_TYPE = "NUM"
                               xWidth = DE_NUM_FLD13_WIDTH
                               xDec   = DE_NUM_FLD13_DECIMALS
   Thisform.CONTAIN_TXTLBL_201.Text13.Value = STR( ;
                        &DE_TABLE_FLD_NAME_13, xWidth, xDec)
 CASE DE_TABLE_FLD13_TYPE = "DATE"
   Thisform.CONTAIN_TXTLBL_201.Text13.Value = DTOC( ;
                                            &DE_TABLE_FLD_NAME_13)
 ENDCASE
Endif


If DE_QTY_TXTFLDS >= 14
 DO CASE
 CASE DE_TABLE_FLD14_TYPE = "CHR"
   Thisform.CONTAIN_TXTLBL_201.Text14.Value = ;
                                             &DE_TABLE_FLD_NAME_14
 CASE DE_TABLE_FLD14_TYPE = "NUM"
                              xWidth = DE_NUM_FLD14_WIDTH
                              xDec   = DE_NUM_FLD14_DECIMALS
   Thisform.CONTAIN_TXTLBL_201.Text14.Value = STR( ;
                        &DE_TABLE_FLD_NAME_14, xWidth, xDec)
 CASE DE_TABLE_FLD14_TYPE = "DATE"
   Thisform.CONTAIN_TXTLBL_201.Text14.Value = DTOC( ;
                                            &DE_TABLE_FLD_NAME_14)
 ENDCASE
Endif

If DE_QTY_TXTFLDS >= 15
```

```
 DO CASE
 CASE DE_TABLE_FLD15_TYPE = "CHR"
   Thisform.CONTAIN_TXTLBL_201.Text15.Value = ;
                                            &DE_TABLE_FLD_NAME_15
 CASE DE_TABLE_FLD15_TYPE = "NUM"
                               xWidth = DE_NUM_FLD15_WIDTH
                               xDec   = DE_NUM_FLD15_DECIMALS
   Thisform.CONTAIN_TXTLBL_201.Text15.Value = STR( ;
                         &DE_TABLE_FLD_NAME_15, xWidth, xDec)
 CASE DE_TABLE_FLD15_TYPE = "DATE"
   Thisform.CONTAIN_TXTLBL_201.Text15.Value = DTOC( ;
                                           &DE_TABLE_FLD_NAME_15)
 ENDCASE
Endif

If DE_QTY_TXTFLDS >= 16
 DO CASE
 CASE DE_TABLE_FLD16_TYPE = "CHR"
   Thisform.CONTAIN_TXTLBL_201.Text16.Value = ;
                                            &DE_TABLE_FLD_NAME_16

 CASE DE_TABLE_FLD16_TYPE = "NUM"
                               xWidth = DE_NUM_FLD16_WIDTH
                               xDec   = DE_NUM_FLD16_DECIMALS
   Thisform.CONTAIN_TXTLBL_201.Text16.Value = STR( ;
                         &DE_TABLE_FLD_NAME_16, xWidth, xDec)
 CASE DE_TABLE_FLD16_TYPE = "DATE"
   Thisform.CONTAIN_TXTLBL_201.Text16.Value = DTOC( ;
                                           &DE_TABLE_FLD_NAME_16)
 ENDCASE
Endif

If DE_QTY_TXTFLDS >= 17
 DO CASE
 CASE DE_TABLE_FLD17_TYPE = "CHR"
   Thisform.CONTAIN_TXTLBL_201.Text17.Value = ;
                                            &DE_TABLE_FLD_NAME_17
 CASE DE_TABLE_FLD17_TYPE = "NUM"
                               xWidth = DE_NUM_FLD17_WIDTH
                               xDec   = DE_NUM_FLD17_DECIMALS
   Thisform.CONTAIN_TXTLBL_201.Text17.Value = STR( ;
                         &DE_TABLE_FLD_NAME_17, xWidth, xDec)
 CASE DE_TABLE_FLD17_TYPE = "DATE"
   Thisform.CONTAIN_TXTLBL_201.Text17.Value = DTOC( ;
                                           &DE_TABLE_FLD_NAME_17)
 ENDCASE
Endif

If DE_QTY_TXTFLDS >= 18
 DO CASE
```

```
 CASE DE_TABLE_FLD18_TYPE = "CHR"
   Thisform.CONTAIN_TXTLBL_201.Text18.Value = ;
                                           &DE_TABLE_FLD_NAME_18
 CASE DE_TABLE_FLD18_TYPE = "NUM"
                              xWidth = DE_NUM_FLD18_WIDTH
                              xDec   = DE_NUM_FLD18_DECIMALS
   Thisform.CONTAIN_TXTLBL_201.Text18.Value = STR( ;
                         &DE_TABLE_FLD_NAME_18, xWidth, xDec)
 CASE DE_TABLE_FLD18_TYPE = "DATE"
   Thisform.CONTAIN_TXTLBL_201.Text18.Value = DTOC( ;
                                          &DE_TABLE_FLD_NAME_18)
 ENDCASE
Endif

If DE_QTY_TXTFLDS >= 19
 DO CASE
 CASE DE_TABLE_FLD19_TYPE = "CHR"
   Thisform.CONTAIN_TXTLBL_201.Text19.Value = ;
                                           &DE_TABLE_FLD_NAME_19

 CASE DE_TABLE_FLD19_TYPE = "NUM"
                              xWidth = DE_NUM_FLD19_WIDTH
                              xDec   = DE_NUM_FLD19_DECIMALS
   Thisform.CONTAIN_TXTLBL_201.Text19.Value = STR( ;
                         &DE_TABLE_FLD_NAME_19, xWidth, xDec)
 CASE DE_TABLE_FLD19_TYPE = "DATE"
   Thisform.CONTAIN_TXTLBL_201.Text19.Value = DTOC( ;
                                          &DE_TABLE_FLD_NAME_19)
 ENDCASE
Endif

If DE_QTY_TXTFLDS >= 20
 DO CASE
 CASE DE_TABLE_FLD20_TYPE = "CHR"
   Thisform.CONTAIN_TXTLBL_201.Text20.Value = ;
                                           &DE_TABLE_FLD_NAME_20
 CASE DE_TABLE_FLD20_TYPE = "NUM"
                              xWidth = DE_NUM_FLD20_WIDTH
                              xDec   = DE_NUM_FLD20_DECIMALS
   Thisform.CONTAIN_TXTLBL_201.Text20.Value = STR( ;
                         &DE_TABLE_FLD_NAME_20, xWidth, xDec)
 CASE DE_TABLE_FLD20_TYPE = "DATE"
   Thisform.CONTAIN_TXTLBL_201.Text20.Value = DTOC( ;
                                          &DE_TABLE_FLD_NAME_20)
 ENDCASE
Endif


*=============================================================*
* Procedure  : AOD_03_WRT_VAL                                 *
```

Source Code

```
* Description: Moves values from text boxes to table fields.  *
*              All values are changed to the same type.       *
*=============================================================*
LOCAL x1, x2, x3, x4, x5, x6, x7, x8, x9, x10
LOCAL x11, x12, x13, x14, x15, x16, x17, x18, x19, x20

If DE_QTY_TXTFLDS >= 1
   x1 = Thisform.CONTAIN_TXTLBL_201.Text1.Value
   DO CASE
   CASE DE_TABLE_FLD1_TYPE = "CHR"
        Replace &DE_TABLE_FLD_NAME_1 WITH x1
   CASE DE_TABLE_FLD1_TYPE = "NUM"
        Replace &DE_TABLE_FLD_NAME_1 WITH VAL(x1)
   CASE DE_TABLE_FLD1_TYPE = "DATE"
        Replace &DE_TABLE_FLD_NAME_1 WITH CTOD(x1)
   ENDCASE
Endif

If DE_QTY_TXTFLDS >= 2
   x2 = Thisform.CONTAIN_TXTLBL_201.Text2.Value
   DO CASE
   CASE DE_TABLE_FLD2_TYPE = "CHR"
        Replace &DE_TABLE_FLD_NAME_2 WITH x2
   CASE DE_TABLE_FLD2_TYPE = "NUM"
        Replace &DE_TABLE_FLD_NAME_2 WITH VAL(x2)
   CASE DE_TABLE_FLD2_TYPE = "DATE"
        Replace &DE_TABLE_FLD_NAME_2 WITH CTOD(x2)
   ENDCASE
 Endif

If DE_QTY_TXTFLDS >= 3
   x3 = Thisform.CONTAIN_TXTLBL_201.Text3.Value
   DO CASE
   CASE DE_TABLE_FLD3_TYPE = "CHR"
        Replace &DE_TABLE_FLD_NAME_3 WITH x3
   CASE DE_TABLE_FLD3_TYPE = "NUM"
        Replace &DE_TABLE_FLD_NAME_3 WITH VAL(x3)
   CASE DE_TABLE_FLD3_TYPE = "DATE"
        Replace &DE_TABLE_FLD_NAME_3 WITH CTOD(x3)
   ENDCASE
Endif

If DE_QTY_TXTFLDS >= 4
   x4 = Thisform.CONTAIN_TXTLBL_201.Text4.Value
   DO CASE
   CASE DE_TABLE_FLD4_TYPE = "CHR"
        Replace &DE_TABLE_FLD_NAME_4 WITH x4
   CASE DE_TABLE_FLD4_TYPE = "NUM"
        Replace &DE_TABLE_FLD_NAME_4 WITH VAL(x4)
   CASE DE_TABLE_FLD4_TYPE = "DATE"
```

```
        Replace &DE_TABLE_FLD_NAME_4 WITH CTOD(x4)
    ENDCASE
Endif

If DE_QTY_TXTFLDS >= 5
    x5 = Thisform.CONTAIN_TXTLBL_201.Text5.Value
    DO CASE
    CASE DE_TABLE_FLD5_TYPE = "CHR"
        Replace &DE_TABLE_FLD_NAME_5 WITH x5
    CASE DE_TABLE_FLD5_TYPE = "NUM"
        Replace &DE_TABLE_FLD_NAME_5 WITH VAL(x5)
    CASE DE_TABLE_FLD5_TYPE = "DATE"
        Replace &DE_TABLE_FLD_NAME_5 WITH CTOD(x5)
    ENDCASE
Endif

If DE_QTY_TXTFLDS >= 6
    x6 = Thisform.CONTAIN_TXTLBL_201.Text6.Value
    DO CASE
    CASE DE_TABLE_FLD6_TYPE = "CHR"
        Replace &DE_TABLE_FLD_NAME_6 WITH x6
    CASE DE_TABLE_FLD6_TYPE = "NUM"
        Replace &DE_TABLE_FLD_NAME_6 WITH VAL(x6)
    CASE DE_TABLE_FLD6_TYPE = "DATE"
        Replace &DE_TABLE_FLD_NAME_6 WITH CTOD(x6)
    ENDCASE
Endif

If DE_QTY_TXTFLDS >= 7
    x7 = Thisform.CONTAIN_TXTLBL_201.Text7.Value
    DO CASE
    CASE DE_TABLE_FLD7_TYPE = "CHR"
        Replace &DE_TABLE_FLD_NAME_7 WITH x7
    CASE DE_TABLE_FLD7_TYPE = "NUM"
        Replace &DE_TABLE_FLD_NAME_7 WITH VAL(x7)
    CASE DE_TABLE_FLD7_TYPE = "DATE"
        Replace &DE_TABLE_FLD_NAME_7 WITH CTOD(x7)
    ENDCASE
Endif

If DE_QTY_TXTFLDS >= 8
    x8 = Thisform.CONTAIN_TXTLBL_201.Text8.Value
    DO CASE
    CASE DE_TABLE_FLD8_TYPE = "CHR"
        Replace &DE_TABLE_FLD_NAME_8 WITH x8
    CASE DE_TABLE_FLD8_TYPE = "NUM"
        Replace &DE_TABLE_FLD_NAME_8 WITH VAL(x8)
    CASE DE_TABLE_FLD8_TYPE = "DATE"
        Replace &DE_TABLE_FLD_NAME_8 WITH CTOD(x8)
    ENDCASE
```

```
Endif

If DE_QTY_TXTFLDS >= 9
   x9 = Thisform.CONTAIN_TXTLBL_201.Text9.Value
   DO CASE
   CASE DE_TABLE_FLD9_TYPE = "CHR"
        Replace &DE_TABLE_FLD_NAME_9 WITH x9
   CASE DE_TABLE_FLD9_TYPE = "NUM"
        Replace &DE_TABLE_FLD_NAME_9 WITH VAL(x9)
   CASE DE_TABLE_FLD9_TYPE = "DATE"
        Replace &DE_TABLE_FLD_NAME_9 WITH CTOD(x9)
   ENDCASE
Endif

If DE_QTY_TXTFLDS >= 10
   x10 = Thisform.CONTAIN_TXTLBL_201.Text10.Value
   DO CASE
   CASE DE_TABLE_FLD10_TYPE = "CHR"
        Replace &DE_TABLE_FLD_NAME_10 WITH x10
   CASE DE_TABLE_FLD10_TYPE = "NUM"
        Replace &DE_TABLE_FLD_NAME_10 WITH VAL(x10)
   CASE DE_TABLE_FLD10_TYPE = "DATE"
        Replace &DE_TABLE_FLD_NAME_10 WITH CTOD(x10)
   ENDCASE
Endif

If DE_QTY_TXTFLDS >= 11
   x11 = Thisform.CONTAIN_TXTLBL_201.Text11.Value
   DO CASE
   CASE DE_TABLE_FLD11_TYPE = "CHR"
        Replace &DE_TABLE_FLD_NAME_11 WITH x11
   CASE DE_TABLE_FLD11_TYPE = "NUM"
        Replace &DE_TABLE_FLD_NAME_11 WITH VAL(x11)
   CASE DE_TABLE_FLD11_TYPE = "DATE"
        Replace &DE_TABLE_FLD_NAME_11 WITH CTOD(x11)
   ENDCASE
Endif

If DE_QTY_TXTFLDS >= 12
   x12 = Thisform.CONTAIN_TXTLBL_201.Text12.Value
   DO CASE
   CASE DE_TABLE_FLD12_TYPE = "CHR"
        Replace &DE_TABLE_FLD_NAME_12 WITH x12
   CASE DE_TABLE_FLD12_TYPE = "NUM"
        Replace &DE_TABLE_FLD_NAME_12 WITH VAL(x12)
   CASE DE_TABLE_FLD12_TYPE = "DATE"
        Replace &DE_TABLE_FLD_NAME_12 WITH CTOD(x12)
   ENDCASE
 Endif
```

```
If DE_QTY_TXTFLDS >= 13
   x13 = Thisform.CONTAIN_TXTLBL_201.Text13.Value
   DO CASE
   CASE DE_TABLE_FLD13_TYPE = "CHR"
        Replace &DE_TABLE_FLD_NAME_13 WITH x13
   CASE DE_TABLE_FLD13_TYPE = "NUM"
        Replace &DE_TABLE_FLD_NAME_13 WITH VAL(x13)
   CASE DE_TABLE_FLD13_TYPE = "DATE"
        Replace &DE_TABLE_FLD_NAME_13 WITH CTOD(x13)
   ENDCASE
Endif

If DE_QTY_TXTFLDS >= 14
   x14 = Thisform.CONTAIN_TXTLBL_201.Text14.Value
   DO CASE
   CASE DE_TABLE_FLD14_TYPE = "CHR"
        Replace &DE_TABLE_FLD_NAME_14 WITH x14
   CASE DE_TABLE_FLD14_TYPE = "NUM"
        Replace &DE_TABLE_FLD_NAME_14 WITH VAL(x14)
   CASE DE_TABLE_FLD14_TYPE = "DATE"
        Replace &DE_TABLE_FLD_NAME_14 WITH CTOD(x14)
   ENDCASE
Endif

If DE_QTY_TXTFLDS >= 15
   x15 = Thisform.CONTAIN_TXTLBL_201.Text15.Value
   DO CASE
   CASE DE_TABLE_FLD15_TYPE = "CHR"
        Replace &DE_TABLE_FLD_NAME_15 WITH x15
   CASE DE_TABLE_FLD15_TYPE = "NUM"
        Replace &DE_TABLE_FLD_NAME_15 WITH VAL(x5)
   CASE DE_TABLE_FLD15_TYPE = "DATE"
        Replace &DE_TABLE_FLD_NAME_15 WITH CTOD(x15)
   ENDCASE
Endif

If DE_QTY_TXTFLDS >= 16
   x16 = Thisform.CONTAIN_TXTLBL_201.Text16.Value
   DO CASE
   CASE DE_TABLE_FLD16_TYPE = "CHR"
        Replace &DE_TABLE_FLD_NAME_16 WITH x16
   CASE DE_TABLE_FLD16_TYPE = "NUM"
        Replace &DE_TABLE_FLD_NAME_16 WITH VAL(x16)
   CASE DE_TABLE_FLD16_TYPE = "DATE"
        Replace &DE_TABLE_FLD_NAME_16 WITH CTOD(x16)
   ENDCASE
Endif

If DE_QTY_TXTFLDS >= 17
   x17 = Thisform.CONTAIN_TXTLBL_201.Text17.Value
```

```
   DO CASE
   CASE DE_TABLE_FLD17_TYPE = "CHR"
        Replace &DE_TABLE_FLD_NAME_17 WITH x17
   CASE DE_TABLE_FLD17_TYPE = "NUM"
        Replace &DE_TABLE_FLD_NAME_17 WITH VAL(x17)
   CASE DE_TABLE_FLD17_TYPE = "DATE"
        Replace &DE_TABLE_FLD_NAME_17 WITH CTOD(x17)
   ENDCASE
Endif

If DE_QTY_TXTFLDS >= 18
   x18 = Thisform.CONTAIN_TXTLBL_201.Text18.Value
   DO CASE
   CASE DE_TABLE_FLD18_TYPE = "CHR"
        Replace &DE_TABLE_FLD_NAME_18 WITH x18
   CASE DE_TABLE_FLD18_TYPE = "NUM"
        Replace &DE_TABLE_FLD_NAME_18 WITH VAL(x18)
   CASE DE_TABLE_FLD18_TYPE = "DATE"
        Replace &DE_TABLE_FLD_NAME_18 WITH CTOD(x18)
   ENDCASE
Endif

If DE_QTY_TXTFLDS >= 19
   x19 = Thisform.CONTAIN_TXTLBL_201.Text19.Value
   DO CASE
   CASE DE_TABLE_FLD19_TYPE = "CHR"
        Replace &DE_TABLE_FLD_NAME_19 WITH x19
   CASE DE_TABLE_FLD19_TYPE = "NUM"
        Replace &DE_TABLE_FLD_NAME_19 WITH VAL(x19)
   CASE DE_TABLE_FLD19_TYPE = "DATE"
        Replace &DE_TABLE_FLD_NAME_19 WITH CTOD(x19)
   ENDCASE
Endif

If DE_QTY_TXTFLDS >= 20
   x20 = Thisform.CONTAIN_TXTLBL_201.Text20.Value
   DO CASE
   CASE DE_TABLE_FLD20_TYPE = "CHR"
        Replace &DE_TABLE_FLD_NAME_20 WITH x20
   CASE DE_TABLE_FLD20_TYPE = "NUM"
        Replace &DE_TABLE_FLD_NAME_20 WITH VAL(x20)
   CASE DE_TABLE_FLD20_TYPE = "DATE"
        Replace &DE_TABLE_FLD_NAME_20 WITH CTOD(x20)
   ENDCASE
Endif
```

```
*=============================================================*
* Procedure   : AOD_04_VALIDATE                               *
* Description: Occurs after doing a click on the Save Push    *
*              Button.                                        *
*=============================================================*
LPARAMETERS p1
LOCAL valid_ok, mode , vf

VALID_OK = 'Y'

*-------------------------------------------------
* Validate Duplicate Record:
*-------------------------------------------------
mode = Thisform.LABEL_MODE.Caption

IF mode = "ADD" OR mode = "CPY"

       vf = Thisform.B20_VALIDATE_DUPLICATE_REC()

       IF vf = .F.
                  valid_ok = "N"
       ELSE
                  valid_ok = "Y"
       ENDIF
ENDIF

* ON ERROR DO ERROR_PROC_01

*-------------------------------------------------
* Field #1 Validation:
*-------------------------------------------------
IF LEN(TRIM(Thisform.CONTAIN_TXTLBL_201.Text1.Value)) > 0
                    *=========================
ELSE
         valid_ok = "N"
         Thisform.CONTAIN_TXTLBL_201.Text1.Setfocus()
                 *=========================
         =MessageBox("Must not be blank.")
ENDIF
*-------------------------------------------------
* Field #2 Validation:
*-------------------------------------------------
 IF LEN(TRIM(Thisform.CONTAIN_TXTLBL_201.Text2.Value)) > 0
                    *===================
 ELSE
         VALID_OK = "N"
         Thisform.CONTAIN_TXTLBL_201.Text2.Setfocus()
                 *=========================
         =MessageBox("Must not be blank.")
 ENDIF
```

```
*------------------------------------------------
IF valid_ok = "Y"
  RETURN .T.
ELSE
  RETURN .F.
ENDIF


*==============================================================*
* Procedure: AOD_05_INIT_SET_FOCUS                             *
*                                                              *
*==============================================================*
LOCAL mode
mode = Thisform.label_mode.Caption

*----------------------------------------------------
IF mode = "ADD"  or mode = "CPY"
    Thisform.Contain_TXTLBL_201.Text1.Readonly = .F.
            *==========================
ELSE
    Thisform.Contain_TXTLBL_201.Text1.Readonly = .T.
            *==========================
ENDIF

*----------------------------------------------------
*
*----------------------------------------------------
On Error return

IF mode = "ADD"  OR mode = "CPY"
    Thisform.Contain_TXTLBL_201.Text1.SetFocus()
            *=========================
ELSE
    Thisform.Contain_TXTLBL_201.Text2.SetFocus()
            *==========================
ENDIF


*==============================================================*
* Procedure: AOD_06_TEXTBOX_VALUE                              *
*                                                              *
*==============================================================*
Lparameters textbox_id, textbox_val

DO CASE
CASE textbox_id = "TXTBOX_0?"                    &&
*     Thisform.Contain_TXTLBL_201.TEXT?.Value = textbox_val
              *=========================

* CASE textbox_id = "TXTBOX_0?"                  &&
```

```
*     Thisform.Contain_TXTLBL_201.TEXT?.Value = textbox_val
             *========================

* CASE textbox_id = "TXTBOX_0?"                       &&
*     Thisform.Contain_TXTLBL_201.TEXT?.Value = textbox_val
             *=========================
ENDCASE



*==============================================================*
* Procedure: AOD_07_TEXTBOX_VAL_RTN_INF                        *
*                                                              *
*==============================================================*
LPARAMETERS textbox_id, textbox_val, fld_seq

*DO CASE
*CASE textbox_id = "TXTBOX_0?"
*    Thisform.Contain_TXTLBL_201.TEXT21.Value = textbox_val
           *==========================

*CASE textbox_id = "TXTBOX_0?"
*     Thisform.Contain_TXTLBL_201.TEXT22.Value = textbox_val
             *=========================

*CASE textbox_id = "TXTBOX_0?"
*   Do Case
*   Case fld_seq = 1
*     Thisform.Contain_TXTLBL_201.TEXT23.value = textbox_val
             *=========================
*   Case fld_seq = 2
*     Thisform.Contain_TXTLBL_201.TEXT24.value = textbox_val
             *=========================
*   Case fld_seq = 3
*     Thisform.Contain_TXTLBL_201.TEXT25.VALUE = textbox_val
             *=========================
* Endcase

*ENDCASE




*==============================================================*
* Procedure: AOD_08_KEY_FLD_TXT_VALUE                          *
*                                                              *
*==============================================================*
Lparameters na

LOCAL  txt_val
```

```
    txt_val = Thisform.Contain_TXTLBL_201.text1.Value
                      *=========================

RETURN txt_val



*==============================================================*
* Procedure   : AOD_09_KEY_VALUE                               *
* Description: Key value obtained from file, converted to      *
*              character string.  For example:                 *
*                                                              *
*                  key_val = STR(vnd_code, 3, 0)               *
*                                                              *
*==============================================================*
Lparameters na

LOCAL key_val

DO CASE
CASE DE_TABLE_FLD1_TYPE = "CHR"

  key_val = &DE_TABLE_FLD_NAME_1
          *====================

CASE P_TABLE_FLD1_TYPE = "NUM"

  key_val= STR(&DE_TABLE_FLD_NAME_1, DE_NUM_FLD1_WIDTH, ;
                                     DE_NUM_FLD1_DECIMALS)
              *====================

CASE DE_TABLE_FLD1_TYPE = "DATE"

  key_val = DTOC(&DE_TABLE_FLD_NAME_1)
                *====================

ENDCASE


RETURN key_val
```

```
*==============================================================*
* Procedure  : AOD_10_GET_NEXT_SEQ                             *
* Description: Used with the ADD Mode, to compute next         *
*              sequence number.                                *
*==============================================================*



*==============================================================*
* Procedure: AOD_11_COPY_CLEAR_KEY                             *
*                                                              *
*==============================================================*

Thisform.Contain_TXTLBL_201.Text1.Value = ""
       *========================



*==============================================================*
* Procedure: AOD_31_GRID_PROPERTIES                            *
*                                                              *
*==============================================================*



*==============================================================*
* Procedure: AOD_32_GRID_COLUMN_PROP                           *
*                                                              *
*==============================================================*



*==============================================================*
* Procedure: AOD_33_GRID_COL_HEADER_PROP                       *
*                                                              *
*==============================================================*
```

Source Code Example for the Contain_txtlbl_20 Control

```
*=================================================================*
* Object    : Text1                                               *
* Procedure : DblClick                                            *
*=================================================================*
 LOCAL  TXTBOX_ID, MODE

 TXTBOX_ID = "TXTBOX_01"
             *===========

 MODE = THISFORM.LABEL_MODE.CAPTION

 DO CASE
 CASE MODE = "ADD"
    THISFORM.B05_PICKLIST_RUN(TXTBOX_ID)
 CASE MODE = "CHG"
    THISFORM.B05_PICKLIST_RUN(TXTBOX_ID)
 CASE MODE = "CPY"
    THISFORM.B05_PICKLIST_RUN(TXTBOX_ID)
 ENDCASE


*=================================================================*
* Object     : Text1                                              *
* Procedure  : Valid                                              *
*=================================================================*
 LOCAL RTN, TXTBOX_ID, MODE

 TXTBOX_ID = "TXTBOX_01"
             *===========

 MODE = THISFORM.LABEL_MODE.CAPTION

 IF MODE = "ADD" OR MODE = "CHG"

   RTN = THISFORM.B06_TEXTBOX_VALID_RTN_VALUE(TXTBOX_ID, ;
                                              THIS.VALUE)
   IF RTN = .F.
     THISFORM.B05_PICKLIST_RUN(TXTBOX_ID)
   ELSE
     RETURN .T.
   ENDIF

 ENDIF
```

Source Code Example for the Pbg_chg_mode Control

```
*==============================================================*
* Class    : Pbg_chg_mode                                      *
* Object   : Commandgroup1                                     *
* Procedure: Click                                             *
*==============================================================*
 LOCAL CMD_G

 CMD_G = THIS.VALUE

 DO CASE
 CASE CMD_G = 1
   Thisform.B75_PB_CHG_MODE_DSP
 CASE CMD_G = 2
   Thisform.B77_PB_CHG_MODE_CHG
 CASE CMD_G = 3
   Thisform.B76_PB_CHG_MODE_ADD
 CASE CMD_G = 4
   Thisform.B78_PB_CHG_MODE_DEL
 CASE CMD_G = 5
   Thisform.B79_PB_CHG_MODE_CPY
ENDCASE
```

Source Code Example for the Pbg_navigation_h Control

```
*==============================================================*
* Object   : Pbg_navigation_h                                  *
* Procedure: Click                                             *
*==============================================================*
 LOCAL CMD_G

 CMD_G = THIS.VALUE

 Thisform.B02_PBG_NAVIGATION_CLICK(CMD_G)
```

Source Code for the Pbg_save_cancel_more Control

```
*==============================================================*
* Object   : Pbg_save_cancel_more                              *
* Procedure: Click                                             *
*==============================================================*
LOCAL CMD_G

CMD_G = THIS.VALUE

Thisform.B02_COMMAND_GROUP_CLICK(CMD_G)
```

Source Code

The C_DE Class Form contains a label with the following properties:

```
Name    = label_mode
Caption = The Caption changes depending the parameter.
          For example: "ADD", "CHG", "DSP"
Height = 16, Left = 3, Top = -20, Width = 72
```

www.ingramcontent.com/pod-product-compliance
Lightning Source LLC
Chambersburg PA
CBHW051231050326
40689CB00007B/880

* 9 7 8 1 4 4 9 0 7 0 5 5 7 *